D0906334

ORWELL

ORWELL

A Man Of Our Time

Richard Bradford

BLOOMSBURY CARAVEL
LONDON · OXFORD · NEW YORK · NEW DELHI · SYDNEY

BLOOMSBURY CARAVEL
Bloomsbury Publishing Plc
50 Bedford Square, London, WC1B 3DP, UK

BLOOMSBURY, BLOOMSBURY CARAVEL and the BLOOMSBURY CARAVEL logo are
trademarks of Bloomsbury Publishing Plc

First published in Great Britain in 2020

A catalogue record for this book is available from the British Library

ISBN: HB: 978-1-4482-1768-7; eBook: 978-1-4482-1770-0

2 4 6 8 10 9 7 5 3 1

Typeset in Perpetua by Deanta Global Publishing Services, Chennai, India
Printed and bound in Great Britain by CPI Group (UK) Ltd, Croydon, CR0 4YY

To find out more about our authors and books visit www.bloomsbury.com
and sign up for our newsletters

For Amy Burns

CONTENTS

PREFACE AND ACKNOWLEDGEMENTS

All quotations below are from texts by Orwell and others cited in the Bibliography. Orwell was of course born Eric Arthur Blair, but for the sake of convenience I will refer to him throughout as 'Orwell' or 'George Orwell' and to the married couple Eric and Eileen as the 'Orwells'. In the preparation of the book thanks are due to the staff of the Library, Ulster University, and to Lisa Verner. Dr Amy Burns, an Orwell fan, has been of great help, as has D. J. Howells, for the same reason. My editor at Bloomsbury, Jayne Parsons, has been a gem.

INTRODUCTION

Biographies, by their nature, are about the past, but this life of Orwell will be a little different. It will bring him into the present day and in so doing show that questions he asked of his generation remain unanswered and sometimes unaddressed.

No author can predict the future, yet Orwell's talent as a foreseer is extraordinary. From the early 1930s onwards he was astute in picking out things about us that would endure and resurface many decades later: antisemitism – especially on the extreme left; the toleration by the free world of authoritarian regimes, now because we need them economically; dim-witted materialism; populist politics; brainless nationalism; doublethink as the motor for political discourse – that is, outright lying; the resurgence of seemingly endemic xenophobia; and, of course, Brexit. Most of the usual suspects weren't alive when Orwell left us in January 1950 but he would not have been surprised by their appearances as players in revivals of his dramas: May, Trump, Johnson, Gove, Corbyn, Farage, Putin, Xi Jinping *et al*.

As a young man Orwell was antisemitic but, unlike almost everyone equally disposed, then and today, he took a step outside himself, recognised what he saw as evil, confronted its causes, and eventually repented. His atonement involved both self-loathing and a terrible recognition that many of his fellow countrymen were as bad as he had been. Anyone who believes that an occupied Britain would have protected its Jews should read his wartime journalism and reconsider. Orwell's assessment of true antisemitism as a form of calculated doublethink tells us a good deal about the state of Corbyn's Labour Party.

In Spain he was a hero, risking his life on numerous occasions leading attacks against Falangist trenches and machine-gun posts. He was shot in the throat and rewarded by being accused of treachery by the Soviets and their fellow travellers in the West. He and his wife Eileen went into hiding in Barcelona and escaped execution by the NKVD, the Russian secret police, by fleeing across the border into France. Briefly, he had experienced a version of what had been happening under Stalin for almost a decade: dissent leading to a show trial and execution.

Orwell loathed poverty but held in equal contempt the inflexibility of Marxism and communism as solutions; systems and ideologies which deny human beings the quixotic opportunity to live and think as they wish are, in his view, almost as cruel as inequality. Travelling among the English working classes he encountered men and women reduced almost to the condition of animals but, despite himself, he also detected a mixture of apathy and grim resignation; something quite different from the wild energy of revolutionary Catalonia. The proles of *Nineteen Eighty-Four* were born out of the sad figures of *Down and Out in Paris and London* and *The Road to Wigan Pier*. He expected that their conditions would improve, but he was not optimistic regarding a change in a collective state of mind. The cheers that greeted Mosley at a packed speech in Lancashire would be echoed decades later by followers of Farage's Brexit Party. Most importantly, he diagnosed a state of introversion and xenophobia that transcends classes and is quintessentially English: Brexit existed long before the Common Market had been invented.

And of course we have doublethink, the use of language to distort objective reality. Today, it is not a tool of the Inner Party but rather a co-operative condition; we don't *mind* being lied to. But we have eradicated the nightmare of *Nineteen Eighty-Four*, haven't we? On the contrary. We hold out our begging bowls, as global trading partners, to China, whose ruling Communist Party might well have made use of Orwell's novel as an instruction manual.

Orwell's novels of the 1930s — *Burmese Days*, *A Clergyman's Daughter*, *Keep the Aspidistra Flying* and *Coming Up for Air* — are fine pieces of writing, but one also feels a tension between them and the three books published in the same period (*Down and Out in Paris and London*, *The Road to Wigan Pier* and *Homage to Catalonia*) which are equally compelling because they are based exclusively on lived experience. Once the Second World War broke out Orwell decided that truth-telling was more important than making things up. His journalism of the 1940s is angry and confrontational because it is based on facts he observed and reported, which virtually everyone else preferred to ignore. As such it was a rehearsal for his two best-known dystopian novels, *Animal Farm* and *Nineteen Eighty-Four*. Both epitomise his theory of what literature should do, laid out in *Inside the Whale*. It should not be a diversion, should not be a branch of the 'arts'. It must show us at our worst and warn us of what we are capable of creating. The Cold War is over but we still need to heed his warning. China's version of Big Brother's totalitarianism is horrifying and not only because it is worse than anything Orwell imagined. In Orwell's day the liberal left deluded themselves about the reality of Stalin's regime. Today we know what happens under Xi Jinping and for the sake of economic expediency we don't care. Orwell said of his last novel: 'don't let it happen'. Seemingly we now aid and abet it. We might suppose Orwell can rest easy in Sutton Courtenay churchyard given that we've prevented it from happening here and in the rest of the 'free world'. But go to his descriptions of the ritual of the Two Minutes Hate, look at recordings of Trump conducting chants of 'Lock her up! Lock her up!' and think again.

THE MISFIT AND THE PURE HELL
OF ST CYPRIAN'S

That Orwell became something of an oddball, a misfit, is not at all surprising given the first ten years of his life. During this period his father, Richard Walmsley Blair, was absent. He was alive and he was not separated from his wife, Orwell's mother Ida Mabel (née Limouzin), but Orwell only met him properly when he was nine years old and even then they switched places; Orwell would thereafter spend less than half the year in the family home after being sent to board at St Cyprian's Preparatory School in 1911. Richard Blair had been an 'Opium Agent' with the British administration in India since 1875 and he only returned to England permanently in 1912. He had met Ida, eighteen years his junior, in India in 1896 and married her the same year, after she had been jilted by a charming suitor of her own age. Richard had gone out to India in 1875, the year of Ida's birth. In 1904, eight years after their marriage, Ida chose to move back to England with their two children. Marjorie, the eldest, was six years old and Eric Arthur Blair (Orwell's birth name) was still a baby, having been born in a whitewashed brick bungalow in Motihari in 1903 less than twelve months before his mother's departure. Ida settled with the children in a comfortable, modestly appointed house in Henley-on-Thames and Richard visited his family there, briefly, in the summer of 1907. Their third child, Avril, was born in April 1908, roughly seven months after his return to India. It is likely that Orwell, then four years old, would have been introduced to his father but there is no record of how anyone in the household felt about a patriarch whose fleeting appearances seemed to involve little more than procreation. It is possible that Richard wrote to his son, but unlikely. Correspondence from a parent thousands of miles away is, generally speaking, retained, but none from Richard to Orwell survives and the latter never refers to any kind of communication between himself and his father during this period.

When Richard retired after thirty-seven years of colonial service in 1912 he would have been a complete stranger to his son, and not only because of his physical absence. Blair senior was a quintessential Victorian. He was born in 1857, eleven years before public hangings were abolished in Britain; prior to 1868 these had rivalled football and cricket as the most popular form of mass entertainment. He came into the world shortly before Queen Victoria's last child, Princess Beatrice, and less than a year after the end of the Crimean War. Changes within the social fabric of England between 1875 and his return to the homeland had largely passed him by: in the Empire time stood still. Richard had risen from Sub-Deputy Opium Agent 3rd Grade to Sub-Deputy 1st grade, busily supervising Indian plantations and organising supplies of the drug to China where addicts were providing the imperial government of India with their most profitable income from exports. The precise nature of his job seemed not to concern him and he gave primary attention to securing a decent retirement pension. £438 per year in 1912 was something of a success in this regard.

Henley in 1912 was a quiet Edwardian Oxfordshire town, not the metropolitan suburb of today, yet it was informed by an easy conviviality that made it almost modern. The rigid class structure of the previous century was gradually eroding. The young Orwell played games with the son of the local plumber and farmers drove their cattle along the main street before joining the professional classes for a drink in the town pubs. But his father was an anachronism. Richard's arrival was an exercise in time travel, causing the older residents of the town to wonder if the previous four decades had been an illusion. He joined the Conservative Club but rarely spoke to other members, and went to the cinema as a dutiful recognition that the twentieth century had arrived, sleeping through most films and speaking of none of them to friends or family. In local pubs he drank cider and sometimes played bridge but no one recalls him ever opening a book. Indoors he insisted that the fire in the front room should be kept blazing all day even during spring and summer. No other members of the family could stand the airless oven-like atmosphere – he also demanded that all doors be kept firmly closed – and it became gradually apparent that his bizarre, seemingly masochistic behaviour had a simple motive. He wanted to recreate the tropical climate of northern India which expatriates, like himself, found all but unbearable but treated as a necessary burden of colonial service. When he did venture outdoors other aspects of India came with him. The local tailor made his suits but his attempts to engage his client in anything close to conversation when measuring him and choosing material were met with gruff monosyllabic responses. Richard saw his tailor as belonging to a lower caste, and if they encountered each other in the street he refused to acknowledge his presence. His only notable attempt to associate with others in the neighbourhood came when he joined the golf club and even then he was less interested in the game or socialising in the clubhouse than with taking control. Within a year he had become remunerated secretary and ran the club, as one member recalled, in a 'terribly autocratic manner ... if anyone got in his way ... they'd get it in no uncertain terms'. Once more he was recreating a feature of India. Since Henley did not offer him a readily subservient indigenous population he would make do by bullying members of the golf club.

At home the tables were turned in that Ida treated him with a mixture of condescension and deprecation. She mocked him when she heard him desperately poking the fire, and she seemed to carry on much as she had when he was abroad, visiting friends in central London and attending events such as the Chelsea Flower Show and the Wimbledon Tennis Tournament, never bothering to ask Richard if he would care to accompany her. Her diary for the summer of 1905 recorded that she 'went to the theatre and saw Sarah Bernhardt, went swimming ... Went to Wimbledon ... Spent all day on the river ...' (Meyers, 2008, p 8). It hardly seems the routine of a woman stoically making do while her husband serves the Empire thousands of miles away. She was having a good time and when Richard returned following his retirement nothing changed. She tolerated his presence but in all other respects saw him as the equivalent of a distant relative. Within a year of Richard joining the household they had moved into separate bedrooms.

Three years before Richard's retirement rumours had circulated throughout Henley that Ida — still in her thirties, vivacious and proud of her appearance — was having an affair with the local general practitioner, Dr Dakin. They would, it was said, meet at the golf club and he would offer to accompany her home, a journey which sometimes took several hours. The doctor's son, Humphrey Dakin, who would eventually marry Marjorie Blair, stated in an interview in 1965 that his father had 'received no encouragement from Ida' and that his jealous mother had spread false rumours as an act of revenge. Notably he did not deny that there had been an affair and he left open to speculation the cause of his mother's jealousy. One has to wonder if Richard's behaviour at the golf club, which another member described as 'tyrannical', was some kind of oblique act of vengeance, directed at the adulterers' meeting place rather than the individuals themselves, one of whom, his wife, he seemed to fear.

In 1914 the Blairs moved to nearby Shiplake, a small, attractive, chocolate-box village overlooking the Thames. Their house was a little smaller but nothing else changed, with Richard and Ida leading separate lives and the former treating his children as the unfortunate outcomes of a marriage that neither party seemed to enjoy but were unable to completely abandon. Their neighbours, the Buddicoms, had three children — Jacintha, Prosper and Guinever — with whom Orwell soon became friendly. He introduced himself by standing on his head while announcing that 'you are noticed more if you stand on your head than if you are the right way up'. Jacintha, suitably impressed, became his first girlfriend, though no one who knew them doubted her insistence that their relationship, which lasted until their late teens, was strictly platonic. She later recalled that while Orwell was always amusing and good company, this persona would fade when his father was present. The Buddicoms' garden was adjacent to the Blairs' and was much more spacious, but Orwell's time with his new playmates would be abruptly interrupted by a summons to supper or homework by a disembodied growl from the hedge. Richard would then slam the door without having acknowledged the Buddicom siblings as fellow human beings, let alone his son's closest friends.

The Buddicom children provided a refuge for Orwell from the atmosphere of cold alienation that pervaded his home. He would later concede that his mother had treated him as her favourite child but at the time she seemed more concerned with creating a life for herself beyond the ossified figure of her husband. Richard was in his mid-fifties but he dressed, behaved and carried himself like someone fifteen years older, a man beset with introspective bitterness. In Henley Ida had mildly discouraged her son from associating with the plumber's children — while more outgoing than her husband she was still a snob — but when Richard returned from India he sternly forbade his son from even speaking with the sons and daughters of the lower orders. This was Orwell's first lesson in the strict ordinances of class distinction, a very English form of apartheid that would preoccupy him for the rest of his life. The youngsters he was allowed to spend time with were a 'gang' comprised of middle-class boys led by the doctor's son Humphrey Dakin. They would go fishing, hunt with air guns and build wigwams in the wooded outskirts of the town, but Orwell's desperate attempts to fit in were thwarted by Dakin. He was annoyed by Orwell purely because his

attempts to court Marjorie seemed continually to be obstructed by
her younger brother's refusal to go away. In 1965 Dakin, despite
Orwell's established reputation as one of Britain's greatest novelists,
remembered him as 'stinking little Eric', the infuriating child 'full of
"nobody loves me" and torrents of tears' (Shelden, p 13). With the
young Buddicoms Orwell seemed at last to have found an alternative
home; however in 1915 Mr Buddicom abandoned his family and ran
off to Australia with his mistress. His children were devastated and
began to appreciate Orwell's sense of isolation. Richard had not
disappeared but he might as well have been somewhere else. The
four of them, during school holidays, created a world for themselves
which marked the genesis of Orwell's literary ambitions. Aged eight
he had stolen a copy of Swift's *Gulliver's Travels* and while over the
next five years he would read much of Shakespeare, H. G. Wells,
Poe, Dickens and Kipling, Swift's volume remained his favourite,
a book that he would re-read continually during the following four
decades. He found it fascinating and addictive because Swift had
at once defied credulity while offering a ghastly mirror image of
aspects of humanity that humans would prefer to ignore. He would
read passages to Jacintha and each regarded Swift as an inspiration
for their own exercises in telling fantastic stories. Much later in
his essay 'Why I Write' (1946) he recalls his time with Jacintha.
'I had the lonely child's habit of making up stories and holding
conversations with imaginary persons, and I think from the very
start my literary ambitions were mixed up with the feeling of being
isolated and undervalued.' In her memoir *Eric & Us* (1974) Jacintha
still appears dumbfounded by the breadth and outlandishness of her
friend's imaginings. On several occasions he speculated as to whether
the people they saw in the streets of Shiplake or Henley were real
or ghosts. He seemed to her to be going beyond storytelling and
genuinely posing the question of whether it might be impossible
to distinguish between actual human beings and spectral figures.
'In town [he said] so many [people] would be strangers that we
wouldn't know whether they were ghosts or not, if they walked

about like anyone else!' Sometimes, after they'd played hide and seek in the Buddicom garden, he would talk about disappearance and concealment as a potential means of passing into oblivion. 'How can you be sure I'm me? ... [when] I might have been *got into* by the shadow of a shadow.' (Shelden, p 57).

Friends of the Blairs remembered Orwell as a boy who was reluctant to associate with other middle-class children, a shy and withdrawn figure who, when the Buddicoms were not available, preferred to spend time with an imaginary friend whom he referred to as 'Fronky'.

His friendship with Jacintha's brother, Prosper, was not imagined but they enjoyed slipping towards a private world of their own. They loved fishing the Thames at a spot above Shiplake that was away from the footpaths and enclosed by willows, where they seemed to have left the rest of mankind behind. When they returned, their activities suggested that they cared little about what everyone else thought of them. At the time bicycle and hardware shops could sell gunpowder and basic firearms over the counter, irrespective of the age or apparent intention of the purchaser. Orwell bought his first 'saloon rifle' when he was ten years old. It was a single-shot smooth-bore weapon but quite capable of killing a human being at up to thirty paces. He and Prosper took it with them on their fishing expeditions and at home they had near-fatal fun with their considerable stock of gunpowder. In the Buddicom kitchen they constructed a whisky still from old pots, pans and used pipes, and assumed that they could speed up the distilling process by spreading gunpowder across the hob of the stove. The predictable resulting explosion singed their eyebrows and blackened their clothes. Fascinated by the strength of their new toy they compressed the powder into sackcloth bags which they tossed onto a bonfire in the garden. Neighbours wondered if the Germans had begun an invasion.

In the Blair garden Orwell had set up something resembling a private commune. No one was certain where the chickens and the goat came from but he tended them devotedly during school holidays and secured a promise from the maid to look after them when he was away. As well as his animals he grew potatoes, turnips, cabbages and carrots in his own plot, as a means of paying the maid for her help. His father, deliberately or not, adopted a stance of obliviousness, while his mother got on with her own life and treated Orwell's activities with benign tolerance. During his years at Prep School he wrote letters only to his mother and not once in them does he mention his father.

Since 1911, Orwell had attended St Cyprian's Preparatory School in Eastbourne, founded in 1899 by Lewis Wilkes and his wife Cicely, both in their twenties at the time. They first made use of a large suburban house and other rented property, but by 1906 the institution was sufficiently profitable for them to move into a new purpose-built facility with extensive playing fields on what had previously been agricultural meadows.

The school's educational model was based on the regime of Thomas Arnold of Rugby. Intellectual advancement was seen as a necessary expediency. The Wilkeses wanted their pupils to obtain places at the best public schools, preferably Eton or Harrow, and then to proceed to Oxford or Cambridge: a conveyor belt to positions of power in the nation and the Empire. Speculative thinking and the questioning of orthodox truths were not indulged. Such activities ran against the spirit of Muscular Christianity that informed the principles of the school: moral inflexibility, integrity and strength of character.

The main building was destroyed by fire in 1939 and St Cyprian's relocated to West Sussex, but numbers began to dwindle and eighteen months later the school closed. Recollections of the school are found in the memoirs of a number of esteemed alumni but its most enduring memorial is a scathing essay by Orwell called 'Such, Such Were the Joys', drafted during the 1940s but not published until 1952, two years after his death. His publisher Fredric Warburg said it was potentially libellous and that even if the names of the Wilkeses were changed there would have been sufficient evidence for them to take a civil action.

It is customary to praise Orwell for the unburdened simplicity of his prose, and while he loathed stylistic flamboyance we should think again before treating him more as a craftsman than an artist. 'Such, Such Were the Joys' is a masterpiece; its use of a gradual accumulation of detail to create a vividly grotesque image is the literary equivalent of Brueghel. He offers us some 'good memories': swimming in the sea beyond the playing fields, walking through these same fields in early summer when time allowed, or snatching an hour's undisturbed reading in the sunlit dormitory. But then: '... the pewter bowls out of which we had our porridge ... had overhanging rims, and under the rims there were accumulations of sour porridge, which could be flaked off in long strips. The porridge itself, too, contained more lumps, hairs and unexplained black things than one would have thought possible, unless someone were putting them there on purpose. It was never safe to start on that porridge without investigating it first.' Next we encounter the slimy water of the plunge bath, in which 'I once saw floating a human turd', damp towels with their 'cheesy smell', the greasy basins of the changing rooms leading onto a row of 'filthy, dilapidated lavatories', none of which had doors, so that 'someone was sure to come crashing in'.

> It is not easy for me to think of my schooldays without seeming to breathe in a whiff of something cold and evil-smelling – a sort of compound of sweaty stockings, dirty towels, faecal smells blowing along corridors, forks with old food between the prongs, neck-of-mutton stew ... the echoing chamberpots in the dormitories.

By the time he wrote this he had witnessed much worse in terms of human degradation in Lancashire, Yorkshire, Paris and Spain, but he gives special emphasis to the petty filth of St Cyprian's because, as he subtly shows, pain and humiliation were key features of the Wilkeses' programme of moral strengthening. We will never know if he recalled authentically the verbal punishments inflicted on the pupils by Cicely, or 'Flip' as the boys referred to her, and her husband Lewis, nicknamed 'Sambo'. But in terms of nuance and cadence they come across as two of the most repulsive sadists in literature. Orwell was not merely revenging himself against a couple who ruined much of his childhood. Rather he was setting the record straight regarding the system which the Wilkeses epitomised, that remained largely unaltered in the 1940s and endures, far more hygienically, in Britain in 2019. Floating turds rarely feature in the *Spectator*'s gorgeously illustrated education supplements, dedicated to prep, private and public schools, but one can still detect the Wilkeses' promise of disciplined advancement.

Orwell's near contemporaries at St Cyprian's have, since their time there, variously disparaged and questioned his representation of the place and the Wilkeses. In his biography of Cecil Beaton, Hugo Vickers quotes his subject describing Orwell's account as 'hilariously funny – but it is exaggerated'. Beaton, for Vickers, claims never to have seen faeces in the bath and implies that Orwell's other anecdotes on the school are erroneous. Beaton was also less than impressed by Orwell's later writings, concluding that 'Orwell made a fetish of the sordid and enjoyed playing up the horror of life among the miners, or the down-and-outs in any city of the world.' In other words, Orwell was a middle-class writer who salved his conscience by self-flagellation and slumming with the lower orders. But as an unapologetic snob and social climber, Beaton would say this.

Orwell's closest friend at the school was Cyril Connolly and even he expressed unease at the latter's recollection of the place as an upper-class borstal. Yet Connolly, albeit inadvertently, provides evidence that the teenage Orwell loathed the place as vehemently as the middle-aged writer. In June 1916 'Flip' Wilkes asked the boys to compose a poem in memory of Lord Kitchener who had died at the beginning of the month. Of the fifty presented Connolly's was ranked third while Orwell trailed a little further behind at eighth. Nonetheless Orwell's 'Kitchener' was the only one that got into print, appearing in the *Henley and South Oxfordshire Standard* on 21 July. The opening stanza is as follows:

> No stone is set to mark his nation's loss,
> No stately tomb enshrines his noble breast;
> Not e'en the tribute of a wooden cross
> Can mark this hero's rest.

The fact that his body was never recovered from the North Sea might cause an ungracious reader to regard this as a statement of the morbidly obvious. But as we read on we also begin to detect a note of, if not quite irony, then at least disrespectful ambiguity regarding the young poet's expression of loss. The closing stanza begins with 'Who follows in his steps no danger shuns,' which might just be taken to imply that Kitchener's successor might not be so content to 'shun' the hideous fate of those he'd encouraged to serve on the Western Front. The subsequent three lines are intriguing:

> Nor stoops to conquer by a shameful deed,
> An honest and unselfish race he runs,
> From fear and malice freed.

Goldsmith's *She Stoops to Conquer* is a classic comedy in which a woman deceives her sister by pretending to be someone else. Surely the thirteen-year-old was not suggesting that Kitchener's propaganda-driven recruitment campaign was a little disingenuous? Perhaps the 'honest and unselfish race' is made up of the poor volunteers he has duped; let us not forget that until his death he effectively 'ran' the propaganda war. Death has, apparently 'freed' him from 'fear and malice', emotions that he might well have stirred among a people who were beginning to tire of the seemingly limitless death toll. Less than two years earlier, shortly after enrolling at St Cyprian's, Orwell's first published poem had appeared in the same *Henley and South Oxfordshire Standard*. 'Awake! Young Men of England' seems,

on the surface, to be another hymn to selfless patriotism but unless
Orwell, and indeed the newspaper's editor, had blinded themselves
to inadvertent double entendres one has to wonder:

Oh! think of the War lord's mailed fist,
That is striking at England today;
And think of the lives that our soldiers
Are fearlessly throwing away.

Wilfred Owen did not open his 'Anthem for Doomed Youth' with
'What passing-bells for these who die as cattle?' until 1917, but it is
eerily prefigured by the image of soldiers 'fearlessly throwing away'
their lives.

Sceptics might treat the notion of an early-teenage version of
Bertrand Russell – dismissed from Trinity College, Cambridge, and
imprisoned for his opposition to the war – as ludicrous, but Cyril
Connolly gives us cause to think otherwise. The following is from
Connolly's *Enemies of Promise* (1938):

I was a stage rebel, Orwell a true one ... he was one of those
boys who seem born old ... Alone among the boys he was an
intellectual and not a parrot for he thought for himself ... and
rejected not only [St Cyprian's], but the war, the Empire, Kipling,
Sussex [home to Kipling and St Cyprian's] and Character.

'Of course, you realise, Connolly,' said Orwell, 'that, whoever
wins this war, we shall emerge a second-rate nation.'

Connolly goes on to tell of how his friend introduced him to H. G.
Wells' 'The Country of the Blind', the story of an explorer who
discovers in the Andes a kingdom in which all citizens are blind and
who as a consequence believe that blindness is superior to sight,
especially for those who govern them. The two boys regarded it
as an appropriate analogy for the state of Britain at war in 1916.
The phrase 'lions led by donkeys' was becoming a commonplace

among disgruntled troops at the Front. Connolly and Orwell also enjoyed Compton Mackenzie's *Sinister Street*, in which Michael Fane experiences prep and public school followed by Oxford, a journey the boys were likely to take themselves. But Mackenzie (St Paul's School and Magdalen College, Oxford) puts a twist on the ideal of the morally upright 'Character' who would be formed by these institutions, with Fane giving himself up to the counterclaims of sodomy, womanising and low-life hedonism.

'Flip' Wilkes adopted a policy of grading pupils according to their chosen reading matter, aside from work on the curriculum, and Orwell took particular pleasure in announcing his fondness for *Sinister Street*, banned from libraries since its publication in 1914. He was awarded zero for his literary tastes and publicly reprimanded for conniving in degeneracy.

Despite his loathing for the school and all it stood for, Orwell excelled academically. In 1916 St Cyprian's employed a Fellow of All Souls College, Oxford, to assess the four principal examination papers and in Greek, Latin, French and English, Connolly and Orwell competed for first and second places. They were the two best pupils in the school and Orwell, accompanied by 'Sambo' Wilkes, went to Eton to take his scholarship exam, an ordeal which lasted for two and a half days and involved a three-hour viva conducted by the Provost, Vice-Provost, Headmaster, Master in College, and six Fellows of Eton representing its various disciplinary areas. He passed, but since there was no scholarship available that year he spent the subsequent twelve months in a form of limbo at Wellington College, a public school of reasonable standing but self-evidently regarded as at best a waiting room for the far more esteemed Eton.

On the day he left St Cyprian's Orwell donned his Old Boy's tie more as an announcement of his escape from the place than an acknowledgement of any debt to it. It was a week before Christmas 1916 and he observed convention by visiting 'Flip' Wilkes to say goodbye; he later commented that he would rather have gone directly to the railway station without having even a brief encounter with this 'vile' individual. He wrote that her 'parting smile' seemed to say: 'We know you disbelieve in everything we've taught you, and we know you aren't in the least grateful for all we've done for you.'

> [H]ow happy I was, that winter morning, as the train bore me away … The world was opening before me, just a little, like a grey sky that exhibits a narrow crack of blue.

He never visited the school, or Eastbourne, again.

2

ETON

Today seven per cent of the population of the UK attend, or have attended, a private school, and these schools, like St Cyprian's in its day, are a key part of the competitive entrepreneurial sector; as individual money-making enterprises they outnumber funeral directors and dentists. The ancient top-ranking public schools – notably Eton, Harrow and Winchester – cater for less than three per cent of the populace but their alumni make up more than one third of members of the House of Commons, along with seventy-four per cent of senior judges, seventy-two per cent of senior officers in the armed forces, sixty-eight per cent of Oscar winners, forty-two per cent of Russell Group and Oxbridge Vice-Chancellors and forty-nine per cent of the captains of industry, businessmen and businesswomen in the top half of the *Sunday Times* Rich List.

Orwell, in *The Road to Wigan Pier*, reflected on the years shortly before the First World War when prep schools and public schools saw themselves as ante-rooms for a life of unhindered privilege. They would condition the sons and daughters of the elite for lives of graceful indulgence – this was the Edwardian era – ensuring that these lucky youngsters dealt with their legacy of entitlement in an appropriately civilised manner. By the time he wrote 'Such, Such Were the Joys' he felt confident in rejoicing in the demise of this conspiracy of exclusion by which the private education system and the upper classes ensured that the proles would not even be able to conduct themselves in the same way as the ruling elite let

alone become guests at the party. The post-war Labour government
would put an end to that. How naive he was.

In *The Road to Wigan Pier* he wrote, of Eton:

> I suppose there is no place in the world where snobbery is quite
> so ever-present or where it is cultivated in such refined and
> subtle forms as in an English public school. Here at least one
> cannot say that English 'education' fails to do its job. You forget
> your Latin and Greek within a few months of leaving school –
> I studied Greek for eight or ten years, and now, at thirty-three,
> I cannot even repeat the Greek alphabet – but your snobbishness,
> unless you persistently root it out like the bindweed it is, sticks
> by you till your grave.

He treats Eton as having had a malign and ineradicable effect on his
character, and the passage is underpinned by his confident belief
that before too long others will not be similarly deformed. '… I
believe there is some hope that when Socialism is a living issue,
a thing that large numbers of Englishmen genuinely care about,
the class-difficulty [enshrined in the private education system]
may solve itself more rapidly than now seems thinkable.' This was
written in 1937, and a decade later – following the trauma of being
almost defeated by the Nazis – Britain did elect something close to
a socialist government, but let us jump forward more than seventy
years beyond the post-war Labour victory. Someone in particular is
brought to mind by Orwell's presentation of the obsessive learning
of Latin and Greek as a token of a public schoolboy's exclusivity,
enabling its beneficiary to claim superiority, despite no practical
gain coming from it. This person is of course the politician-with-no-
surname: Boris. Of late he has become a little more crowd-friendly
but previously, in his columns in the *Daily Telegraph* and elsewhere,
in his speeches in the Commons and on the hustings, and in his
interviews in the media Johnson never tired of reminding us that
he has acquired a skill that most of us will never master. He can

enrich his platitudes and shallow rhetoric with the magic dust of a dead language.

There are intriguing parallels between Johnson's and Orwell's experiences at Eton, at which both arrived aged thirteen. Johnson soon became secretary of the school debating society, editor of the school newspaper, and at seventeen, a member of the exclusive Eton Society, an elite-within-an-elite, whose members are allowed to wear multi-coloured waistcoats and houndstooth trousers rather than the black and pinstripe of the rest of the school. Members of the Society are familiarly known as 'Poppers', self-appointed prefects who monitor boys in chapel and at other formal gatherings and enforce discipline in ways that often seem arbitrary. It is informally accepted that Poppers can behave much as they wish to, including showing each other nepotistic favouritism during their school years and thereafter.

Orwell too entered Eton as part of an elite-within-an-elite. He arrived in 1917 as one of seventy King's Scholars, or 'Collegers'. Connolly described them as a kind of monastic order, conducting themselves in a manner that was as formal, hierarchical and ritualistic as the Spanish Court in the age of Velázquez. They lived in a house that was separate from the rest of the college, part-Victorian, part-Tudor. They were, to an extent, a society of their own with conventions and practices they closely guarded as a sign of their separateness from the rest of the College, which at the time numbered around 1,000 pupils.

Orwell, together with fellow Etonians Roger Mynors and Denys King-Farlow, set up the first independent school newspaper, initially called the *Election Times* – in reference to the internal electoral system by which the Collegers established their own hierarchical structure. It was a crude, hand-written affair sold exclusively to other Collegers for a penny, and in 1920 it gave way to *College Days*, commercially printed, sold within the College and also stocked for its snob-appeal by local newsagents. It carried paid-for advertisements from, amongst others, Pears Soap and Eno's Fruit Salts. Orwell was a regular contributor and King-Farlow later claimed that he and his partners made a profit of around £100 on the 1920 copies.

But while Johnson and Orwell seemed to enjoy the opportunities for self-advancement offered by this assembly of the elect, look closer and the apparent similarities between them begin to break down.

The Poppers come close to being a parody of the College they represent and the society their members will police and dominate following their departure. They are unapologetically and openly corrupt in terms of reserving places for those they assume will reward them in the future, or to whom they owe favours. They are a microcosm of the infrastructure that effectively regulates and governs Britain, from the political hierarchy through the judiciary to the arts and the media. Johnson was fully aware of this as he took his first step towards what he hoped would be ultimate power, and as this book goes to press he has become the leader of the Conservative Party and prime minister, carrying into his Cabinet those whose votes he had bought during the Commons stage of the party leadership election. Equally, his role as secretary of the debating society was his rehearsal for the Presidency of the Oxford Union, the breeding house for the barbed rhetorical exchanges of Commons debates, in which sound, fury and spittle displace anything resembling transparency or truth-telling. And as he took up the editorship of the school newspaper he did so with one eye on the organs of Tory propaganda. He has served as editor of the *Spectator* and writes a weekly column for the *Telegraph*, now regularly referred to as the 'Daily Borisgraph'. It is evident that the adolescent Leviathan has changed little during his journey into middle age. His insistence that the prorogation of Parliament has nothing to do with Brexit – delivered with an artful smile – and his addiction to dissembling at Prime Minister's Questions and during speeches delivered around the country demonstrate that he expects his listeners to share his disrespect for transparency. In the school that nurtured him there was, is, a conspiracy of entitlement.

Lies are the gift of the elite and everyone else has to put up with a conspiracy of untruth. Eton today has come to resemble the training camp for the Inner Party of *Nineteen Eighty-Four*, an assembly of figures who, for no other reason that they *belong*, seem able to control our destiny. The eventualities of the 2016 EU Referendum will leave an ineradicable imprint on our society for a generation, and what faces us was engineered exclusively, albeit sometimes haplessly, by Etonians. David Cameron initiated the Referendum, but not because he felt that those disgruntled by the EU should be allowed to speak for themselves. He took the result for granted and wanted in victory to muzzle the 'swivel-eyed' nutcases of UKIP who threatened the Tory command of the electorate. Cameron misread the mood of the country, but Johnson saw amongst the voters an inclination to accept self-delusion and fabrication. Jacob Rees-Mogg, leader of the Conservative European Research Group (ERG), was UKIP's ally in the Tory party and ensured that Theresa May would fail in her attempt to get a relatively merciful withdrawal agreement through the Commons. On becoming prime minister Johnson brought Rees-Mogg into the Cabinet as Leader of the House of Commons. His first initiative was to issue a code of practice for all answerable to him regarding unsuitable linguistic behaviour. Bad grammar seemed to Rees-Mogg to be the verbal equivalent of wearing a black tie before 6 p.m. The use of 'hopefully' as an adverb was outlawed despite it being a commonplace since the seventeenth century, and while he has yet to sentence transgressors to public canings these are early days. In March 2019 an Eton man, Sir Oliver Letwin, tabled an amendment to enable MPs to take over from the Executive; he came close but failed. During Johnson's coronation as the contestant almost certain to win favour amongst Tory MPs, the only person likely to cause party members to think again was another Old Etonian, Rory Stewart, engagingly eccentric and sometimes realistic but destined to extinction by his blustering co-Etonian rival. Stalinism was far more horrific than anything we are asked to confront today, but while Etonians don't despatch us to labour camps they do run our lives. Eton seems to incite profligate sovereignty, even beyond politics. Hugh Fearnley-Whittingstall did not choose Westminster as his route to power but he has shown an almost colonial tendency to own, command, or – more subtly – demand respect from places and people. 'River Cottage' is his oligarchy, something he has transformed and improved, and his prole-like neighbours appear suitably grateful.

Orwell paid his dues to the closed hierarchical society of Eton, while at the same time he subverted and mocked all that it represented. It was a tradition that on their arrival in the lower sixth form pupils would recite an extract from a work, usually a poem, that evoked their sense of optimism and courage as they entered the senior level of their esteemed College. Typically two of his peers chose Tennyson's 'Ulysses' and Matthew Arnold's 'The Scholar Gipsy'. Orwell recited a lengthy passage from Robert Louis Stevenson's novella *The Suicide Club*. The *Eton College Chronicle* was impressed by his delivery but appeared somewhat reluctant to comment on the suitability of the piece. The eponymous club is an occult group patronised by people of the moneyed classes and aristocrats. The act of suicide is not something that its members always undertake voluntarily but each seems aware that an organisation that involves at least the likelihood of self-inflicted death is somehow appropriate to their lifestyle and standing. Orwell must have taken some time in choosing a work that, to him at least, appeared so well suited to the club of which he was a member. One of Orwell's contemporaries at Eton was Sir Steven Runciman, a minor aristocrat who would become a distinguished historian. Much later when recalling their time together he presents Orwell as someone he found intriguing but whom he never really knew. 'Eric [had] much the most interesting personality. I enjoyed his company. His mind worked in rather different ways, his reactions were different from ordinary schoolboys … he loved airing his knowledge, particularly to the masters who were slightly shocked to find someone so well read.' But, 'he was a curious boy. He did not really *like* other people. He liked their intellectual side, someone to talk to, but friends didn't really mean anything to him.' (Meyers, 2000, p 35). Runciman's opinion that he 'did not really *like* other people' should be looked at in context, given that the 'other people' he appeared to dislike were his fellow Etonians.

Cyril Connolly and Orwell had formed an alliance of mild rebellion at St Cyprian's but the former suggests in *Enemies of Promise* that at Eton he had begun to detect something disagreeable in his erstwhile friend. He was, Connolly claimed, determinedly 'aloof' and self-contained. He spent his time 'perpetually sneering at "They" – a Marxist-Shavian concept which included Masters, Old Collegers, the Church, and Senior reactionaries'.

Orwell would welcome new boys with seemingly kind, avuncular enquiries as to their faith: 'Cyrenaic, Sceptic, Epicurean, Cynic, Neoplatonist, Confucian or Zoroastrian?' Puzzled by this catalogue of obscure and extinct avocations the youngsters, or most of them, would commit themselves to the one Orwell had left out: 'I'm a Christian!' to which he'd reply 'Oh, we haven't had that before.' Some might see this as absurdist humour but there is evidence to suggest that it was part of Orwell's contemptuous assault upon the intellectual laziness of the Christian establishment. He told a friend that 'there are at least six members of staff [clergymen] who make a very good living out of the Crucifixion. It's worth over £2,000 a year between them ... I reckon that must be the most profitably-exploited event in history – and they all have to talk as if they wish it hadn't happened.' (Meyers, 2000, p 34).

Among the staff, Orwell's counterpart as an outsider was Aldous Huxley, then unpublished. In his second novel, *Antic Hay* (1923), he tells of his despair at teaching at a public school, a thinly disguised version of Eton. His class of arrogant, aggressive pupils bully him and regard his willingness to espouse unorthodox ideas as a sign of weakness. Sir Steven Runciman recalled that 'He stood there, looking something of a martyr but at the same time extraordinarily distinguished.' According to Runciman the only pupil who went against the mob-rule tendency to humiliate and deprecate him was Orwell who enjoyed Huxley's 'use of *words*, the phrases he used and that was a thing that Eric Blair very much did appreciate … He rather stood up for Huxley because he found him interesting' and, as he might have put it, he recognised him as a fellow misfit.

Following the disclosure of the so-called 'Orwell's List' to the *Independent* in 1996 it became commonplace among politically correct liberals to treat him as homophobic. There are a number of occasions on which, in letters and conversation, he referred, less than favourably, to individuals as 'pansies' or 'nancy boys', notably the poets Stephen Spender and W. H. Auden. In 1949 his friend, the beautiful Celia Kirwan, to whom he once proposed marriage, asked him to prepare the 'list' of people he knew, or knew of, that he thought might be sympathetic to Stalin and the USSR. Kirwan worked for the Information Research Department (IRD), a part of the Foreign Office that was established to monitor, and counter, pro-Soviet propaganda; it was set up by the Labour government. Alongside the names on the list he appended very brief comments on his reason for including them and several, including Spender and also the politician Tom Driberg, were present because of their homosexual tendencies. Some commentators, including Paul Foot, Richard Gott and Alexander Cockburn, treated the list as proof that Orwell in middle age had become 'McCarthyite' and 'bigoted', particularly regarding his apparent implication that homosexuality inclined men towards treachery and left-wing extremism. Timothy Garton Ash has defended him, albeit half-heartedly, by suggesting that homosexuality, illegal in 1949, could have been used by Russian agents as a means of blackmailing their sympathisers. It should be pointed out that the purpose of the list was to advise the IRD on who could be trusted as writers of government-sponsored articles on what was soon to be the Cold War, that the IRD was not a branch of MI5 or MI6 and that those named by Orwell were in no danger of being monitored by the security services. They would simply not be considered as potential pro-government propagandists. Nonetheless, since the disclosure of the list there has been a general consensus that while Orwell might not have been rabidly homophobic, he harboured a few knee-jerk prejudices that were standard issue for white, middle-class men born in the Edwardian era.

I mention this because both his defenders and critics mislead us on it, as a number of incidents during Orwell's years at Eton show. Connolly would marry Jean Bakewell but he made no secret of his previous and ongoing homosexual relationships. Whether he was bisexual or whether Bakewell, slightly more affluent, provided him with the opportunity to maintain his itinerant, hedonistic lifestyle remains a matter for speculation. He had affairs with several boys at Eton, one in 1920 with the fourteen-year-old Christopher Eastwood. Orwell wrote to Connolly affirming that he too was attracted to this boy, three years his junior. The letter no longer exists but Connolly quoted it verbatim in a letter of his own to T. E. Beddard. Biographers have treated Connolly's report in an elephant-in-the-room manner – it exists but we'd prefer not to comment on it – for the simple reason that it is inexplicable. Neither prior to it nor later did Orwell disclose or show attraction to men and it is ludicrous to imagine that for three decades after Eton he remained devoutly in the closet. The letter reveals much, not because of what it says but in its manner. Connolly was bright, but Orwell outshone him spectacularly and the former's assumption, in the letter to Beddard, that his friend was attempting to steal his young lover is proof of his self-absorbed intellectual limitations. Throughout the letter, as quoted by Connolly, Orwell refers to him as 'proprietary', and it is evident – though apparently not to Connolly – that Orwell was turning himself into a caricature of the kind of boy who might have been envious of Connolly's success as a molester of juniors.

I am afraid I am gone on Eastwood (naughty Eric) ... I am not jealous of you (noble Eric). But you, though you aren't jealous, are apt to be what one might call 'proprietary'. (Shelden, p 76).

Orwell is playing the role of Connolly's rival while at the same time quietly mocking the system of bullying and 'owning' younger boys in Eton. Eastwood, shortly before he died in 1983, spoke of his memories of his Eton contemporaries, including Orwell. He confessed, with regret, that he had hardly known Orwell, by then a globally renowned author, but recalled him as a boy prone to 'standing aside from things a bit, observing – always observing'.

The Master in College, J. F. Crace, was a bachelor who, according to King-Farlow, had 'a tendency to be overfond of some boys'. Orwell devised an advertisement for *College Days* which read 'A.R.D. – After rooms – JANNEY'. Janney was the familiar version of Crace's Christian name which he invited his favourite pupils to use, especially during private tuition periods known as 'after rooms'. Orwell did not hate homosexuals per se, even the moderately paedophiliac types with a particular taste for younger men and teenagers. Rather, he was enraged by the appropriation of homosexuality by the upper classes as yet another affirmation of their immunity from the rules that everyone else had to observe.

Orwell regarded homosexuality not as something that repulsed him but as a further confirmation that those who went through St Cyprian's, Eton, Oxford and Cambridge could do as they wished with their assumed subordinates. He did not see being gay as an affirmation of liberalism but as a confirmation of privilege. The system of 'fagging' in public schools, particularly Eton, involved a micro-drama enacted by the apprentice ruling classes in preparation for adulthood. 'Fags' were always the youngest boys, treated by their elders as servants and, even in Orwell's times, obliged to deal with such humble tasks as boot-blacking, the brushing and laying out of clothes, and cooking breakfasts. If the senior, or 'fagmaster', thought his fag deserved a lesson in humiliation his duties might be extended to include the warming of lavatory seats or wiping the backside of his senior, post-defecation. Fags were also the victims of what we would today treat as sexual abuse. They were conditioned to obey orders from their seniors and therefore became easy targets for young men who wanted sex without the tiresome conventions of equality and consent.

In 1921, when he was eighteen, Orwell was charged by his fellow pupils for being late for prayers. His accusers alleged that this went beyond fecklessness, that he was making a deliberate protest against Anglicanism in particular and Christianity in general. Orwell's so-called equals, the 'super-seniors', condemned him to a flogging which would be delivered by a pupil of the same age; all involved were in their final year at Eton. Connolly seemed astonished and dumbfounded by Orwell's refusal to appeal against the verdict or to ask the masters to intervene in this case of an adult being assaulted by his peers. Orwell's biographers are equally puzzled by his decision to take the beating. His willingness to experience pain was not, however, some kind of perverse masochism. Entreating his fellow pupils for mercy involved a display of respect for the public school system that could take the law into its own hands. He wanted the boy, in fact the *man*, who beat him to recognise that assumed superiority was a short step from tyranny. When he wrote *Animal Farm* and *Nineteen Eighty-Four* he had witnessed terrifying spectacles in Spain, predicted the horrors of Fascism in Germany and had become contemptuous of the British left who thought that Stalin's communist regime was but a slightly flawed utopia. Long before this he had experienced a parochial, very English, brand of totalitarianism in Eton. He was overjoyed by the election of a post-war Labour government but angered by its apparent reluctance to eradicate aspects of British society that, in his view, buttressed its inequalities. Labour's decision not to abolish public schools enraged him.

Denys King-Farlow and Orwell did become friends, of sorts, but the former remained wary of and puzzled by him. Orwell's habit of mocking the visiting parents of fellow pupils seemed to King-Farlow arbitrary and unmotivated; he picked his targets at random rather than as a means of revenging himself against their particularly irritating offspring. King-Farlow regarded his 'jeering comments' as symptomatic of a general loathing for conventions. 'For my generation the precept of honouring your mother and father at least in public was very much ingrained in everyone.' But 'Blair', he reflected, 'always enjoyed playing the lone wolf'. At St Cyprian's Orwell had been bullied by an older boy who was athletically built and enjoyed displaying his talents for roughing-up his peers on the rugby field and in the boxing ring. In 'Such, Such Were the Joys' he recalled he'd taken revenge in a manner that most would have seen as unsportsmanlike. '[I] walked up to Burton with the most harmless air I could assume, and then, getting the weight of my body behind it, smashed my fist into his face.' Burton had to be treated by a local GP but felt too humiliated to name Orwell as the aggressor. Orwell repeated the exercise at Eton, laying out an unsuspecting senior boy who had been tormenting Connolly.

In the summer of 1920 he spent a week at the Eton Officer Training Corps (OTC) camp on Salisbury Plain and then joined his family who were on holiday at Looe in Cornwall. Having changed from his school uniform into an OTC second lieutenant's khaki kit he had to borrow casual clothes from friends of the family in Looe. For his return to Eton he dressed again in the OTC uniform but missed the connection at Plymouth railway station. With only a small amount of change he wandered the streets of the town, being mistaken on two occasions for a recently demobbed veteran of the war. He slept under a bridge and later that summer, in August, he wrote to Runciman, enthusing about his 'first adventure as an amateur tramp'. He commemorated the other aspect of the adventure, his being taken for a demobbed subaltern, in *Coming Up for Air* by having the recently commissioned George 'Tubby' Bowling receive 'a wire from the War Office telling [him] to take charge of the stores at Twelve Mile Dump [in Cornwall] and remain there till further notice', which he duly does, relieved at missing front line service in France. There's a degree of self-caricature here but the portrait of Bowling as an unheroic toiler serving well behind the lines carried other resonances. Richard, Orwell's father, decided in 1917 to seek an army commission and was, to everyone's amazement, accepted. He was sixty and, while no reliable records survive, thought to be the oldest subaltern in the services. He was assigned to the 51st India Labour Company in Marseilles and made chiefly responsible for the care and feeding of army mules. The first time Orwell saw him after the end of the war was during his visit to Cornwall.

The night in Plymouth enabled him for the first time, as an adult, to revisit the games of role-playing that he enjoyed so much as a child in Henley and Shiplake and which had allowed him some relief from a home life that discomforted and frustrated him. The week after his return he inscribed a copy of a book with 'Presented to College Reading Room, June 1920, by E. A. Blair'. It sat on the shelf where he had placed it, apparently unopened, until in 1972 a boy flicked through it, read the inscription and recognised its significance. It is a seemingly random collection of works by Shaw called *Misalliance, the Dark Lady of the Sonnets, and Fanny's First Play, with a Treatise on Parents and Children*. The literary pieces are of slight significance and we have to wonder why Orwell thought the volume would interest his successors at his alma mater, at least until we reach the essay with which it closes, the *Treatise on Parents and Children*, particularly the explosive sub-sections called 'School':

> None of my schoolmasters really cared a rap (or perhaps it would be fairer to them to say that their employers did not care a rap and therefore did not give them the necessary caring powers) whether I learnt my lessons or not, provided my father paid my schooling bill, the collection of which was the real object of the school ... My schooling did me a great deal of harm and no good whatsoever: it was simply dragging a child's soul through the dirt ...
>
> And this is what happens to most of us. We are not effectively coerced to learn: we stave off punishments as far as we can by lying and trickery and guessing and using our wits.

Shaw's most memorable passage involves his comparison of school with prison:

> But it is in some respects more cruel than prison. In a prison, for instance, you are not forced to read books written by the wardens and the governor … and beaten or otherwise tormented if you cannot remember their utterly unmemorable contents. In the prison you are not forced to sit listening to turnkeys discoursing without charm or interest on subjects that they don't understand and don't care about, and are therefore incapable making you understand or care about.

All of Orwell's contemporaries at Eton judged him to be intellectually gifted, if unorthodox, and most of his tutors, notably Andrew Gow, felt that he was extraordinarily clever but calculatedly feckless. In the exams that ended the school year in 1920 he came 117th out of the 140 boys in the lower sixth form. Among the King's Scholars who sat for examinations that year he was last. This did not mean that he had excluded himself from Oxford or Cambridge. In 1920–21 neither university was particularly concerned with the documented academic credentials of their freshmen; however, Orwell would need to obtain a scholarship to enter a college, given his family's modest financial state. He had expressed his contempt for Eton by showing indifference to its examinations but there was no reason why he could not marshal his considerable talents to win an Oxbridge scholarship. Oxford, for some reason, was regarded as his most suitable destination and there are conflicting accounts of why he did not even try for a place. Jacintha Buddicom later recounted how Ida and her own mother had made a 'vigorous' case to Richard Blair that his son should be encouraged to go for a scholarship. Gow, when consulted by Blair senior on the matter had allegedly told him that 'Eric did not stand a chance of getting a scholarship,' but we have to consider this alongside Gow's other comments on Orwell's apparent brilliance.

Perhaps Gow's comment almost sixty years later sheds some light on this: Orwell he reflected, would have 'brought disgrace on the College [because] he had done absolutely no work for five years'. Gow didn't think that Orwell was beneath the standards required of Oxford scholarship undergraduates; quite the contrary. But he wanted to punish him – deny him the opportunity of Oxford – because of his rebellious attitude towards Eton and all it stood for.

3

BURMA

A question raised and then brushed over by Orwell's biographers is why he became a member of the Indian Imperial Police Force in Burma. Shelden cites a recollection of Jacintha Buddicom that Richard Blair was determined that his son should follow him as a member of the Colonial Service. Given Richard's general indifference to whatever his son got up to and his enervated state of mind it is difficult to imagine that he would insist on anything. No one else remarked on him playing any part in Orwell's decision to go abroad and Orwell himself never commented on why he did so.

When he rejoined his family after Eton they had moved from Shiplake to the seaside town of Southwold on the Suffolk coast. It was a popular resort for middle-class retirees, particularly those who had worked on the Indian sub-continent. In January 1922 Orwell registered at 'Craighurst', a crammer designed to coach young men for entry-level examinations for all manner of professional careers, including the civil service. It was certainly not exclusively dedicated to preparation for a life in the Colonial Services, and the purpose of his enrolment was only evident to Orwell's friends and family when he took the train to London in June to sit for examinations at the Civil Service Commission – and even then he only disclosed the specific nature of his application when he returned to Southwold. He was, he announced, hoping to become an officer in the Indian Imperial Police Force. Much of the examinations curriculum was ludicrously irrelevant to maintaining order in the Oriental colonies. Technical Drawing hinted at pragmatism but its relevance to the policing of an indigenous population remained open to speculation. English (principally literature), History (British and European), Geography (begrudgingly global) and Maths might well, in the deranged conceptions of Empire builders, have been thought useful as a means by which colonial subjects could be improved by those who policed them. But it is difficult to see how an officer's proven expertise in Greek, Latin and French would cause the natives of Bangalore to treat him with greater respect. Orwell recorded the highest score in Latin among those who sat the examinations and came bottom in the only non-written examination, horse-riding.

Steven Runciman recalled that at Eton '[Orwell] used to talk about the East a great deal, and I always had the impression that he was longing to go back there ... It was a sort of romantic idea.' (Shelden, p 86). It is difficult to imagine any 'longing' on Orwell's part to 'go back' to a place where he had spent only the first twelve months of his life. His cultivation of a 'romantic idea' of 'the East' could well have been a parodic jibe at his friend's precocious affection for the Byzantine period and the Orient, subjects in which he would become a renowned scholar. He was playing games with Runciman's perception of him, much as he did with most of his peers at Eton.

There is no evidence that Orwell aspired to follow in his father's footsteps. Indeed there is no record of any of the Blair family or anyone who knew them speaking or writing of Richard's career in India. Orwell himself, in a brief autobiographical note in 1947, wrote of his father's years as 'an official in the English administration' of India but said nothing more specific. Ida would have known of his role as a late-Victorian equivalent of a heroin dealer, albeit fully sanctioned by the authorities, and it is difficult to imagine that Orwell remained ignorant of what exactly his father did.

Up to this point, his nineteenth year, Orwell had shown an increasing tendency towards disrespecting and sometimes treating with contempt the orthodoxies of the British establishment and middle-class life. It thus seems unlikely that he was motivated to enrol for the Colonial Police Force as an act of patriotism, let alone paternal allegiance. His decision to go to Burma, rather than the far more agreeable environment of India, is equally fascinating. From his brief period of training he would have known how the various parts of the Empire had been acquired and as a consequence how they were governed, and even though these apprentice servants of the imperial enterprise would not have been encouraged to make moral judgments it would have been evident to all that Burma had experienced an extraordinary history of ruthless suppression. Britain had fought two wars against the Burmese in the early to mid-nineteenth century, mostly as a means of ensuring that the country would remain supplicant as a trading hub adjacent to the far more significant Indian sub-continent. In the 1860s however, a British Expeditionary Force, led by Sir Harry Prendergast and acting on the orders of Lord Randolph Churchill, had brushed aside all military resistance and demanded immediate and unconditional surrender from the Burmese king, Thibaw, who would spend the rest of his life exiled in India. Rather than imposing a protectorate with a proxy administration answerable to Westminster, or even governing the territory by direct rule from a body in London specifically responsible for the country, Churchill turned the area into a money-making enterprise. There was a police force which was, when Orwell decided to move there, made up of 13,000 men, largely British officers and mixed other ranks, mostly Indians, and this was also effectively the country's government. No other body of administration existed to decide on how the indigenous population should exist or what their future might involve. Burmese small traders, fishermen and farmers were, within limits, allowed to conduct their business – otherwise the population would go naked or starve – but aside from these economic contingencies the nation was an early twentieth-century version of a slave plantation.

Orwell had chosen his location with masochistic precision. He knew he was on his way to a version of Conrad's *Heart of Darkness.*

Two events are referred to dutifully by his biographers. On his liner the SS *Herefordshire* he witnessed the British quartermaster furtively stealing a custard cake. On the high seas this was class discrimination writ large: the quartermaster, the worker, was not starving, but his envy of the passengers who consumed such delicacies caused him to risk humiliation and punishment. Next, when the liner docked in Ceylon, Orwell saw a coolie, a native Indian/Sri Lankan, mishandle and drop the luggage of a party of disembarking Europeans. The young man was brutally kicked by a police sergeant who was supervising the arrival of the ship, to the applause of all the white passengers who witnessed the assault. Orwell recorded these events in 1940 and 1947 respectively but we have no reason to suspect that he had made use of his twenty years of accumulated anti-colonialism and guilt to displace teenage indifference. He began his first novel only six years after his return from colonial service; *Burmese Days* is driven by a virulent loathing for the whites who administered the country. Ellis is a violent, racist manager of a timber company and Lieutenant Verrall a military policeman of aristocratic background who treats the other Europeans as only slightly superior to the Burmese. When Ellis learns that Verrall, who is not a member of the run-down European Club, has kicked the Indian butler for failing to put ice in his whisky and soda, a darkly farcical exchange takes place:

'Who are *you* to come kicking our servants?'

'Bosh my good chap. Needed kicking. You've let your servants get out of hand here.'

'You damned, insolent young tick, what's it got to do with *you* if he needed kicking? You're not even a member of this Club. It's our job to kick the servants, not yours.'

It is almost certain that Orwell used the incident he witnessed in Ceylon as the basis for this. On the liner the sergeant acts according to the roles designated by the social and ethnic hierarchy: the middle-class, white passengers could hardly be expected to kick the coolie themselves. In the novel Orwell injects a brilliant note of caricature into the scenario as the two men argue over which of them has the right – by membership of the Club, or by virtue of aristocratic hauteur – to do the kicking.

In November 1922 Orwell enrolled at the Burma Provincial Police Training School in Mandalay. His training would involve nine months of instruction in law, languages (mostly the basics of the predominant local language), police accounts and procedure. After that he would spend fifteen months on probation at his first posting in the frontier outpost of Myaungmya. Aged twenty he was expected to run the headquarters and the region, since the notoriously indolent Superintendent of the Police spent most of his time touring the locality in his car, with his servants, shooting wildlife. Orwell oversaw the headquarters staff of more than forty men, supervised the recruitment and training of constables from the indigenous population and was responsible for arranging police escorts for trials. Most importantly he was responsible for planning night patrols. The British were primarily concerned with the protection and profitable management of their own enterprises, notably oil and timber. As a result officers such as Orwell, stationed in the hinterland, were expected only to ensure that the anarchic condition of these regions remained self-contained and did not encroach on the urban centres inhabited by the Europeans. There were some anti-colonial activists abroad but they were of slight significance compared with internecine violence and outright criminality. The night patrols in Orwell's district were sent out as an attempt to subdue the so-called 'dacoit' gangs. These groups of men would burgle the houses of families in other villages, and their sense of being ungoverned, aside from the peripheral presence of the colonial police, caused them to commit horrific crimes against those who resisted them, including burning opponents to death. Patrols were comprised of locally recruited constables who made only token attempts to apprehend the dacoits; they feared for their own safety.

His next posting in 1924 was to Twante, a location even more remote than Myaungmya. Aside from his senior officer there were only two or three Europeans in the area. Orwell spent much of his time travelling from village to village and acting as an intermediary in disputes on alleged criminal acts or matters of ownership that could no longer be dealt with by tribal headsmen – the latter were now subject to British jurisdiction. Two years after leaving school he had become a colonial autocrat, able to impose rulings on matters that affected the lives of his subjects and largely accountable to no one but himself.

A year later his next position, in Syriem, drew him closer to the European infrastructures of the colony. It was only ten miles by river from Rangoon, which Orwell visited regularly to dine in restaurants, visit acquaintances from the Training School – he had few 'friends' – and most of all to call in at Smart and Mookerdum's bookshop where the latest novels and collections of verse arrived from London, albeit several months after publication. Three further postings after Syriem, at Insein, Moulmein and Katha, shifted him closer still to Eurocentric urban areas, each surrounded by lush tropical forests, which would provide the setting for *Burmese Days*.

Orwell's maternal grandmother, Mrs Limouzin, lived in Moulmein in great comfort, one might say luxury, as did his aunt who was married to a major figure in the forestry service. The Limouzin family had been in Burma before the British began to make colonial inroads in 1824, prior to the accession of Queen Victoria. They made a considerable fortune exporting teak and other hard woods to European furniture producers but much of this was lost during a period of rash speculation on the rice market. Nonetheless in the 1920s they remained within the top ten per cent of the wealthiest Europeans. A street in Moulmein was named after the family. Much later one of Orwell's colleagues recalled coming across him at a social event with two older ladies, one of whom asked him about 'Eric's prospects'. This is the only piece of flimsy circumstantial evidence that Orwell made an attempt to contact his mother's family. If the two ladies were his aunt and grandmother it is odd that he did not introduce them as such to his colleague.

Despite living within a mile of his grandmother's house for six months during his period in Burma, not once does Orwell refer to her by name in either his published or unpublished writing or in any recollected conversations thereafter. His only recorded reference to her was to a correspondent, twenty years later: 'My grandmother lived forty years in Burma and at the end could not speak a word of Burmese – typical of the ordinary Englishwoman's attitude [and the] disgusting social behaviour of the British.' Orwell would have known her by reputation – everyone in the town did, especially for her select parties and her refusal to acknowledge that the non-Europeans spoke different languages – and a few years later a figure who closely resembles her would feature in his work. Mrs Lackersteen (surname only) of *Burmese Days* is a sniffy, etiolated memsahib, 'yellow and thin, scandalmongering over cocktails – living twenty years in the country without learning a word of the language'.

In Twante Orwell attended the village churches of the Karens, a tribe which originated in China. Many were converted to Christianity by missionaries in the mid-nineteenth century. Orwell had gone to chapel services at Eton because he had no choice and by 1924 his interest in Christianity was slight; he was certainly not a regular churchgoer. His purpose was to mix with the locals and he began to communicate reasonably fluently with the Karens in their own language, or rather languages, a collage of linguistic variants for which there were no printed guides in English.

Roger Beadon was the same age as Orwell, a fellow police trainee, and they remained in regular contact throughout the latter's years abroad. Beadon recalls Orwell's ability to mix easily with the local population.

> We saw each other every day [at the training school], we attended instructions in law, Burmese and Hindustani ... But what shattered me more than anything else was that, whereas I found it [learning the languages of the locals and socialising with them] difficult, it didn't seem to worry him at all ... before he left Burma, he was able to go into a Hpongyi Kyaung, which is one of those Burmese temples, to converse in a very high-flown Burmese with the Hpongyis, or priests, and you've got to be able to speak Burmese very well to be able to do that. (Crick, p 148).

He was, as Beadon indicates, deliberately setting himself against the standard expatriate attitude to the native Burmese population. Even those who stopped short of treating the Burmese with brutality and contempt foreswore actually mixing with them, let alone absorbing their languages and culture. Beadon also presents a portrait of Orwell as a man who had decided from the start to avoid becoming part of the social circuit of the Europeans:

> He didn't speak very much about his past ... he was very quiet ... he was a very pleasant fellow to know, but he kept very much to himself. I was fond of going down to the club and playing snooker and dancing and what have you, but this didn't seem to appeal to him at all, he wasn't what I would call a socialite in any way, in fact I don't think he went to the club very much ... I think he mostly read ... or stayed up in his room. (Crick, p 144).

Despite Beadon's impression of Orwell as an introvert he did, during their first months in Mandalay, 'socialise' but his choice of company was unorthodox to say the least. In *Burmese Days* Mandalay is described by the narrator as 'a rather disagreeable town – it is dusty and intolerably hot, and it is said to have five main products all beginning with P, namely, pagodas, pariahs, pigs, priests and prostitutes', but the novel's author seemed more content with the place, seeking out areas of the city, and their personnel, that suited his temperament. He wandered through districts inhabited only by the Burmese and sometimes visited women specified by the final 'P'. He was particularly interested in a legendary figure spoken of at the training school as a man who had gone beyond native. H. R. Robinson was a former Indian army captain who had been dismissed from his position in the Burma police service for behaviour deemed to bring it into disrepute. He had associated regularly with the native Burmese populace, befriended local men, had affairs with women, and by the time he reached Mandalay, become an opium-addict. Orwell sought his company with the same perverse determination with which he avoided that of his aunt and grandmother. The European establishment treated Robinson as a dissolute hedonist but Orwell was not trying to become a fellow traveller in depravity. Rather, he was fascinated by stories of the earlier Robinson, or 'Robbie' as he was known. When Robinson served as a magistrate in North Borneo he had slept with a native woman accused of murdering her husband. She admitted to him that she was guilty and explained why, in terms of Buddhist 'right mindfulness', the act was justified. She was acquitted and Robinson became a devotee of Buddhism. The apparent motive for Orwell's determination to become fluent in Burmese, so that he could talk with Buddhist monks, left Beadon dumbfounded. Orwell was prompted to do so by Robinson, not because he wished to espouse Buddhism, but rather because he was fascinated by Robinson's hybridised Western version. This involved nothing resembling self-denial – aside from his opium habit Robinson had taken on a regular Burmese concubine and drank anything available. Two years after they first met, when Orwell had departed for remote postings, Robinson decided on a shortcut to nirvana, a mystical state in which one is released from such carnal instincts as desire and even inclinations involving love and commitment. The most elementary English translation of nirvana is 'to blow out' and, in 1924, this is what Robinson attempted to do, literally, by shooting himself in the head with his old service revolver. He recovered, although he managed to remove both of his eyes, and survived in a state of fatalistic contentment until 1965 when, in a North London suburb, he finally succeeded in taking his own life. Orwell admired him greatly though he rarely spoke of their friendship to his colleagues in the police force or to other Europeans he met in Burma, and only publicly disclosed their association when he reviewed Robinson's memoir in 1942 and confessed he was 'glad to receive evidence of his continued existence'. Robinson was Orwell's anti-establishment talisman. He had not as yet decided on how he would make use of his equally contrarian inclinations, but he was concerned with little else.

In Burma Orwell began to adopt different personae, sometimes acting out fundamentally opposed states. In 1925 Christopher Hollis passed through Rangoon on his way back to London from an Oxford Union debating tour of Australia and New Zealand and was told that Orwell, who had been two years ahead of him at school, was stationed close by. Hollis sought out his fellow Old Etonian, and much later, in the mid-1950s, recalled their conversation:

> In the side of him which he revealed to me at that time there was no trace of liberal opinions. He was at pains to be the imperial policeman, explaining that these theories of no punishment and no beating were all very well at public schools but that they did not work with the Burmese ... He had an especial hatred ... for the Buddhist priests, against whom he thought violence especially desirable – and that not for any theological reason but because of their sniggering insolence. (Crick, p 159).

In 1956, when he published this, Hollis was a Conservative MP with well-established opinions against the dissolution of the Empire and on the evils of socialism, but he was also fully aware that Orwell was equally well known as someone who had expressed his contempt for colonialism.

We have no reason to doubt the authenticity of his account of their conversation but what is equally evident is that Orwell was playing Hollis for a fool. He was fully aware of the reactionary Old Etonian's views on British rule in Burma and he fed him similarly intransigent prejudices. Why? Orwell already had literary ambitions. In Burma he produced several poems which mocked the knee-jerk racism of the Europeans, and fragments survive, written on imperial police stationery, of what appears to be a piece of Burma-set prose fiction. For Hollis he reinvented himself as everything he loathed, much in the manner that a novelist would make nastiness believable. He was rehearsing in real life the more ghastly aspects of *Burmese Days*. Several years earlier he had played the same trick against Cyril Connolly at Eton, involving the latter's use of privilege to force himself on younger boys.

When Beadon visited Orwell, uninvited, at his house in Insein he caught a glimpse of the figure who had isolated himself from the culture of expatriate clubs. 'He had goats, geese, ducks and all sorts of things floating about downstairs … it rather shattered me, but apparently he liked that – and that was his sort of idea of … Oh, of living naturally as some people call it … Not going native mind. I don't mean that; more "bohemian"… Didn't seem to give a damn … Seemed a ruddy mess to me.' (Crick, p 163). This was Orwell's version of going not-quite-native, a nod of respect towards Robbie, but something he tried to keep to himself. In his essay 'Shooting an Elephant' (1936) he wrote:

> In Moulmein, in Lower Burma, I was hated by large numbers of people … in an aimless, petty kind of way anti-European feeling was very bitter. No one had the guts to raise a riot, but if a European woman went through the bazaars alone somebody would probably spit betel juice over her dress. As a police officer I was an obvious target and was baited whenever it seemed safe to do so …

The subtext is clear. Along with the hint of guilt and self-loathing comes a sense of bitterness. 'In the end the sneering yellow faces of young men that met me everywhere, the insults hooted after me when I was at a safe distance, got badly on my nerves.' In other words: I deserved it but resented it too – out of this conflict, involving guilt, conscience and a grim legacy bred into him from his father, his mother's family and his school, comes Flory, the anti-hero of *Burmese Days*. Flory, like his author, hates the colonial system that pays his salary and obliges him to associate with sadistic racists. But he does not quite have the courage to act on his feelings. He loathes his work as a timber merchant who has exploited the natural resources of Burma; a trade by which Orwell's maternal ancestors built their fortune. He 'goes native' by taking a Burmese mistress but seeks recognition by the colonial establishment in his pursuit of Elizabeth Lackersteen, a girl from a wealthy European family. After his Burmese mistress discloses his secrets in front of a church congregation, he shoots himself – the parallels with Robinson's failed attempt are not coincidental. Robinson beguiled Orwell because he had gone native but not by default. It was his decision to befriend and have relationships with the Burmese and he did so openly, accepting his dismissal from the service as a natural consequence of his actions. His attempted suicide was not brought on by shame or his sense of feeling excluded from the European establishment. He had spent several years trying to seek out his own quasi-Buddhist version of the secret of the universe with the assistance of opium-induced trances but after each, when he 'came down', he found that the elusive nirvana had disappeared. Eventually he gave up and sought it out in whatever state awaited him after death. Robinson might appear ludicrous to some, but Orwell saw him as heroic because he had rejected the orthodoxies of the colonial ruling class while refusing to conceal his other life. He was the antithesis of Flory and as such his inspiration.

The characters and many of the events that make up *Burmese Days* were distilled from what Orwell had witnessed, heard and experienced, but the book is not in the strictest sense of the word 'true'. But what of his two other famous accounts of his time in Burma, 'Shooting an Elephant' and 'A Hanging'? Both were published as travel essays (respectively in 1936 and 1931), but many commentators have brought into question their authenticity as stories of actual events. This is partly because there is little documentary evidence to substantiate Orwell's accounts. Biographers seem especially troubled by the manner in which Orwell tells us what occurred. Both essays are 'literary' in the sense that Orwell deploys his considerable skills as a prose stylist to bring the figures involved alive and to convey to the reader the emotional dilemmas he faces and cannot properly resolve. 'A Hanging' is the most problematic in this regard because we join the narrator, Orwell, as he and his fellow officers convey the condemned man to the gallows and watch the execution:

> It is curious but till that moment I had never realised what it means to destroy a healthy, conscious man. When I saw the prisoner step aside to avoid the puddle, I saw the mystery, the unspeakable wrongness, of cutting a life short when it is in full tide. This man was not dying, he was alive just as we were alive. All the organs of his body were working – bowels digesting food, skin renewing itself, nails growing, tissues forming – all toiling away in solemn foolery. His nails would still be growing when he stood on the drop, when he was falling through the air with a tenth of a second to live.

As we follow this man to his death, Orwell quite brilliantly weaves into the account details that are both mundane and horrifying, particularly the 'large woolly' stray dog that 'pranced round us … made a dash for the prisoner … and … tried to lick his face'.

There are hundreds of other stories by Orwell about his experiences as a tramp, a miner, a hop-picker and a fighter in Spain which he offers to us as transparent and genuine and where we

take his honesty on trust. Why is it, then, that 'A Hanging' – and
slightly less so 'Shooting an Elephant' – have proved so magnetic
to commentators seemingly obsessed with the distinction between
truth and believability? I am convinced that Orwell attended the
hanging reported in the essay. The most telling circumstantial
evidence for this is that all new police officers in Burma were
expected to witness an execution as a macabre form of initiation,
a rite of passage designed to numb their potentially hazardous
sensitivities – all of the individuals executed in the country in the
1920s were Burmese, Indian or Chinese. More significantly, why
did he write about it? The critic David Lodge was so impressed by
the quality of the piece, and its capacity to make us feel as though
we are present, that he wonders if it should be treated as a short
story, irrespective of what Orwell actually saw. Much later, in 'Why
I Write', Orwell tells how in *Homage to Catalonia* he conveyed
unpleasant truths about his experiences in Spain. 'I did try very
hard in it to tell the whole truth without violating my literary
instincts ... If I had not been angry ... I should never have written
the book.' This is equally relevant to 'A Hanging'. What he saw that
day convinced him that capital punishment was vile and inhumane,
as much a disgrace to those who approved and perpetrated it as a
hideous experience for the condemned. He used his best resources
as a writer to force anyone who reads it to feel they too are there
on that day, to become a proxy witness and to confront themselves
with a question. How would we feel if we were Orwell, witness to
and complicit in the killing of 'a healthy conscious man'? This is why
so many commentators have been magnetised and discomforted by
the piece. They have been obliged to face this dilemma, to cross the
line between reading the story and becoming, like its author, part of
the dreadful act of judicial killing. Orwell brings us in – some might
say ghoulishly – and won't allow us to leave.

Orwell is a writer for our time because the issues he foregrounded
and tackled in his work are timeless. Of the 193 members of the
United Nations, twenty-three states retain the option of execution

for murder or other crimes. More than two thirds of these are constitutionally aligned towards a religious doctrine, predominantly Islam, but in statistical terms China – still a quasi-Maoist tyranny despite its economic power – by far exceeds any other nation in terms of the number of people killed by state authority (more than one thousand in 2017). In the so-called 'first world' of economically advanced countries who have supposedly improved themselves since the Enlightenment and the Second World War in terms of thoughtful humanitarianism, the US stands out as the robust defender of the right to kill its own citizens.

The last execution in the UK took place in 1964 and the following year capital punishment was abolished for murder. In 2003 the abolition of the death penalty became a basic precondition for membership of the EU. One of the most widely quoted mantras among Leave supporters during and after the 2016 Referendum has been 'taking back control'. Five UKIP MEPs, one of whom was, briefly, the party leader, have been outspoken supporters of the UK making use of its 'independence' from the EU as a route to restoring hanging. A large number of supporters of Farage's new Brexit Party maintain that this is a key element of our new separateness. A YouGov poll in 2017 showed that fifty-three per cent of Leave voters, irrespective of their other political allegiances, were pro-death penalty, and a poll held by Queen Mary University, London, in 2018 found that fifty-four per cent of members of the Conservative Party were in favour of the return of the death penalty. The present Home Secretary, Priti Patel, is a populist Brexit supporter who announced her support for capital punishment shortly after her election as an MP; of late she has been obliged to renounce her avocation but only as a token gesture towards the liberal consensus. There is a clear correlation between the 'taking back control' state of mind and a commitment to reaffirming our right to execute people.

Orwell in 'England Your England' (*The Lion and the Unicorn*, 1941) foresaw Brexit and the mindset of largely working-class UKIP supporters. '[T]he famous "insularity" and "xenophobia" of the English is far stronger in the working class than in the bourgeoisie ... The English working class are outstanding in their abhorrence of foreign habits ... the insularity of the English, their refusal to take foreigners seriously, is a folly that has to be paid for very heavily from time to time.' I'll say much more on this later but I bring it up now because 'A Hanging' is not just an account of men perpetrating a terrible act against a fellow human being. Orwell does not tell us outright that the condemned is a non-European. Rather, we learn of this through nuances and most of all from the subtly implied mannerisms of the Westerners involved in the execution: they behave less as though they're killing a man than a member of a sub-species. In 'Shooting an Elephant' he invites us, implicitly, to compare his killing of this elegant docile creature with his account of the hanging. He clearly feels distaste for the Burmese spectators, 'the sea of yellow faces ... all happy and excited over this bit of fun ...' There is a suggestion here of a scale of superiority, with the Europeans at the top, animals – such as the elephant – at the bottom, and the indigenous population somewhere in between, but tinged with elements of the human and the bestial.

We, he implies, have the right to treat the locals as animals, and as a consequence they establish their own status by imitating us when they take pleasure in the killing of an elephant, their inferior. When Orwell returns to the officers' mess a number of his colleagues tell him that 'it was a damn shame to shoot an elephant for killing a coolie, because an elephant was worth more than any damn Coringhee coolie'. If you systematically dehumanise people you become the equivalent of an animal.

There is a close correlation between the notion of racial superiority implicit in colonialism and the desire by many to retain or restore capital punishment. In the first instance what we might crudely refer to as civilisation, a collective sense of the intrinsically just set against the innately evil, has resulted in a global consensus on race and colonialism: both are seen as ineluctably loathsome at least among those who do not seek fame via ludicrous extremism. In the second there is no such consensus. Opinions on capital punishment transcend boundaries between nations and political ideologies. States which maintain the death penalty might be in a minority but they and the citizens of other nations who advocate its return share a sense of making a stand against an interfering, sometimes alien, liberal establishment. This was a notable feature of the Referendum Leave campaign in which the European Court of Human Rights was presented as having undermined the independence of the British judiciary, and indeed the law-making provision of Parliament. For example, Paul Nuttall MEP, one-time leader of UKIP, was happy to appear in the media and volunteer as the executioner of convicted child killers. The question of whether colonialism or the concept of racial superiority is acceptable is no longer seriously raised, or at least those who raise it are no longer bestowed respect. But with the death penalty there are still a considerable number of individuals and nations who endorse its implementation and who are treated with grudging tolerance. For Orwell the execution of a man and the social and political acceptance of the evils that come with colonialism were interwoven. He did not believe that any decent human society could abolish one and not the other because both were based on the premise that one group could treat a person in a manner that is self-evidently cruel and inhumane. The following is from his final notebook of 1949.

> When a murderer is hanged, there is only one person present at the ceremony who is not guilty of murder. The hangman, the warders, the governor, the doctor, the chaplain [in the margin: 'other prisoners?'] – they are all guilty: but the man standing on the drop is innocent. Everyone who has ever seen an execution knows this, and indeed even the public which gloats over the reports in the *News of the World* knows it after a fashion; the vast bulk of what is said is simply a hypercritical [sic] cover for

continuing to enjoy the pleasures of being guilty and indulging in murder, while remaining respectable.

'A Hanging' is about the grotesque, immoral parallels between colonialism and capital punishment. In the late 1940s when he wrote this he foresaw the tensions between self-aggrandisement and self-pity that afflict Britain now; he knew that the Empire was over. Today we still regard the Commonwealth as some kind of guarantee of our past grandeur: we don't govern them anymore but perhaps they'll rescue us from being part of a club of lesser nations otherwise known as the EU, and, for some, Brexit will enable us to enjoy the 'pleasures of being guilty and indulging in murder': the European Court of Human Rights and the EU will no longer prevent us from treating judicial killing as a political option.

Orwell wrote in 'Shooting an Elephant' of his hatred of the job he was doing and his rejection of the racial intolerance it involved.

> ... I had already made up my mind that imperialism was an evil thing and the sooner I chucked up my job and got out of it the better ... The wretched prisoners huddling in the stinking cages of the lock-ups, the grey, cowed faces of the long-term convicts, the scarred buttocks of the men who had been flogged with bamboos – all those oppressed me with an intolerable sense of guilt.

In early 1927, after serving for five years, Orwell was due for leave, which he took. He opted for sick-leave, stating dengue fever as the cause, probably because he could then cite this as the reason for his departure from the police and avoid unnecessary paperwork. Once back in England he tendered his resignation later that year.

4

SLUMMING IT

Anyone treating Orwell's expressions of guilt and shame regarding Burma as cases of false contrition should look at his behaviour once he returned to England in 1927. After five years of service his salary was £660, roughly forty per cent above his father's reasonably comfortable pension. He could have extended his sick leave on full salary until the end of March 1928, but instead he requested that his resignation should take effect at the earliest opportunity on 1 January. He had no other plans for gainful employment and he was deliberately denying himself £165. He did not hate the Colonial Police Service quite enough to risk becoming destitute but he was not prepared to take any more of its money than he needed simply to survive during the first few months of his time in England.

His family, still in Southwold, were shocked by the changes in him. He'd grown a moustache and was much thinner, and from the sharply defined bone structure of his face he appeared to have aged, appearing at least ten years older than the teenager who had gone out East in 1922. Also he was distracted, seeming almost feckless, caring little about his clothes and appearance and prone to treating the Blair household as a necessary stop-over, and not a place he would have chosen to live. He rarely joined his parents and sister Avril for meals, and left cigarettes burning in ashtrays and half-consumed snacks on tables. His father was disappointed at his decision to leave the Colonial Service and dismayed that he had no plans for another career, but worse was to come. When he announced to his parents that he intended to become a writer, his father and mother were, according to Avril, 'rather horrified'. Later, an acquaintance of Richard Blair recalled that he had expressed disgust at his son's decision to become 'a dilletante'.

Later that summer, out of politeness, Orwell joined the family for a holiday in Cornwall and in autumn visited the Buddicoms in Shropshire, although Jacintha was away. Later their aunt Lilian, in whose house they were staying, described Orwell as 'very different'. Esmé May, then twelve, was the daughter of the Blair's daily helper and cleaner, and regarded the family as 'high class' and Richard as 'a gentleman'. The son, however, she found to be 'a loner ... not quite there'. Once term began in Cambridge Orwell arranged to visit his ex-Eton tutor Gow who had become a Fellow of Trinity. Gow welcomed him briefly in his rooms and then took him to dinner at High Table. According to his later recollections the sole purpose of Orwell's visit was to inform him of his decision to become a writer and to seek basic advice as to how to establish himself in the profession. Gow might seem an odd choice in this respect because in 1927 he had not yet published anything – it would not be until the 1930s that he produced edited versions of the texts of ancient Greek poets such as Theocritus and Nicander, not the sort of thing that anyone apart from other classical scholars would read, let alone buy.

Gow told Orwell that it would probably be a good idea for him to make contact with members of the literary establishment – editors of magazines and newspapers, commissioning editors for book publishers and so on. 'I said in a rather non-committed way that he might as well have a try.' In other words Gow, good-naturedly enough, provided the same kind of common sense platitudes that Orwell might have received had he sought advice from a stranger on the train to Cambridge. The whole episode is dutifully recounted by biographers but without comment, probably because it appears faintly bizarre, rather like a passage abandoned by Wodehouse because of its lack of humour and credibility. In my view the strange

visit was part of Orwell's private rite of passage. All he did was to
announce to Gow his decision on his future, with the enquiry on his
thoughts as a polite addendum. He would cross paths, sometimes
befriend, quite a number of his Eton contemporaries later in life
but he did so, mostly during the war years, when he had no other
option – they and others like them ran the cultural establishment.
Orwell was trying to say goodbye to all that he had been, much of
which he had come to loathe, and to prepare himself for something
very different.

As soon as he returned to Southwold Orwell wrote to a friend
of the family, Ruth Pitter, whom he'd met only once and briefly,
asking if she could find him a room to rent in West London. Pitter
and her friend Kathleen O'Hara lived in Notting Hill. The letters
do not survive but it is evident from Pitter's later account to Crick
that he had made it clear that he was unable to afford anything
beyond the kind of dwelling used by manual workers. 'We found
a bedroom in a poor street,' she recalled. She said he seemed far
from well, struggling to cope with a sudden transformation from
the tropics to the onset of what would be a very cold winter. She
added: '… he was also sick with rage. He was convinced that we had
no business to be in Burma, no right to dominate other nations. He
would have ended the British Raj there and then.' (Crick, p 179).
O'Hara and Pitter lent him an oil-stove – apart from an open
fireplace, the room was unheated – and he would supplement this
by using candles to warm his fingers well enough to allow him to
practise his new trade, writing. Pitter, a published poet, confessed
that she and O'Hara 'used to laugh until we cried at some of the
bits he showed us', and admitted that at first they saw him as a
'wrong-headed' young man who had thrown away a good career in
the vain pursuit of a vocation that was evidently beyond him. 'He
wrote so badly. He had to teach himself writing. He was like a cow
with a musket.' Eventually, however, she began to detect something
else about him. 'But the formidable look was not there for nothing.
He had the gift, he had the courage, he had the persistence to go

on in spite of failure, sickness, poverty ...' One fragment from this period survives – a plan for a play with some brief attempts at dialogue – but Pitter remembers that he also attempted short stories. All depicted working-class figures enduring various forms of exploitation, suppression and deprivation, but apart from his struggles with the mechanisms of prose and dialogue he had major problems with his preferred topic. As he admitted of this period in *The Road to Wigan Pier*:

> But I knew nothing about working-class conditions. I had read the unemployment figures but I had no notion of what they implied; above all, I did not know the essential fact that 'respectable' poverty is always the worst. The frightful doom of a decent working man suddenly thrown on the streets after a lifetime of steady work, his agonised struggles against economic laws which he does not understand, the disintegration of families, the corroding sense of shame ...
>
> I was conscious of an immense weight of guilt that I had got to expiate ... I felt that I had got to escape not merely from imperialism but from every form of man's dominion over man. I wanted to submerge myself, to get right down among the oppressed, to be one of them and on their side against their tyrants.

Orwell's first excursion was to the East End, specifically to Limehouse Causeway where he entered a common lodging house advertising 'Good Beds for Single Men', which made his Notting Hill room seem luxurious by comparison. He had roughed up his least respectable clothes and no one suspected that he was anything other than destitute, like the rest of the residents. A drunken stevedore staggered towards him and he later wrote of this as 'a kind of baptism'. He expected that the man would attack him but he was offering comradely hospitality: ''Ave a cup of tea chum! ... 'ave a cup of tea.'

A year and a half earlier the General Strike of 1926 had been the one time in British history when the 'ordinary people', the working classes, had come close to forcing a reversal in government policy, almost overturning the government itself. Nearly two million workers in transport and heavy industry went on strike in support of coalminers who faced lock-outs, wage reductions and worsening labour conditions. Within nine days the government, assisted by middle-class volunteers who feared a socialist revolution, had defeated the Trades Union Congress. When Orwell decided to disguise himself as a down-and-out the government victory had resulted in manual and industrial workers having no say in matters such as wage levels and redundancy. Large numbers of men, already poorly paid, who had survived above the poverty line before the strike, now joined the ranks of the unemployed.

During December 1927 and January 1928 Orwell ventured further downward into the world of London's dispossessed. He disguised himself as a tramp, making use of clothes given away by charities or which, because of their grim condition, could be bought for token amounts, mere pennies. His first significant publication would be an essay, 'The Spike', which appeared in the *Adelphi* magazine in 1931. It was a rehearsal for the London-based section of *Down and Out in Paris and London.* The eponymous Spike was the twentieth-century version of a workhouse, effectively the last resort for men on the brink of malnutrition or those who feared that another night in the open might mean they would freeze to death. As Orwell reports, residents were treated as cattle but the most interesting passage involves his conversation with 'a rather superior tramp, a young carpenter who wore a collar and tie … and carried several of Scott's novels in his frayed bag.' The man is drawn to Orwell, probably because of his accent. He didn't doubt that he was genuinely destitute – there were plenty of 'middle-class' men who had fallen on bad times – but now he had the opportunity, as Orwell put it, to keep 'himself aloof from his fellow tramps' by forming an alliance with one of his own. Orwell complains of the wastage of food in the workhouse kitchen. 'And at this he changed his tune immediately. I saw that I had awakened the pew-renter who sleeps in every English workman.' Orwell's new friend explains that the workhouse must throw food away because if an abundance of decent edible meals became known among the tramps 'you'd have all the scum of the country flocking into them. It's only the bad food as keeps all that scum away. These tramps are too lazy to work, that's all that's wrong with them. You don't want to go encouraging them. They're scum.' Orwell comments: 'His body might be in the Spike, but his spirit soared far away, in the pure aether of the middle classes.' It is evident from Orwell's rendition of his dialect that the man is working class, but he aspires to a condition of moral superiority, irrespective of the fact that he has no immediate prospect of a job.

Fast-forward eighty-five years to a Channel 4 series of documentaries called *Benefits Street* (2014) which focuses on the residents of a street in Winson Green, Birmingham, where, allegedly, ninety per cent of the residents live on the dole and other benefits provided by the Welfare State. The accuracy of the filmmakers' depiction of James Turner Street remains open to debate, though the individuals who appear in it rarely if ever dispute their status as entirely dependent on state subsidies and seem proud of their expertise in minor criminality, shoplifting in particular. More significant was the backlash provoked by the documentaries. Channel 4 and the media regulatory body Ofcom were bombarded with online complaints, some of which accused the programme makers of 'poverty porn', exaggerating the outlook and lifestyle of the residents to create a freakshow. These were by far outnumbered by complainants who bore a startling resemblance to Orwell's 'pew-renter who sleeps in every English workman'. The word 'scum' appeared in numerous messages, but only from the more tolerant. The majority were less restrained and on Twitter, named residents were threatened with violence and death. A debate in the House of Commons was held during which Iain Duncan Smith, the Conservative Secretary of State for Work and Pensions, claimed that the programme fully justified the changes being implemented by the 2012 Welfare Reform Act which would make it extremely difficult for individuals to claim any benefits without providing irrefutable proof that they were concurrently in the process of applying for jobs or seriously disabled. As Orwell's new friend put it, 'these tramps are too lazy to work, that's all that's wrong with them'.

In 1932, when Orwell was writing regularly for the *Adelphi*, he reviewed a book on France and included an anecdote of his own. On his voyage home from Burma his ship had docked for a few days in Marseilles where newspaper and wireless reports were dominated by the imminent execution in the US of Sacco and Vanzetti, anarchists who had been convicted for murder during an armed robbery that appeared entirely unrelated to their political activities. Orwell witnessed demonstrations by tens of thousands of people in the city, convinced that there had been a deliberate miscarriage of justice designed to instil fear among other political radicals. Orwell felt that this kind of protest 'might have [been] seen in England in the eighteen forties, but surely never in the nineteen twenties'. He watched the protesters from the steps of one of the city's British banks and the clerks who joined him confirmed his suspicion that while much of the rest of Europe was aghast at what was taking place in America his own country was blighted by supine conservatism:

> It was instructive to hear the clerks (English) saying 'Oh, well, you've got to hang these blasted anarchists,' and to see their half-shocked surprise when one asked whether Sacco and Vanzetti were guilty of the crime for which they had been condemned.

By February Orwell had seen the worst of what awaited men who chose to avoid the regimented humiliations of the Spike and slept rough, which involved a number of grotesque options. The Thames

Embankment was favoured by most, since tramps who spent the night there were, through some bizarre by-law, exempt from a regulation that covered all other districts of the capital and allowed destitute individuals to sit or lie more or less where they wished, provided that they did not invade private spaces or obstruct thoroughfares. What they could not do, however, was sleep. If they fell asleep policemen must wake them and insist that they move on. The rationale for this nineteenth-century provision was that it would prevent indigents from dying of exposure. Refusal to move, or wake up, could result in arrest. As Orwell made clear in *Down and Out in Paris and London* the homeless were being treated as inconveniences and the legal and social infrastructure had done all it could to ensure they were made to 'disappear', without actually disposing of them. In December 2018 the *Guardian* disclosed that since 2015 almost 7,000 travel tickets – including for trains, aeroplanes and buses – had been purchased by eighty-three councils in England and Wales to 'encourage' rough sleepers in their boroughs to go somewhere else. Famously, the leader of Windsor Council expressed his wish that the town should sweep itself clean of the homeless in preparation for the wedding of Prince Harry and Meghan Markle in 2018. More recently, a man found sleeping on the platform of Sutton railway station in Surrey had dirty water from a floor-cleaning bucket thrown over him by railway employees to encourage him to wake up and go away. It was later disclosed that he suffered from a long-term medical condition but he was, according to a railway spokesman, causing offence to fare-paying passengers.

Orwell tells of how those who elected to avoid the Embankment dealt with the 'wake up' law. At the so-called 'Twopenny Hangover', 'lodgers' sat in a row on a bench, leant on a rope and somehow managed to sleep upright. The police, apparently, felt it difficult to prove that sleeping in such a posture was an offence. The other option was 'The Coffin', where, for fourpence a night, residents could insulate themselves against the cold by sleeping in a wooden box covered with tarpaulin. Orwell found the prospect macabre and horrifying but those who chose it could claim to the police that they were not asleep 'outdoors'.

My comparisons of Orwell's experiences with present-day down-and-outism might strike some as a little unfair. True, the various branches of the Welfare State have been battered by the 'austerity' policies of the Conservative government of late but surely they provide a more secure safety net for the homeless and unemployed than was available in the years following the General Strike. A recent book, however, shows that things have got worse. In *Hired* (2018), James Bloodworth tells of his experiences working in the most demeaning, poorly paid and sometimes dehumanising jobs that contribute to the government's proud boast of 'record' levels of employment. Just as enlightening, and horrifying, are his encounters with those suffering the collateral damage of recent policies, especially those without jobs or homes. Gary in Blackpool once had a 'normal' life earning £400 a week to keep himself and his family in modest accommodation, but by the time Bloodworth met him he was sleeping rough in a mixture of plastic and cardboard. There are many more like Gary on the pavements of the town where the Northern proletariat once spent their summer holidays; now the place has become a dumping ground for the unemployed and a playground for those of the same class who, after a night drinking, take pleasure in assaulting or urinating on them. Gary hadn't squandered his opportunities, but losing his job had sent him into a downward spiral, with the social services unable and unwilling to treat his route to destitution as anything other than inevitable. He tells Bloodworth of his failed suicide attempt and his ongoing treatment for cancer – he is eligible for chemotherapy but not accommodation – and most of all of his sense of feeling like a sub-human. Drunks would kick him and spit on him and those charitable enough to throw him some coins felt it their duty to order him to not spend their contributions on drink. Orwell's 'pew-renters', albeit secular but equally contemptuous of their inferiors, are certainly still with us today. No one, including the former Chief of Staff to Theresa May who offered a cover blurb, doubted the authenticity of Bloodworth's account.

Those who elected to sleep upright at the 'Twopenny Hangover' were often involved in skirmishes with the police regarding the manner in which the 1824 Vagrancy Act should be interpreted and enforced; uprightness might just be regarded as proof that vagrancy had not occurred but the matter remained open to debate. On 20 June 2019 the *Guardian* reported that Westminster Council had boarded up sections of pavement and put up notices stating that anyone trespassing on Council property would face prosecution. The only individuals tempted to cross the barriers to the cordoned-off areas of the pavement would be those who needed to sleep on them; all others would use the non-cordoned parts of the walkway as a means of proceeding from one place to another. If the 'Twopenny Hangover' seemed bizarre then the Westminster Council policy appears to be another variation on the game of incitement-and-deterrence played by the authorities against the homeless. According to the Combined Homeless and Information Network, 8,855 people were recorded as bedding down on London's pavements in 2018, a record high.

In April 1928 Orwell boarded the train to Dover, and then travelled from Calais to Paris, where he took a room at 6 Rue du Pot de Fer in the 5th arrondissement, which he describes in *Down and Out in Paris and London* as made up of 'leprous houses, lurching towards one another in queer attitudes, as though they had all been frozen in the act of collapse'. It was not a particularly fashionable location for Parisians, but for American, and some British expatriates it was a magnet. Bohemian artists and writers were conspicuously present. A few years before Orwell's arrival Ernest Hemingway had installed his wife and firstborn child in an apartment less than 200 metres away, above a timber mill, with a 'lavatory' that amounted to a hole in the floor surrounded by a curtain. He could have afforded a much better place but for many of the Paris-based modernists, roughing it was *de rigueur*. Ezra Pound had lived close by, as had American novelist John Dos Passos. There is no evidence that Orwell wanted to join the circle of aesthetic radicals who had flocked to Paris in the 1920s. At the time he seemed to have no knowledge of their existence. Later, when questioned on this, he said that he might have seen James Joyce in the street but since he didn't know him, or what he looked like, he could not be certain. Orwell never commented on why he chose to go to Paris and all we can infer is that he was continuing with his experiment of living among the poor.

The Paris section of *Down and Out in Paris and London* points up the difference between the French capital and its British counterpart. In London, he and his fellow tramps, unemployed and homeless, are not simply members of a different social substratum; they've been cut adrift. Orwell had to become someone else, and Ruth Pitter remembers laughing at him as he 'unpacked' his 'suit' of ragged filthy clothes, and changed into them, with him 'looking daggers at us, daring us not to laugh, but we did'. In the slums of the 5th arrondissement, he didn't need to disguise himself. No one doubted that he was a bilingual Englishman of reduced circumstances who had come to Paris to make enough francs to live on by teaching English. Not being an outright imposter seemed to confer on Orwell a sense of macabre good-fellowship with figures by parts eccentric and thoroughly unpleasant. 'Charlie', whose anecdotes pepper the book, comes from an educated, middle-class family and doesn't bother to explain his present circumstances. He does, however, beguile his friends with a story that makes Nabokov's *Lolita* seem like a fairy tale, telling in lurid detail of how he gained access to a brothel for men with particular tastes. These involve the gratification of customers who enjoy sex with the young and unwilling; in short, he takes grisly satisfaction in his account of how he paid to rape a girl. Then we come to Orwell's own stories of working as a *plongeur* – a dishwasher and general dogsbody – in the Hotel X, where the cook will not only spit in the soup sometimes, but as a matter of routine. He licks the steak and slaps it with his unwashed hands 'like an artist judging a picture' and then places it lovingly onto the plate with his 'fat pink fingers, every one of which he has licked a hundred times that morning'. Then the waiter joins the ceremony and 'dips *his* fingers into the gravy – his nasty, greasy fingers which he is forever running through his brilliantined hair'. For morning patrons their toast is 'buttered' with forehead sweat, after its brief acquaintance with the sawdust on the kitchen floor. Orwell reports this dispassionately or at least he does his best to do so. It is evident that he feels a comradeship with the French lower orders, compared with pity and infuriation at the supine resignation of the British. The French workers' fouling of the food is a gesture of which he approves unconditionally. However, he observes that 'in very cheap restaurants it is different': chefs and waiters respect diners as their equals. 'Roughly speaking, the more one pays for food, the more sweat and spittle one is obliged to eat with it.'

Orwell lived in Paris for more than eighteen months, returning to England in December 1929. His worst time in France was, according to his 'How the Poor Die', a period he spent in the Hôpital Cochin suffering from what he claimed was pneumonia. He was surprised that he'd survived, given that such public hospitals seemed to him undignified waiting rooms to oblivion for those who could not afford private care.

There has been a good deal of speculation on how much Orwell exaggerated facts, made them up or left them out completely, particularly the grotesqueries of his time in Paris. He hadn't yet published any fiction but the vividness of his depictions of other slum residents makes them both breathtaking and a little less than credible, especially when compared with the hopeless mundaneness of the English tramps. Aside from Charlie, whose description of his rape of the virgin is a masterclass in lush verbosity, we also encounter the most colourful of Orwell's associates, Boris, one-time captain in the Russian army and now exiled by the Bolsheviks. 'He was,' Orwell states, 'my close friend for a long time.' Update *War and Peace* to the

early twentieth century and Boris could have walked straight out
of it:

> Voilà, mon ami! There you see me at the head of my company.
> Fine big men, eh? Not like those little rats of Frenchmen. A
> captain at twenty – not bad, eh? Yes, a captain in the Second
> Siberian Rifles; and my father was a colonel.

Two figures who were most certainly present in the same Paris
neighbourhood but are conspicuously absent from the book are
Nellie and Eugène Adam, who kept a flat less than half a mile from
the Rue du Pot de Fer. Nellie Adam, née Limouzin, was the aunt
from Burma who had since moved to Paris. Was Orwell making
a point of ignoring members of his maternal family, as he had in
the East? He knew they were there, but irrespective of whether
he made contact with them it is curious that he never referred
to them subsequently in correspondence or conversation; or
rather, not quite. Crick's is the most meticulously researched
biography of Orwell and he tells of how his subject, in his final
years, 'told a friend ... that, as a young man, he had gone to
Paris partly to improve his French, but he had to leave his first
lodgings because the landlord and his wife only spoke Esperanto
– and it was an ideology, not just a language'. Nellie's husband
Eugène, fluent both in Breton and French, had become committed
to communism after a visit to Moscow, chosen Esperanto as the
international language of the coming world of revolution, and
refused to speak anything else in his home. Orwell, while never
referring specifically to his uncle, consistently regarded left-
wing Esperantists as 'cranks'. Does this matter? It does if we
are to believe that Orwell had descended into a netherworld of
poverty with little hope of returning, following the theft of what
little money he had saved, and had as a consequence come close
to death. The Adams would have been, had he chosen to contact
them, a very convenient safety net.

5

WAS ORWELL AN ANTISEMITE?

Documentary realism allows for degrees of overemphasis and quietly hidden opportunities for evasion but there is little doubt that much of the Paris-based account is authentic, which brings us to a feature of it that has since hung like a shadow over Orwell's reputation as the 'conscience of the twentieth century'. Shortly after *Down and Out in Paris and London* came out in 1933 its publisher, Victor Gollancz, received a letter from a reader who stated that '... I am appalled that a book containing insulting and odious remarks about Jews should be published by a firm bearing the name Gollancz.' Boris is unapologetically antisemitic, weeping at having to share rooms with a Jew and cursing the man for daring to exist. He tells Orwell of how during the war 'a horrible old Jew, with a red beard like Judas Iscariot', sneaked into his billet and offered him the use of a 'beautiful young girl only seventeen ... [for] only fifty francs'. She was the man's daughter. 'That is the Jewish national character for you.' It was, he adds, considered 'bad form' for a Russian officer to spit on a Jew: 'a Russian officer's spittle was too precious to be wasted on Jews ...' Orwell doesn't comment but in Chapter Three he describes having to sell some of his clothes at a shop in the Rue de la Montagne Ste-Geneviève kept by a 'red-haired Jew, an extraordinarily disagreeable man' and, without explaining why this man is any more disagreeable than the many others who variously defraud and exploit their fellow human beings in that part of the city, he adds: 'It would have been a pleasure to flatten the Jew's nose, if only one could have afforded it.' It is interesting that he chose the man's nose as his preferred target because soon after his return to London he enters a café at Tower Hill where 'in a corner by himself a Jew, *muzzle down* [my emphasis] in the plate, was guiltily wolfing bacon'.

There was more than one letter of complaint to Gollancz and they seemed to have had some effect since thereafter Orwell exerted a notable degree of self-control in his presentation of Jews in his work. Beneath the surface, however, something else was going on. In his – then unpublished – diaries which record his experiences with working-class hop-pickers, effectively his next stage of 'going native', he tells of how (on 28 August 1931) he came upon 'a boy of twenty named Young Ginger, who seemed rather a likely lad'. He takes a liking to Ginger, but rather less so to Ginger's companion:

> ... a little Liverpool Jew of eighteen, a thorough guttersnipe. I do not know when I have seen anyone who disgusted me so much as this boy. He was as greedy as a pig about food, perpetually scrounging round dustbins, and he had a face that recalled some low-down carrion-eating beast. His manner of talking about women, and the expression of his face when he did so, were so loathsomely obscene as to make me feel almost sick. We could never persuade him to wash more of himself than his *nose* [my emphasis] and a small circle around it, and he mentioned quite casually that he had several different kinds of louse on him.

In terms of his habits and hygiene he is no worse than many of the other homeless figures with whom Orwell shares various levels of deprivation. So why does he reserve such contempt for the 'Jew'? A clue might lie in the fact that he never refers to him by name. This is consistent with *Down and Out in Paris and London* where, apart from the figures mentioned above, one memorable episode involves a 'Jew' who cons his fellow slum-dwellers by selling them cocaine which turned out to be face powder. It is difficult to imagine that Orwell did not know the given names of these individuals but he only ever refers to each of them as 'the Jew'. Even in the *Diaries* he continues this practice. On 19 September 1931 he tells of the people he meets in a 'kip' in Tooley Street, East London. One is a thief who steals from shops, houses and cars, and sells 'the stuff to a Jew in Lambeth Cut'. In the so-called Morocco Diary, covering the period when Orwell and his wife Eileen spent time in North Africa after the Spanish Civil War, Orwell takes a particular interest in the considerable population of Jews, some of whom he speaks to, but again he never once shows any interest in their names. It was almost as though Orwell could not confer upon these 'Jews' the entitlement to individuality enjoyed by everyone else and preferred to see them part of a collective condition.

Once the Nazis had taken power in Germany and made clear that antisemitism would be the official government policy Orwell made his disapproval clear enough in articles and book reviews. As he published more and became a member of the literary establishment he also formed friendships with a considerable number of Jews. With his first publisher, Victor Gollancz, he remained on terms of if not amiability then at least mutual respect, as he did with others – writers, intellectuals and publishers. The writers and political agitators, Tosco Fyvel and Arthur Koestler, were probably his two closest friends during the war years. Fredric Warburg was as much his trusted confidant as his publisher and he respected and enjoyed the company of journalists Jon Kimche and Evelyn Anderson.

Orwell's most outspoken piece on antisemitism was published in the *Contemporary Jewish Record* in April 1945, less than a month before the end of the war in Europe. The full, horrific nature of the Holocaust was not yet known to the public but there had been no reporting restrictions on the pre-war Nazi policy of the repression, persecution and deportation of Jews, and accounts on the liberation of Belsen by American and British forces had already appeared in the press. Orwell's reputation as an obstinate prevaricator – less a man who sits on the fence than one who refuses to accept that either side of it is satisfactory – is well established and his 'Antisemitism in Britain' gives credence to this. It also, however, shows that despite what was known of what had happened in Germany, antisemitism remained an endemic feature of British society, and he offers verbatim records of remarks made to him by individuals from across the socio-economic spectrum of London 'during the past year or two'. There's the 'middle-class woman' who claims that 'no one could call me antisemitic, but I do think the way these Jews behave is too absolutely stinking. The way they push their way to the head of queues and so on. They're so abominably selfish. I think they're responsible for a lot of what happens to them.' There's a chartered accountant, a milkman, a woman ('intelligent') buying a book, a young intellectual ('communist'), a tobacconist and a middle-aged office worker. All of them hate Jews and while it is impossible to disprove Orwell's claim that their statements are authentic, one can't dispute that many bear a remarkable resemblance to Orwell's own sense of revulsion at the 'little Jewish guttersnipe' from Liverpool and other Jews he encounters in his *Diaries*. It is quite likely that these people were real but one might also suspect that he was also recognising, with horror, something of his past in them.

Orwell goes on to explore the nature and causes of antisemitism, telling of how from Chaucer onwards English literature has reflected the attitude to Jews in Britain as a whole, with Shakespeare, Smollett, Thackeray, Shaw, H. G. Wells, T. S. Eliot, Huxley, Belloc and Chesterton exhibiting unapologetic antisemitic tendencies. He does not express his own opinions on these writers, only that 'Anyone who wrote in that strain *now* would bring down a storm of abuse upon himself, or ... would find it impossible to get his writings published.' Normally a defender of free speech, irrespective of the vile nature of the message, he does not regret the fact that since the war a form of censorship had become a matter of course.

He admits that he has 'no hard-and-fast theory about the origins of antisemitism'. He offers a variety of contributing factors such as medieval prejudice, modern nationalism, capitalist and anti-capitalist scapegoating, etc., but he seems content with it as a form of 'neurosis' or schizophrenia. The most compelling passage is:

> What vitiates nearly all that is written about antisemitism is the assumption in the writer's mind that *he himself* is immune to it. 'Since I know that antisemitism is irrational,' he argues, 'it follows I do not share it.' He thus fails to start his investigation in the one place where he could get hold of some reliable evidence – that is, in his own mind.

Particularly telling is his assumption that balanced, intelligent writers – unlike the knee-jerk antisemites whose expressions he records – immunise themselves from their prejudice by treating it as irrational and therefore beneath their elevated intellectual and moral position. On the surface he is addressing this with cool objectivity, but read the passage in relation to what we know of his own transgressions and it is evident that he is talking to, even interrogating, himself. To adapt and extend an old adage: alcoholism and antisemitism have much in common – to deal with either you must first acknowledge that you have a problem. Throughout the essay he returns to the tension between deep-seated, perhaps instinctive, antisemitism and the reluctance or inability of antisemites to face up to their prejudices. He tells of how in 1943 a multi-faith service was held in St John's Wood to show the sense of solidarity felt by Londoners for recently arrived Jewish refugees. 'On the surface it was a touching demonstration of solidarity ... But it was essentially a conscious effort to behave decently by people whose subjective feelings must in many cases have been very different.' Orwell follows this with more examples of people he knew, though who he does not name, who will maintain an allegiance to persecuted Jews while harbouring a private distaste for their presence. He does not name them because, as is evident in an entry in his *Diary* of 25 November 1940, he is one of them.

> The other night I examined the crowds sheltering in Chancery Lane, Oxford Circus and Baker Street stations. Not all are Jews, but, I think, a higher proportion of Jews than one would normally see in a crowd of this size. What is bad about Jews is that they are not only conspicuous, but go out of their way to make themselves so. A fearful Jewish woman, a regular comic-paper cartoon of a Jewess, fought her way off the train at Oxford Circus, landing blows on anyone who stood in her way ... What I do feel is that any Jew, i.e. any European Jew, would prefer Hitler's kind of social system to ours, if it were not that he happens to persecute them ... They make use of England as a sanctuary, but they cannot help feeling the profoundest contempt for it. You can see this in their eyes, even when they don't say it outright.

On five other occasions in his 'As I Please' pieces he addresses antisemitism directly, continually finding evidence that the British public would have co-operated with the Nazis if the nation had been occupied. (See especially 'As I Please', 11 February 1944.) He was exposing something distasteful and at the same time engaging in a private exercise in repentance. On 19 May 1944 he offered a specimen of the correspondence he regularly received:

> TO THE JEW-PAID EDITOR
> TRIBUNE
> LONDON
>
> YOU ARE CONSTANTLY ATTACKING OUR GALLANT POLISH ALLY BECAUSE THEY KNEW HOW TO TREAT ... ALL JEW-PAID EDITORS ... WE KNOW YOU ARE IN THE PAY OF THE YIDS ... YOU ARE A FRIEND OF THE ENEMIES OF BRITAIN! THE DAY OF RECKONING IS AT HAND.

BEWARE. ALL JEW PIGS WILL BE EXTERMINATED THE
HITLER WAY – THE ONLY WAY TO GET RID OF THE YIDS.
PERISH JUDAH.

In any other circumstances this piece of spittle-flecked sub-literacy
might have caused laughter (today we encounter brilliant caricatures
of similarly cretinous social-media ranters in *Private Eye*), but in
1944 Orwell displayed it to shame those who might share the
writer's opinions or even be tempted to laugh at him. Was this
hideous figure an invention? Possibly, but if so Orwell created him
as a painful, grotesquely exaggerated version of himself. If there
are any doubts that 'Antisemitism in Britain' should have been
retitled 'Antisemitism in Orwell' the following passage should
remove them.

> It will be seen, therefore, that the starting point for any investigation
> of antisemitism should not be 'Why does this obviously irrational
> belief appeal to other people?' but 'Why does antisemitism appeal
> to me? What is there about it that I feel to be true?' If one asks this
> question one at least discovers one's own rationalisations, and it
> may be possible to find out what lies behind them.

Six months after the *Jewish Record* article he wrote a piece for the
Tribune called 'Revenge is Sour' in which he tells of his visit to a
recently liberated concentration camp. He comes upon 'a little
Viennese Jew', a translator who had been enlisted in the branch of
the American army which deals with the interrogation of prisoners.
This 'Jew' comes upon a senior Nazi officer and begins to kick him.
Orwell is horrified, feeling that the liberators have sunk to the
same level as the Nazis, but his focus is upon how the 'Jew' takes
pleasure in revenging himself against the SS officer 'with the same
air of working himself into a fury [to kick the SS man] – indeed
he was almost dancing up and down as he spoke – the Jew told us
the prisoner's history'. Not, the 'soldier' or even 'the translator';

the 'Jew'. Evidently Orwell's attempt at a self-administered 'talking cure' in the earlier article had been only partially successful.

I stress this issue because it is of immense relevance to the present day. From his period in the East End and Paris onwards Orwell became more and more committed to the objectives of the Independent Labour Party (ILP). In Burma he found that the Empire was intrinsically racist and by the time he returned to England social injustice and inequality were his exclusive concerns. How could he reconcile these commitments and principles with an apparent contempt for Jews? Today, the Labour Party is riven with accusations of antisemitism against a large number of hard-left figures. Those among its moderate faction – notably its former deputy leader Tom Watson – advocate ruthless expulsions of members who have made anti-Jewish comments online or at meetings or been proved to be involved with campaigns against Jewish Labour supporters or MPs. Of the latter Luciana Berger, MP for Liverpool Wavertree, is the most prominent victim. She, along with six other Labour MPs, resigned from the party in February 2019, for a number of reasons, including the policy of the leadership regarding Brexit; she has recently joined the Lib Dems. In October Dame Louise Ellman, Jewish and a Labour MP for more than twenty years, resigned from the party because of its endemic antisemitism. Each was particularly unsettled by evidence that the party had not dealt severely enough with expressions of antisemitism from within its own ranks. In March 2018 Berger asked the leader Jeremy Corbyn why he had in 2012, prior to his election as leader, objected to the removal of a mural in Tower Hamlets depicting a group of individuals sitting around a Monopoly board. The US Holocaust historian Deborah E. Lipstadt had stated that the figures were almost identical to caricatures of Jews that appeared in the Nazi propaganda weekly *Der Stürmer*. It might be added that the mural also brings to mind Orwell's verbal portrait of a Jew in an East End café with his 'muzzle down in the plate'. The artist, Mear One, all but agreed, claiming that the work depicted 'an elite banker cartel', particularly the Rothschilds and Rockefellers, and added that 'some of the older white Jewish folk in the local community had an issue with me portraying their beloved #Rothschild or #Warburg etc as the demons they are'. Corbyn had responded to the artist's online comments, claiming that the plan to remove the work went against the principle of freedom of expression, adding 'Why? You're in good company. Rockerfeller [sic] destroyed Diego Viera's mural because it includes a picture of Lenin.' At the time Corbyn was a backbencher little known outside Westminster but with a long history within it as the supporter of radical left-wing causes, particularly involving pro-Palestinian anti-Israel organisations. Berger's tweet caused a firestorm, with a large number of the party leader's previous comments and actions being brought to public attention. He had in 2012 attended a conference in Doha hosted by Hamas, an Islamist group dedicated to the destruction of Israel, and hosted a panel discussion which included the senior Hamas member Husam Badran who had orchestrated a series of bombings in Israel between 2001 and 2002 that resulted in seventy-nine civilian deaths. Corbyn said later that he was 'friends' with both Hamas and Hezbollah, the Lebanon-based group which also mounts attacks against Israel. In 2010 Corbyn co-chaired an event in the Commons with anti-Zionist Auschwitz survivor Hajo Meyer during Holocaust Memorial Week. Meyer's talk was entitled 'The Misuse of the Holocaust for Political Purposes', specifically the foundation and perpetuation of Israel as a state. In January 2013 Corbyn defended the statement by Manuel Hassassian, the UK Palestinian Authority representative, that Israel should be prevented from 'building its messianic dream of Eretz Israel,' adding that 'Zionists ... have two problems ... One is that they don't want to study history and secondly, having lived in this country for a very long time ... don't understand English irony either. Manuel does understand English irony and uses it very, very effectively ...'

The exposure of Corbyn's past caused numerous similar activities by party members to come to light. Kayla Bibby, a prominent activist, had in 2016 posted a picture of an alien imprinted with the Star of David attacking the Statue of Liberty and added the caption: 'The most accurate photo I've seen all year!' In March 2018 Christine Shawcroft resigned from her post as head of the

Labour Party's Disputes Sub-Committee after it was revealed that in 2015 she had opposed the suspension of Peterborough council candidate Alan Bull in 2015. Bull had supported an article that declared the Holocaust a hoax. In March 2018 Damien Enticott, Labour councillor for Bognor Regis, made a number of blatantly antisemitic online posts including the suggestion that 'Hitler would have a solution to the Israel problem'. Andrew Slack, Labour councillor in Luton, commented on his Facebook page in 2016 that 'Israel was created by the Rothschilds, not God … and what they are doing to the Palestinian people now is EXACTLY what they intend for the whole world'. He illustrated his words with a cartoon caricature of an Israeli soldier with blood dripping from his hands and mouth. Also in 2016 Aysegul Gurbuz announced on Twitter that 'if it wasn't for my man Hitler these Jews would've wiped [out] Palestine years ago,' and hoped that Iran's ongoing nuclear programme would enable them to 'wipe Israel off the map'. The Luton-based Labour councillor prefaced this in 2011 and 2014 with praise for Hitler as the 'greatest man in history'. It hardly seems necessary to point out the similarities between these deranged utterances and the letter received by the 'JEW-PAID EDITOR', Orwell, in 1944.

The two most prominent Labour antisemites are Ken Livingstone and Naz Shah. Livingstone, one-time Labour leader of the Greater London Council, Labour MP and Mayor of London, accused the *Evening Standard* photographer Oliver Finegold of 'harassing' guests at a 2005 political event, and asking him if he had been 'a German war criminal'. When Finegold pointed out that his age and being Jewish made this unlikely, Livingstone replied that you are 'just like a concentration camp guard, you are just doing it because you are paid to, aren't you?' A year later, during a conflict regarding a building project, he advised the Jewish businessmen David and Simon Reuben that 'they can go back to Iran and try their luck with the ayatollahs'. Most famously, in 2016 Livingstone claimed on BBC Radio London that in 1932, after his election, Hitler was an ardent Zionist, advocating that European Jews should be deported to Israel. 'He [Hitler] was supporting Zionism before he went mad and ended up killing six million Jews.'

Shah was active in 2016 too. As Labour MP for Bradford West she had sent out an online image of Israel's geographical outline superimposed on the US and added the caption: 'Solution for the Israel-Palestine conflict – relocate Israel into United States.' Since 2012 there have been more than one hundred recorded speeches or statements online by Labour members and active supporters, many of them elected representatives of the party, which equal the savagery of the cases reported above.

Berger, Watson and a number of other Labour moderates were appalled by the nature of these outbursts but disgusted even more by their party's apparent reluctance to discipline antisemites. Livingstone, for example, was placed on temporary suspension after 2016, pending an investigation, a seemingly interminable period brought to a close only by his voluntary resignation from the party in 2018. Labour councillor and former Mayor of Blackburn, Salim Mulla, called Jews a 'disgrace to humanity', blamed Israel for organising school shootings in the US and said that 'Zionism' was orchestrating ISIS. He was temporarily suspended from the Party before reinstatement. Bob Campbell, an activist for the Teesside branch of Momentum, the far-left pro-Corbyn group, posted on Twitter an image of a rat marked with the Star of David and claimed that ISIS is controlled by Israel. He was not disciplined by the party. Miqdad Al-Nuaimi, Labour councillor in Newport, Wales, tweeted that Israel was assuming the 'genocidal character of the Nazis' and insisted there was an alliance between Israel and ISIS. He was temporarily suspended and then cleared.

Shortly after Berger's resignation a senior member of her constituency party, Margaret Tyson, accused her of 'supporting the Zionist Israeli government [whose] Nazi masters taught them well'. Other Twitter messages from Labour members included, 'Shame on Luciana Berger, A Zionist Bitch, … I hate her baby [she was eight months pregnant at the time], her Israel', and another included an allegation that she was a 'Fifth columnist' who should be charged with treason for 'acting for a foreign power [Israel]'. One promised to kill both her and her baby, once she had given birth.

Nazism and various post-war far-right organisations in Europe and elsewhere have unashamedly combined outright racism with ludicrous conspiracy theories as the basis for their hatred for Jews. More recently, the left has routinely made a claim that their attitude has nothing to do with what Orwell described as 'irrational' and 'neurotic' tendencies. The standard defence against accusations of antisemitism made by the figures quoted above is that their remarks have been manipulated, taken out of context, that they have nothing against Judaism as an ethnic group, a religion, even a race; rather that the true target of their critique is the state of Israel, specifically its treatment of Palestinians from 1948 onwards. This is the incessant claim of Corbyn supporters, who insist that he does not have 'a racist or antisemitic bone in his body'. Here the distinctions between Orwell's failings and dilemmas and contemporary Labour antisemitism become pertinent. Nazism caused Orwell to confront the fact that his vile prejudices involved something far more than a private transgression. He suddenly recognised that individual bigotry could become the licence for mass murder, that in his personal failings he was complicit in what was going on in continental Europe. Labour antisemites reverse this equation between contrition and collective responsibility. They rehearse a whole gallery of ideological and ethical mantras in order to disguise their loathing for Jews.

Orwell's opinions on Palestine tended to fluctuate. During the 1930s European Jews, terrified by Fascism, swelled the number of those already settled in the region. By 1938 there were more than 500,000 Jews in Palestine and the settlement had the almost unswerving support of the ILP. As early as 1931 the British socialist journalist Henry Noel Brailsford was producing articles based on his recent visits to the area. He reported that 'miracles' were being wrought. The Kibbutzim communes were an organic, liberal alternative to Stalin's brutally enforced schemes of collectivisation.

The vast majority of Labour activists supported Zionism. It was synonymous with democratic socialism, and the 1930s reports on how Kibbutz settlements had transformed acres of previously barren land, virtually desert, into fertile agricultural enterprises were greeted with widespread enthusiasm. The implication was that the Arabs, by neglect or incompetence, had mismanaged their homeland. In November 1939 a police surveillance file on Orwell records him supporting the 'British Committee for Jewish–Arab Solidarity' set up by Labour in June that year. The Committee did not have a specific agenda but it was founded to monitor the hoped-for co-operation between Palestinian Arabs and recently arrived Jews, to campaign against the latter's apparent inclination to transform the status quo. Hence, Orwell's support for it. Later in 'Antisemitism in Britain' he stated that '… many Zionist Jews seem to me to be merely antisemites turned upside-down'; he felt that a long-suppressed group were now becoming colonialist, and since Burma he had loathed colonialism in all its manifestations. In his 'Notes on Nationalism', published close to the end of the war, he states that Zionism 'has the unusual characteristics of a nationalist movement' which 'flourishes almost exclusively among the Jews themselves'. The post-war Conservative Party was resolutely anti-Zionist, fearing that the foundation of a potentially powerful Jewish state in the Middle East would threaten Britain's imperial ambitions in the region. For the Tories the Empire was alive and kicking. Labour, when elected to government, continued with the Conservative policy of a military crackdown against a variety of Zionist groups who sought independence. Throughout the party as a whole, however, there was a feeling that Britain was denying survivors of the Holocaust their inalienable right – a territory of their own where they could protect themselves. Despite the fact that some of his closest friends and political associates were fervently pro-Zionist Orwell held out against supporting the establishment of a Jewish state. During Christmas 1945 he spent time with his friend Arthur Koestler, who argued that the hundreds of thousands of Jewish refugees from the Holocaust should be shipped by the Allies to their 'new home' in Palestine. Orwell was resolutely opposed to the project, so much so that Koestler felt it best to end the dispute rather than endanger their relationship. Later, in his 'As I Please' column in the *Tribune* (November 1946), Orwell seemed to wish to continue their exchange by contending that at least 100,000 Jewish refugees attempting to get to Palestine should be encouraged to settle in Britain. He argued that this would boost the post-war economy that was chronically short of labour. This appears both generous and bizarre given that he had made it clear that in his experience most British working people were virulently antisemitic. In an editorial meeting of the *Tribune* the Labour MP Aneurin Bevan, who was on the board of the magazine, launched into a pro-Zionist speech, only to be informed by Orwell that British Zionists were a 'bunch of Wardour Street Jews who had a controlling interest over the British press'. The man who reported this in his memoir of Orwell was Tosco Fyvel, who remained by equal degrees his devoted friend whilst being profoundly unsettled by his opinions on Palestine and Zionism.

Orwell never opposed outright the foundation of an independent Jewish state and in this respect a comparison between him and the present mood of antisemitism becomes instructive. In 'Antisemitism in Britain' he conducted a secret dialogue with an aspect of himself that he found it difficult to sublimate yet which caused him some self-loathing. Malcolm Muggeridge attended Orwell's funeral and later expressed his surprise at the large number of Jews present, including Zionists such as Fyvel, believing the deceased to be 'strongly antisemitic'. We don't have verbatim records of Orwell's conversations with his Jewish friends but from what we can infer the latter treated him as a man who was struggling with various elements of guilt and uncertainty. Fyvel, for example, remonstrated with him after reading his account of the Jew kicking the ex-SS officer – in the manner of 'what would you do?' – and Orwell accepted his point. In 1946 Koestler published a novel called *Thieves in the Night* in which the decision by a Jewish immigrant to Palestine to join a Zionist paramilitary group is presented sympathetically. Orwell told Koestler's wife that 'I enjoyed reading it, but you know my views, at any rate Arthur knows my views about the terrorism business.' They remained close and Koestler too attended his funeral. Orwell's Jewish friends knew him, better than Muggeridge did, as being a decent man, honest enough to recognise his failings.

In 'Antisemitism in Britain' he is brutally clear about the state of things in his home country:

> There is more antisemitism in England than we care to admit, and the war has accentuated it ... It is at bottom quite irrational and will not yield to argument.

He adds that matters are so unsettling that 'Antisemitism should be investigated – and I will not say by anti-Semites, but at any rate by people who know they are not immune to that kind of emotion.' His readers, many of whom would soon become members of the post-war Labour government, evidently took no heed of his call. Just over seventy years later, however, the same party felt it necessary to conduct just such an investigation, focusing primarily on itself. It was led by Shami Chakrabarti, Labour member and later Shadow Attorney General, an appointment that some felt indicated a careless disregard for impartiality. Chakrabarti found that the party was not overrun with antisemitism, and that antisemitism was not endemic in the culture of Labour, but it should guard against the use of language or images that involved racial stereotypes and distortions of historical fact, notably the treatment of Jews by the Nazis, and should take disciplinary action against those who transgressed against these ordinances. How would Orwell have felt about the findings of a commission issued three generations after he called for it? In 'Antisemitism in Britain', rather eerily, he seems to respond:

> To study any subject scientifically one needs a detached attitude, which is obviously harder when one's own interests or emotions

are involved. Plenty of people who are quite capable of being objective about sea urchins, say, or the square root of 2, become schizophrenic if they have to think about the sources of their own income.

Shortly after delivering her report Chakrabarti was, at the behest of her party leader Jeremy Corbyn, elevated to a peerage in the House of Lords. Following the launch of the inquiry findings Marc Wadsworth, a member of Momentum, accused the Jewish Labour MP Ruth Smeeth of conspiring with the Tory press against Labour. At the launch he had seen her talking with the *Daily Telegraph* journalist Kate McCann and alleged that they were working 'hand in hand' to undermine the party. When discussing the inquiry Corbyn digressed and compared Israel's actions against Gaza with ISIS. He responded to criticism of this by stating that 'our Jewish friends are no more responsible for the actions of Israel or the Netanyahu government than our Muslim friends are for those self-styled Islamic states or organisations'. In short: I respect you as a Muslim provided that you do not support Islamic terrorism and I tolerate your Jewishness so long as you dissociate yourself from Israel. The vast majority of Jews in the UK and elsewhere support Israel, in that they want it to continue as an independent state, but they are radically divided on the policies of its various governments. But, for Corbyn, Jews who do not renounce Zionism are the equivalent of Islamic fundamentalists who conduct gratuitous beheadings as a matter of course. Consider this alongside Wadsworth's Jewish 'conspiracy theory' and we have a fine example of Orwell's notion of the 'schizophrenia' which would evolve into Two Minutes Hate in his final novel.

Orwell's most telling comment on antisemitism is that its adherents can't fully recognise their own prejudices: 'Since I know that antisemitism is irrational … it follows that I do not share it.' This is, as I've pointed out, an admission of his own failings, but it is also horribly prescient. Tony Blair, during a visit to Israel, was asked if he thought Corbyn is an antisemite. 'Some of the remarks are not explicable in any other way ... Does he think he is? No, he doesn't think he is at all.' (*Times of Israel,* 4 June 2019). It is happening today but Orwell gives it particular emphasis in *Nineteen Eighty-Four*, in which 'doublethink' allows people to hold two irreconcilable opinions simultaneously. The most troubling character in *Nineteen Eighty-Four* is Emmanuel Goldstein. We know little about him as an individual, only that he was a former senior member of the Party who has broken away and founded a dissident movement called 'the Brotherhood'. He is routinely identified as a version of Trotsky, partly because both departed from their party and both were Jewish. This is a simplistic reading because we are never quite certain that Goldstein even exists, let alone whether he is responsible for treacherous activities and authorising anti-Party propaganda. All we know is that an image of him is presented regularly on 'telescreens':

> It was a lean Jewish face, with a great fuzzy aureole of white hair and a small goatee beard – a clever face, and yet somehow inherently despicable, with a kind of senile silliness in the long thin nose ... It resembled the face of a sheep, and the voice, too, had a sheep-like quality ... He was the commander of a vast shadowy army, an underground network of conspirators dedicated to the overthrow of the State.

Goldstein encapsulates the contradictions that fuelled post-war antisemitism. Was he a victim (a 'sheep') or a more disturbing presence 'the commander of a vast shadowy army', probably involving bankers and moneylenders? Any tension between sympathy and revulsion was, as Orwell makes clear in his representation, overruled by a single factor. Goldstein was a 'Jew' and fully deserving of the Two Minutes Hate that followed the projection of his image.

Nineteen Eighty-Four beckons us towards the Labour Party today. The Jew, for many of its members, is like Goldstein: transformable, available for endless interpretations of who or what he might represent. Doublethink is alive and well in the culture of the twenty-first-century Labour Party, in which seemingly limitless numbers of activists appear able to switch so easily between their rational opinions on an allegedly colonial state, Israel, and a more feral, instinctive contempt for Jews because they are Jews. Recently the Equality and Human Rights Commission announced that it was launching an inquiry into Labour antisemitism, implicitly, if not specifically, alleging that Chakrabarti had failed in her remit.

The young Orwell was an antisemite, and traces of his prejudices survived until the beginning of the Second World War when no one in Britain was in any doubt about the Nazi programme. He came to loathe himself for what he was and was ashamed by what he saw in his country. Regarding Israel he was uncertain and was concerned primarily with the fate of those Jews who had survived the Holocaust. Most of all he was honest about his failings and alert to the fact that Jews themselves, especially Zionists such as Fyvel and Koestler, had far more right to control their destiny than he did. If only there were more like him now, especially in the Labour Party.

6

HOPELESS

Two weeks before Christmas 1929 Orwell took the train, 3rd class, from Paris to Dunkirk and boarded the ferry to Tilbury. He might have spent a few days in London – the exact records regarding his journey are sketchy – but it is clear that his destination was his parents' house in Southwold, where he arrived shortly before Christmas Day. We do not know if he informed Richard and Ida of his arrival in advance or whether he simply knocked on the door. Avril later reported that during the months that followed the atmosphere was uncomfortable. In Paris he had begun two novels and completed two short stories but the only evidence of these attempts to achieve his objective of becoming a writer was his collection of rejection slips. He had sold a few articles, but nothing more. His father's disapproving response to his announcement of his projected vocation two years earlier hung in the air; it was evident to all that he had failed.

He made no attempt to obtain a job and during 1930 he seemed unfocused and directionless. His mother and sister found him occasional work as a tutor, first for the teenage son of the Morgans, a wealthy local family. Bryan Morgan was crippled by polio and by local consensus 'backward' but he and Orwell seemed well matched, and spent much of their time taking walks in the countryside around Southwold, chatting distractedly. Bryan's sister Dora was sixteen and attractive; she later described Orwell as 'rather an awkward customer … We used to make jokes about him.' One day when he and Bryan were 'playing' on a meadow near the Morgan house she approached them 'to chat'. Orwell smiled and pressed a piece of paper into her hand. On it was a recently composed love poem, 'Ode to a Dark Lady'; clearly Dora. She threw it away after her return to the house.

Orwell had also become friends once more with Brenda Salkeld, whom he'd first met in 1928. She was a gym teacher at a local girls' school, daughter of a Bedfordshire vicar and the same age as Orwell. They shared a laconic sense of humour and talked of novels they enjoyed; and in June 1930 Orwell asked her to marry him. She politely declined. When recalling the proposal in later life she seems not so much aghast at the prospect of a long-term relationship with him as puzzled by the nature of his gesture. Never before had he indicated that he was interested in anything more than companionship. He seemed set upon acting in a deliberately erratic, faintly bizarre manner. She recalled also that, despite his shock declaration, they remained on good terms and that on a number of occasions she invited him to stay at the family home, a Georgian rectory in Bedfordshire. Later in 1930 he resumed his tramping expeditions, albeit for brief periods, and Brenda's mother hardly recognised the filthy individual at her door, who stank and carried several days of beard. She ordered him immediately to take a bath, and to make use of some of her husband's casual clothes. Mrs Salkeld described his behaviour as 'funny' though it is not clear whether she meant farcical or peculiar.

Orwell's mother also found him work tutoring the three boys of her friends, the Peters, during their summer holidays. Richard Peters later became a senior academic and recalled that while they enjoyed their time with him immensely their exchanges seemed unrelated to anything educational. He talked with them about books, but randomly, and instead seemed more concerned with instructing them on the local wildlife. Often he took them fishing for roach at the Walberswick millpond, and one morning announced that he would show them how to do something he'd taught himself when he was their age in Henley: how to make a bomb with gunpowder from shotgun cartridges. It exploded and, as with his childhood experiment with Prosper Buddicom, all were left with singed eyebrows. Their tutor was, as Richard remembered, 'rather strange, but very nice'.

In spring he spent a few weeks with his sister Marjorie and his brother-in-law Humphrey Dakin. Dakin had started a new job in the civil service and they had recently purchased a house in the suburbs of Leeds. Dakin felt a contempt for Orwell that endured long after the latter's death and he later commented that he was struck by how during the visit he seemed snobbishly introverted, notably that he refused to mix with Dakin's friends at the local pub: 'He used to sit in a corner by himself, looking like death.' The visit was his first reconnaissance for his journeys to the working-class heartlands of the North, out of which would come *The Road to Wigan Pier*. Dakin implies that Orwell's standoffish manner in his local pub indicated hypocrisy: he didn't *really* want to mix with ordinary people. In truth, Dakin's fellow drinkers were, like himself, upwardly mobile, lower middle-class professionals. Orwell 'sat in a corner' because this was not the Yorkshire that he wanted to see – Dakin does not mention that his brother-in-law used his time there to take regular bus and train journeys to mining villages outside Leeds.

It is not clear if he had given up on fiction, but over the two years following his return to Southwold he worked relentlessly on what would become *Down and Out in Paris and London*. Mrs May, the Blair's cleaner, asked her daughter to take regular hot cups of tea to him in the upstairs bedroom from which he rarely emerged, and where his presence was evidenced only by the clicking of typewriter keys. 'Poor boy,' she said later, 'I felt so very sorry for him … He always seemed to be three days from a shave … in a dream.'

Orwell did, however, begin to make tentative contacts with members of the literary establishment in London, notably the editors of the *Adelphi*. Founded by Middleton Murry in the 1920s the *Adelphi* was in its early years a typically Bloomsbury Group magazine. It took delight in pieces reflecting the new aesthetic and mood of modernism and cared little that such topics ensured that very few people bought it: its owners, editors and contributors were sufficiently well off not to bother about making money from their project. In 1930 the co-editorship passed to Sir Richard Rees – minor aristocrat and Old Etonian – and Max Plowman, a man from a similar background. Rees and Plowman set about moving the *Adelphi* from the margins to the centre ground of the London literary scene, and Rees arranged a meeting with Orwell in the magazine's offices in May 1930 with a view to taking him on, initially as a book reviewer and potentially as a contributor. Rees later diagnosed him as a 'bohemian Tory', unhappy with his roots and status, but unsure of his political destination. Orwell later confirmed Rees' impression: he did not at the time know enough about socialism to openly espouse it but his experiences with the dispossessed were propelling him towards an empathy with those who offered them a political voice. There is a vivid report by Jack Common, one of the first genuinely working-class figures admitted to British literary culture, who had been taken on, from his Tyneside manual job, as a 'circulation pusher' for the magazine. He would later become a regular contributor. His first encounter with Orwell was at an editorial meeting:

> Already a legend was shaping about him. He was not as other Bloomsbury souls, they said, he was an outsider, a rebel, a tramp, he lived and wrote in the bottom-most underworld of poverty. …
>
> He was sitting in Katherine Mansfield's armchair one dusky afternoon … talking to Max Plowman and Sir Richard Rees, our editors … he looked the real thing: outcast, gifted pauper, kicker against authority, perhaps near-criminal. But he rose to acknowledge the introduction with a hand-shake. Right away, manners – and more than manners, the process euphemistically called 'breeding' – showed through. A sheep in wolf's clothing, I thought … Was Eric just a phoney then? Or anyway an amateur pauper. (Crick, p 204).

The completed draft of *Down and Out*, or *A Scullion's Diary* as it was first called, was rejected first by Jonathan Cape and next by T. S. Eliot, commissioning editor of Faber and Faber (19 February 1932). Eliot's letter is an evasive, vague explanation of why his company did not want it: it was 'decidedly too short' (did he feel that prurient readers had an appetite for more portraits of abject poverty, despair and hopelessness?); 'too loosely constructed, as the French and English episodes fall into two parts with very little to connect them' (an incomprehensible objection – was he not convinced that pauperism in Paris and London might manifest itself differently?). Who knows why Eliot decided to reject it, but it is worth taking a guess. Ten years earlier in his monument to modernist verse, *The Waste Land*, Eliot had dealt with the working classes as sub-human. By bringing the reader into their world and treating them sympathetically, Orwell probably did not endear himself to Faber's editor.

Two months after the book was turned down by Faber, Orwell began work as a teacher at the Hawthorns High School in Hayes, a Middlesex suburb around fifteen miles from the centre of London. Aside from the owner, Mr Eunson, who was too uneducated to do any teaching himself, there was only one other master. There were around fifteen pupils, boys between the ages of ten to sixteen. It was certainly not a version of St Cyprian's. Eunson made a living by offering locals who despised the prospect of their sons going to council schools the most basic form of private education. The only qualifications on offer were the contemporary equivalent of vocational GCSEs, enabling sixteen-year-olds to avoid the trades or manual work and find jobs as clerks in local government or commercial offices. Orwell taught there for almost two years, performing his tasks dutifully, and amusing and engaging the boys, much as he had the Peters brothers in Southwold. On one occasion he arranged a day out and showed a group of Hawthorns pupils how to capture marsh gas from the edge of the Thames in jars and then cause it to explode back in the classroom. The boys weren't well off so they might well wish to forage for free fireworks.

Orwell lived in the school and in June 1932 received a letter there from central London in which Victor Gollancz stated that he would publish *Down and Out in Paris and London*. Gollancz had been influenced most of all by the report from his reader Gerald Gould:

> This is an extraordinarily forceful and socially important document, and I think it most certainly ought to be published ...
> I know nothing about the author but I am convinced of his genuineness. Nobody could have made up the experiences which he describes ...
>
> The picture is convincing and personally, although I found it utterly disgusting, as of course it is meant to be, I also found that it held my attention far more closely than the ordinary novel ...

On the advice of his lawyer, Harold Rubinstein, Gollancz insisted that all of the names of individuals should be changed, and that clues as to the location of filthy cafés or Salvation Army hostels be made more vague so as to see off potential civil actions. Thinly disguised obscenities such as 'f_____' had to be deleted completely. Orwell did not object and hurriedly rewrote the draft in his room at the Hawthorns. Accounts differ as to why he now decided to stop being Eric Blair. The most obvious and probably the most likely reason was that he now knew that he could be a writer and that he wanted, at least on the printed page, to detach himself from his past, some of which he despised. George is a solidly English name and up to his death he could never quite make up his mind about how he felt about England, except that he could not stop being part of it. The river Orwell meanders slowly, almost thoughtfully, through Suffolk, and Eric Blair, as was, had enjoyed walking along its banks. Gollancz's advance of £40 disappointed him but in today's terms it is the equivalent of £3,500–£4,000, not bad for a first non-fiction book by a relatively unknown author.

Down and Out in Paris and London came out in 1933 and virtually all of the reviews were positive. The popular and generally right-wing *Evening Standard*, *Daily Mail* and *Sunday Express* judged it to be shockingly authentic rather than, as Orwell feared they might, warning against it as nourishment for socialist agitators. C. Day Lewis wrote in the *Adelphi* that it should 'shake the complacence of twentieth-century civilisation'. That Day Lewis would within months join the Communist Party is probably a coincidence. The *Manchester Guardian* found it to be 'a book which might work a revolution', and the *Times Literary Supplement* weighed in: 'a vivid picture of an apparently mad world'. J. B. Priestley in his dust-jacket blurb for the American edition pronounced it 'uncommonly good reading. An excellent book and a valuable social document.' Only the anonymous reviewer for the *New English Weekly* ventured doubts as to whether the author had genuinely lost contact with his, presumably more stable, life and circumstances: 'Down certainly, but out?'

His parents expressed relief that Eric was writing under a pseudonym and hoped that he would continue to do so were he to produce similar works, fiction or non-fiction. Ida seemed more puzzled than shocked; the figure who reported these events appeared to her utterly unlike her son, or at least the son she thought she knew. Friends in Southwold of Orwell's age – notably Eleanor Jacques, Dennis Collings and Brenda Salkeld – loved the book and encouraged him to celebrate his success.

Orwell 'courted' Eleanor and Brenda more or less at the same time but in different ways. With the latter he seemed, in part, to be playing the role of a minor-gentry suitor from a Jane Austen novel: any prospect of sex, for either, seemed to be sidelined by his bizarre marriage proposal. At the same time he did make it clear to Eleanor, in a non-aggressive, unassuming manner, that he thought they should have sex, and they did. Biographers have tried to explain this in terms of the alleged differences between the two women, with Brenda as relatively proper and demure and Eleanor her livelier, sexier alternative. Apart from the fact that

Eleanor was a little more attractive than Brenda, they had a great deal in common. Few now dispute that Brenda was the model for the spinsterish Dorothy in *A Clergyman's Daughter* and Eleanor for the more fiery Rosemary in *Keep the Aspidistra Flying*, but in each case the fictional characters incorporated gross exaggerations of aspects of their real-life counterparts. As would soon become his routine, Orwell was becoming a chameleon, acting out roles and, most significantly, involving others as members of the cast, as plans for his fiction evolved.

Shortly before he sent the draft of *Down and Out* to Eliot in autumn 1931 he extended his investigations of life at the bottom of the social scale by joining groups of working-class Londoners – some in casual employment, others unemployed – who at the end of every summer made their way to Kent to pick hops for the brewing industry, for what he describes as 'starvation wages'.

The only record we have of this is in his 'Hop-Picking Diary', published almost sixty years after his death. There are many parallels with *Down and Out*, notably his friendship with 'Ginger' who becomes the English working-class counterpart to Boris, the grand White Russian Cavalryman exiled in Paris. Orwell's empathetic attachment to Ginger is gradual, but self-evident – 'he' mutates into 'we' as the diary proceeds. When not doing casual work Ginger is a petty criminal. For him, theft is a means of survival and Orwell relishes becoming his partner in this: 'Ginger and I had only a blanket each, so we suffered agonies of cold for the first week; after that we stole enough pokes [sacks] to keep us warm.'

> On several nights Ginger tried to persuade me to come and rob the church with him, and he would have done it alone if I had not managed to get it into his head that suspicion was bound to fall on him, as a known criminal. He had robbed churches before, and he said, what surprised me, that there is generally something worth having in the Poor box. We had one

or two jolly nights, on Saturdays, sitting round a huge fire till midnight and roasting apples. One night, I remember, it came out that of about fifteen people round the fire, everyone except myself had been in prison. There were uproarious scenes in the village on Saturdays, for the people who had money used to get well drunk, and it needed the police to get them out of the pub. I have no doubt the residents thought us a nasty vulgar lot, but I could not help feeling that it was rather good for a dull village to have this invasion of cockneys once a year. (8 October 1931)

In *Down and Out* Orwell sometimes lapses into empathy and fellow-feeling with others at the bottom of society, notably Boris, but he does his best to take a step back and present things with as much impartiality as he can. As this passage from his *Diary* shows, the real Orwell wanted to become a member of the club of the dispossessed. He does not judge Ginger on his plan to rob the church, preferring to advise him on the prospect of getting caught. He is frustrated at finding that he is the only one who has not been to prison; he would later get drunk in an attempt to be brought before magistrates and sentenced for being drunk and disorderly. And he clearly enjoys the effect on the village of the presence of 'us'.

The 'Hop-Picking Diary' is important because it became the raw material for key parts of his second novel, *A Clergyman's Daughter*, written when his first, *Burmese Days*, was still being considered by publishers. Orwell later said he hated *A Clergyman's Daughter*, allegedly purchasing and burning as many of the first editions as he could. He certainly did not allow it to be reprinted in his lifetime once the first print run had sold out. D. J. Taylor thinks that Orwell could not quite make up his mind what he was attempting to achieve, causing the eponymous Dorothy to '[fall] in and out of the book, pushed aside by the torrents of reportage'.

I found it rather moving, one of the best of his pre-*Animal Farm* novels. Dorothy Hare is the daughter of a thoroughly disagreeable home-counties rector, for whom she keeps house. The widowed Rev. Hare is the younger son of minor gentry, maintaining the English tradition of the church as the destination of the sibling who does not inherit the title. He loathes virtually all of his parishioners, mainly because he cannot bear having to speak to, let alone baptise and comfort, individuals so far beneath his social standing. Dorothy dislikes her father but endures her life with him for want of an obvious alternative, until one day she finds herself in a London backstreet, sitting on the pavement, unable to remember quite where she came from or who she is. Thereafter, for the substance of the novel, she becomes a female version of George Orwell, or at least Orwell during his hop-picking adventures. The first people she comes across are Nobby and his two friends, Flo and Charlie. Their East End dialect is doubly puzzling to her, first through its unfamiliarity and also because she cannot quite remember the kind of language – educated, lower middle class – that makes her who she is. The 'Hop-Picking Diary' shows that Nobby is a near-exact replica of Orwell's friend Ginger. It would be unjust, however, to regard Orwell as drawing lazily on his then unpublished diary for want of resourceful inspiration. Rather he is experimenting with the relationship between what he had witnessed and the hypothetical and unknown.

As he was preparing the draft, which he completed in a little over six months, he corresponded regularly with Brenda Salkeld and they met on several occasions. Before setting off for Kent he wrote to her to arrange a meeting:

> I don't know what condition I shall be in. I suppose you won't object to a 3-day beard? I will promise to have no lice, anyway. What fun if we could both go hopping together. But I suppose your exaggerated fear of dirt would deter you. It is a great mistake to be too afraid of dirt.
>
> Best Love,
> Eric

He knew that Brenda would treat his invitation to go hopping as a joke and so it is, for her at least. Orwell was thinking about his novel, particularly the 'what if?' direction of the story. Brenda won't come with him in real life, but he'll bring her into the book to replace him. Dorothy hates the hardships of her new existence, the dirt in particular (and here he nods towards Brenda), yet at the same time she begins to feel that Nobby, Flo, Charlie and others treat her with a kind of rough good-fellowship. Gradually, fragments of her memory return and she begins to compare her previous life with her new one as an outcast and there is an extraordinary passage in Chapter Two when the narrator speaks for her:

> Yet you were happy, with an unreasonable happiness. The work took hold of you and absorbed you. It was stupid work, mechanical, exhausting and every day more painful to the hands, and yet you never wearied of it; when the weather was fine and the hops were good you had the feeling you could go on picking for ever and for ever. It gave you a physical joy, a warm satisfied feeling inside you ... The sun burned down upon you, baking you brown, and the bitter, never-palling scent, like a wind from oceans of cool beer, flowed into your nostrils and refreshed you. When the sun was shining everybody sang as they worked; the plantations rang with singing.

Dorothy is neither naively romantic nor condescending about her time with the impoverished hop-pickers. She knows that her occasional moments of elation are rare detours from a state of weary endurance. Nobby, whom she likes, even respects, is arrested. 'He caught Dorothy's eye and winked at her once again before being led away. And that was the last she ever saw of him.' Nonetheless, becoming someone else changes her. She loses her faith, and it testifies to the quality of the novel that Orwell only implies a reason for this while avoiding some weighty notion of cause. Dorothy returns to her role as her father's housekeeper, coordinator of Women's Institute events and proxy for the Rev. Hare when he cannot be bothered to care for his parishioners. She no longer believes in God, but at one point she kneels in church and beseeches Him to help her in dealing with her certainty that He does not exist.

Becoming someone else offers Orwell a route towards tackling the dilemmas he faced as himself. Dorothy's amnesia is uninvited but her creator was continually attempting to distance himself from his past even if he could not remove it from his memory.

Since Eton Orwell had gradually developed an aversion to all forms of established religion but he continued to waver between agnosticism and atheism. In Southwold he attended church, albeit irregularly, refused to take communion, hardly ever spoke with other worshippers, and read the *Church Times* in the same way that an anthropologist would scrutinise tribal rituals. David Astor in an interview in 2000 recalled Orwell telling him that 'I have passed myself off for pious and there is nothing for it but to keep up the deception.' The declaration seems odd until we read the passages where Dorothy is described as conducting the same exercise. She is certainly not attempting to reignite some aspect of her faith – she is content that it is gone forever – but for some reason of her own she returns in disguise to aspects of her past, acting out rites that no longer have any significance.

In his correspondence with Brenda, Orwell offers clues as to the direction and nature of the novel, persistently referring to Joyce's *Ulysses*. In Chapter Three of *A Clergyman's Daughter* he adapts the Joycean technique of stream of consciousness to his memories of Trafalgar Square, where the hop-pickers would assemble for their journey to Kent, mixing with prostitutes, tramps and Covent Garden porters. He is not copying Joyce; his chapter involves what amounts to a naturalistic cacophony of outburst and half-recorded conversations; it is as if he is walking through the district with a microphone picking up more or less at random verbal portraits of human exchange. This is documentary realism, not modernism. The least authentic presence, the one he has clearly invented, is also the most amusing: a rambling defrocked vicar who endlessly recalls his past while betraying his perversions:

> My Boys' Cricket Club, teetotallers only, my confirmation classes – purity lecture once monthly in the Parish Hall – my Boy Scout orgies! The Wolf Cubs will deliver the Grand Howl. Household Hints for the Parish Magazine, 'Discarded fountain-pen fillers can be used as enemas for canaries …'

Orwell knew that despite her father's profession Brenda would enjoy this. Each of them despised the hypocrisies within the Church of England, particularly the High Church. In a letter of June 1933 to Brenda he wrote that 'The *CT* [*Church Times*] annoys me more and more. It is a poor satisfaction even to see them walloping the Romans, because they do it chiefly by descending to their level … I have been told, that *CT* advertisement columns are full of disguised abortion advertisements …' He opens the letter with 'I sent you about two thirds of the rough draft of my novel yesterday' – containing the Trafalgar Square chapter with the defrocked vicar. On 27 July 1934 he tells her that 'I had lunch yesterday with Dr Ede. He is a bit of a feminist and thinks that if a woman was brought up exactly like a man she would be able to throw a stone, construct a syllogism, keep a secret etc.' Brenda was fully aware that in the novel her friend was conducting an experiment similar to Ede's hypothesis, by placing a woman in exactly the circumstances that he, a man, had experienced. His arch account of Ede's ideas shows that he and Brenda had talked of these matters, and that each would treat the doctor's quack liberalism as preposterous. Ede's premise is that women 'brought up' as women are in various ways backward and intellectually inferior.

The principal cause of critics' displeasure with the novel is the apparently arbitrary jump from Dorothy's past to her imminent future. She does not know how or why she ends up in a London backstreet and Orwell denies the reader an explanation. As

an aesthetic gesture the quality of this shift is debatable but as
a moment of autobiographical self-scrutiny it is fascinating.
Dorothy was, like her creator, crossing boundaries between
status, background, dialect, class, prospects, even states of mind.
Orwell casts into his novel questions that troubled him regarding
his non-fictional adventures: principally, can I become part of or
understand a way of life that I can only enter as a pretender? Just
as significant is his enrolment of Brenda as his correspondent and
advisor on the progress of the book. She was his sounding board
for the book's other exercise in becoming someone else, a woman.
A Clergyman's Daughter is a subtly feminist novel. Dorothy is by no
means a cosmopolitan 'new woman', one who might hold a degree
or pursue some career of her own. She is unambitiously intelligent,
with little experience beyond the village of her father's parish, and
in this respect she is Brenda Salkeld. Brenda knew this but was
certainly not insulted by it. Thrown into the world of danger, near-
starvation and manual labour with no hope of returning to her
previous life – she cannot remember what it involved – she shows
innate qualities of endurance and courage. Orwell was saying to his
friend: you would have coped as well as I did.

Brenda had already seen drafts of the work before it was published,
but when Orwell sent her a copy in March 1935 he stated: 'You will
see … that I have employed you as a collaborator in two places.'
She knew he had borrowed from her for the book but the term
'collaborator' is differently nuanced, and 'two places' is intriguing.
In the novel we come across Warburton, a wealthy amoral rake who
lives in the same village as the Hares. He attempts to seduce Dorothy,
who resists his advances and finds him particularly abhorrent.
Thereafter he treats her with a curious blend of condescension and
scorn. And then there is Nobby:

> Nobby had tried to make love to Dorothy, of course, and, when
> she repulsed him, bore her no grudge. He had that happy temp-
> erament that is incapable of taking its own reverses seriously.

Orwell had never tried to persuade Brenda to have sex, but he had shocked her into a response by proposing marriage (and he had rehearsed this with his love poem to the sixteen-year-old Dora). She had 'collaborated' once in life with Orwell himself, and in the novel her proxy had done so in two places by rejecting the repulsive Warburton and, more obligingly, the advances of Nobby.

Orwell was exploring the parallels between proactive seduction and other gestures and roles allocated exclusively to men, specifically proposing marriage or declaring emotional, potentially sexual inclinations in verse. In each instance the woman, especially if not forewarned, is forced into a defensive state; she is obliged to respond while a man is free to make an advance whenever or in whatever form he chooses.

The Me Too movement has enabled women, and some men, to speak out on mainstream and social media and offer accounts of everything from inappropriate double entendres in the workplace or on the street to rape. Aside from allowing individuals to go public with disclosures of what had occurred perhaps decades earlier, it also, within months, created an effect that invites comparison with the far more gradual openings up of the consensually sanctioned secrets, lies and hypocrisies of Western society from the nineteenth century onwards. Obvious examples include the legal recognition in the 1960s that homosexuality is not a crime or a perversion and, since then, a general perception within society of lesbians, gays, bisexuals and transgender individuals as 'us' rather than 'them'. Me Too, far more rapidly, exposed what seems to be the final skeleton in the cupboard of our supposedly liberal First-World society: that in everything from show business to the office or railway carriage, men have been allowed to act as pests and predators and have apparently been sanctioned in doing so by undisclosed social conventions.

I would not venture that Orwell anticipated Me Too, not quite; but he did make a small gesture towards what would become a mass movement more than eight decades later. Consider the ways in which his biographers – all of whom are male – have dealt with

Dorothy. Taylor describes her as 'condemned to a life of spinsterdom owing to her terror of sex'. On what grounds does he present her as such? All we know for certain is that unasked-for physical contact with Warburton makes her feel ill. As far as Nobby is concerned she simply turns him down without damaging their friendship. In Shelden's opinion, 'She likes men as friends, but she cannot bear their physical advances,' and as evidence of this he quotes the passage where Dorothy inwardly fumes at the nature of men after Warburton's advances: 'Why couldn't they leave you *alone*? Why did they always have to kiss you and maul you about?' Clearly, Shelden extrapolates Dorothy's experience with one man to a notion of her as by parts virtuous and frigid. Meyer presents her as 'pale, shy, *repressed* [my emphasis] and overworked … frigid and spinsterish …' In the novel that went to press Warburton's attempt to have sex with her bears a striking resemblance to the majority of allegations made against Harvey Weinstein. Only two women claimed that he had non-consensual sex with them; the rest stated that he demanded they perform sexual acts in return for his decision on whether to advance or ruin their careers. While Warburton has no influence on Dorothy's future both he and Weinstein share a perception of their rank as leaving them unaccountable in terms of how they behave towards women.

I must stress the term 'novel that went to press' because Victor Gollancz insisted that Orwell describe Warburton's act thus: '… [he had] begun making love to her, violently, outrageously, even brutally'. In the original draft Orwell wrote that he 'tried to rape Dorothy'. Gollancz was a social radical who knew that women of all classes in Britain were vulnerable to rape and other forms of sexual assault. But he was also a businessman, aware of the effect that Orwell's first draft would have on even his more liberal-minded readers. Was he over-anxious? The British period drama *Downton Abbey* is set in the same period as Orwell's novel. It has been outstandingly popular in the UK and the US, but in 2014 an episode featured a graphic representation of rape. Violent, horrible presentations of rape have occurred in film and television dramas for some time, and virtually all reflect a broad acceptance that it is a terrible crime which should not be ignored in depictions of our world that make any claim to be realistic. Following the *Downton Abbey* episode, however, social media was swamped with complaints from fans of the programme who seemed shocked and distressed; the overwhelming mood of the complainants was that the rape scene was inappropriate. The popularity of *Downton Abbey* was founded upon the generally reliable appeal of false nostalgia; returning to various periods of the past as a means of escaping our own. The rape did not shock simply because it involved rape; rather it showed that people in the 1920s and 1930s could be as unpleasant as their present-day counterparts. To pretend that life then was utterly different from life now is ludicrous of course, but it is based on the same premise that caused Gollancz to demand that Orwell should revise his wording. *Downton Abbey* fans displaced the present in favour of a past made up of secrets and lies: we know it happens but the modern viewer shares with Gollancz a reluctance to accept that what actually happens does not correspond with our delusion. In the 1920s and 1930s men found guilty of rape faced sentences of life imprisonment, but it was a commonplace presumption among the police and within the judicial system that the victim was subconsciously willing, or 'just asking for it'. Even psychologists of the period held that rape was a 'victim-precipitated crime'. Here we should re-examine Orwell's biographers' presentations of Dorothy as variously spinsterish, terrified of sex, unable to bear the physical presence of men, virtuous and frigid. Up to the late 1970s these same stereotypes informed the consensus of opinion on women who accused men of rape. Warburton is middle-aged, physically unattractive, egotistical and content with his position as a man who can treat women such as Dorothy much as the feral predator treats its prey. Weinstein comes to mind, but so does a more powerful figure who claimed that a particular term – 'the person who got away' – was, 'under the rules of Me Too', one that 'I'm not allowed to use … anymore. I can't do it.' The 'person' was a woman who resisted his sexual advances. He was recorded as saying: 'And when you're a star, they let you do it. You can do anything … Grab them by the pussy. You can do anything.' Trump's manner is certainly more crude and brutish than Orwell's biographers' in their treatment of Dorothy, but they all belong in the same club.

Orwell was baiting contemporary readers, a strategy that Gollancz almost undermined. He wanted them to look behind the delusional conventions of social mores at what could actually occur when men felt empowered to treat women as inferior and as sexual conquests. Later, in *Nineteen Eighty-Four*, he would return to this experiment. The relationship between Winston and Julia is more equitable than that of Warburton and Dorothy, but for Orwell, the author, there is something equally vile about it.

7

BOOKS, MARRIAGE, AND THE JOURNEY NORTH

Orwell left Hawthorns in 1933 and found another job teaching at the slightly more prestigious Frays College in Uxbridge. Little is known of his time there given that he was forced to resign after only a few months. He had bought a second-hand motorbike and spent much of his spare time on excursions through the country lanes surrounding Uxbridge. In mid-December he set off in torrential rain wearing only light clothes, and within a day had come down with a chill that soon developed into pneumonia. His mother and Avril visited him in Uxbridge Cottage Hospital where the doctor informed them that his life was in danger. 'How the Poor Die' (1946) is based largely on his experiences in a Paris hospital but there are a couple of memorable passages that come from his time in Uxbridge. English nurses, he observes, 'are dumb enough, they may tell fortunes with tea-leaves, wear Union Jack badges and keep photographs of the Queen on their mantlepieces, but [unlike their French counterparts] at least they don't let you lie unwashed and constipated on an unmade bed, out of sheer laziness'. Nostalgia and condescension with a hint of patriotism perhaps, but we should also remember that when he wrote this memoir the most radical policy of the recently elected Labour government was the 1946 National Health Service Act. Orwell seemed confident that English nurses would provide excellent services 'free at the point of delivery'. He also tells of how a fellow patient with whom he was drinking tea suddenly died, and of how the nurses removed him so dextrously that no one else in the ward noticed.

He was discharged in January 1934 and returned once more to the family home in Southwold only to receive a letter, later that month, from Gollancz, informing him that they had decided not to publish *Burmese Days*. His agent, Leonard Moore, placed it with Harper Brothers who published an American edition, and eventually Gollancz changed his mind and brought it out in the UK in 1935, after insisting that *every* name be changed, even those of indigenous characters, to avoid libel actions.

Orwell completed *A Clergyman's Daughter* in September and posted it to Moore after leaving Southwold for a new address and a new job in London. The arrangement came about with the assistance of his aunt Nellie, still in Paris, who wrote to her friends Francis and Myfanwy Westrope, who lived on the southern edge of Hampstead. Like the Adamses, the Westropes were ardent socialists and fans of Esperanto as the language which would bring unity and peace to a new world of shared ownership. Nellie asked the Westropes if they might find her nephew some work, however modestly paid, and somewhere to live. They could, and contacted Orwell in Southwold offering him a post in their bookshop, called Booklovers' Corner, in South End Green, Hampstead. He would also be provided with lodgings above the shop in the Westropes' flat.

We have no evidence that Orwell asked Nellie for help but we do not need any. We know that he wanted to move to London and his aunt was not a clairvoyant. Once more he covered his tracks regarding his contacts with the Limouzin branch of the family, and a blend of lying and concealment would be the keynote of this time in the Hampstead bookshop. It was the setting for his most autobiographical novel, *Keep the Aspidistra Flying*, a work that is unmatched in the annals of fiction for its double allegiance to authenticity and disinformation. It was fifteen years before he began to formulate the dystopia of *Nineteen Eighty-Four* but he had this internalised, quixotic exercise in Newspeak to fall back on.

In terms of his temperament and outlook the book's protagonist, Gordon Comstock, is an exact replica of his author – cynical, undemonstrably ambitious as a writer and prone to bouts of introversion and eccentricity. Both work, for very little money, in a North London bookshop, but in every other respect Orwell reinvents himself as everything that he is not, involving features that shame him, that he hopes to rid himself of, and which he fears.

Comstock reserves implacable contempt for the vast majority of his customers, in his view intellectual over-reachers and dull middlebrow timewasters who never tire of sharing their opinions with him. But we only learn of this via the narrator. Orwell was relentlessly polite and obliging, happy to exchange ideas with anyone who had wandered into the shop, irrespective of their cleverness or breadth of reading. Notably, in Orwell's letters to Brenda, we discover traces of Comstock which, perhaps for the sake of decency or keeping his job, the author and his character kept mostly to themselves.

Comstock describes the entire contemporary literary spectrum from lowbrow to highbrow as 'dead stars above, damp squibs below. Shall we ever again get a writer worth reading?' D. H. Lawrence is merely 'all right' and Joyce is 'better before he went off his coco-nut'. One must assume by this that he refers to the Joyce of *Ulysses*, then his most recent novel. It is evident from Orwell's letters to Brenda that he admired it greatly and he marvelled at the anti-establishment endeavours of Lawrence. Most of all Comstock loathed the London literary intelligentsia as the broader network of privilege distilled into the world of publishing, and ensuring the success of 'snooty, refined books ... by those moneyed young beasts who glide so gracefully from Eton to Cambridge and from Cambridge to the literary reviews'. Comstock does his best to advance his literary career without seeking such patronage but despite himself becomes associated with Ravelston, the slick, socialist editor of *Antichrist*. Comstock presents *Antichrist* as being run to salve its editor's conscience: '... it gave the impression of being edited by an ardent Nonconformist who had transferred his allegiance from God to Marx ... Practically anything got printed in *Antichrist* if Ravelston suspected that its author was starving.' Self-evidently Ravelston and his magazine are based on Sir Richard Rees and the *Adelphi*. Orwell formed a close friendship with Rees and was a regular contributor to the *Adelphi*, but does Comstock allow us a glimpse into feelings that caused him disquiet, almost self-loathing?

All of this brings to mind the recollections of the *Adelphi*'s circulation pusher, Jack Common, ex-mechanic and son of a Newcastle engine-driver. Common had no idea when he first met him that Orwell was creating Comstock, his twisted doppelganger, but, inadvertently, he tells us a great deal about what was going on. Common asked him how he came to write for the *Adelphi* and Orwell told him that he first read it in Burma. It was, he said, a relief from 'petty minds ... starved for intellectual debate' but that he came to hate its upper middle-class sanctimoniousness. 'Often the magazine disgusted him. Then he'd prop it up against a tree and fire his rifle at it till the copy was a ruin.' This, apparently, is Orwell speaking to him, but we might easily be listening to his fictional counterpart. Common recalls a conversation with Orwell in which they discussed the 'curse' of Christmas for those who couldn't afford to celebrate it:

> Anyway it is certain that he was tempted to launch out with one of the statements he loved to use for shock value and which made him appear like an over-long *enfant terrible* in decay. 'I would like to spend Christmas in gaol,' he said.

In the novel Comstock drags Ravelston into a foul working-class pub and introduces him to prostitutes. Ravelston has to pay his friend's fine for being drunk and disorderly and have him released from gaol. Orwell was determined to find out what it was like to be in custody and 'Clink', written in 1932 but not published until much later, records his farcical attempts to drink enough to get himself arrested and imprisoned.

Comstock's pursuit of Rosemary combines pathos with desperation; he is an appallingly inept suitor. Orwell, when he wrote the novel, was seeing three women at the same time. Apart from his Southwold friend Eleanor Jacques, whom he'd met several years earlier in Southwold and who was now in London, there was Sally Jerome – privately educated and part South African, part American – and Kay Welton, well read and 'modern' in terms of her attitude to whom she chose to sleep with. According to Mabel Fierz, a friend of Orwell's who also flirted with him, 'Kay had a good figure, useful for sex.' Comstock's 'bitch of a landlady' forbids female visitors to her tenants and when Myfanwy Westrope asked Orwell if he would be receiving women guests he assumed she was about to apply the same edict. He at first said 'no' and she replied, 'I only meant that I didn't mind whether you do or not.'

With regard to his social life Comstock is equally unfulfilled, Ravelston excepted, and it remains unclear if this is due to his decision to isolate himself from a culture that he holds in contempt or whether those he meets simply don't like him. His creator, however, was busily gregarious and enjoyed a wide range of friendships with thinkers and cultural figures similarly concerned with literature and politics. One of these was with his fellow lodger at the Westropes, Jon Kimche, a Swiss Jew who had arrived in England aged twelve. He worked alongside Orwell at the bookshop. Kimche was active in the ILP and would become an influential writer and political activist; he was an ardent supporter of a post-war Jewish state. The two men got on well and would remain friends, despite Orwell's anti-Zionist opinions. Due to Myfanwy Westrope's illness Orwell and Kimche had to find new rooms. Mabel Fierz contacted her friend Rosalind Obermeyer, then studying psychology at University College, London, who owned a flat at 77 Parliament Hill. There Orwell entertained Kay Welton privately and introduced her to two men he had recently met via

Rosalind. Rayner Heppenstall had a degree in English from Leeds University and would go on to write novels and poems and work as a producer for the BBC Third Programme. They would go out for drinks, sometimes with Kay, and Orwell would occasionally host basic dinner parties for them in the shared sitting room of the flat, usually chops cooked on his 'Batchelor Griller'. He had learnt the basics of cooking when working in the hotel kitchen in Paris.

One night at the fashionably bohemian Bertorelli's restaurant in Fitzrovia Orwell dined on the best Italian food – generally unavailable in London at the time – in the company of Rees, Heppenstall and Dylan Thomas; much drink was taken by all and Heppenstall recalls the evening as a bizarre encounter between two men whose impact on literature would be great but who were too incapacitated by cider and gin to talk of it. Heppenstall also introduced Orwell to T. Sturge Moore and the poet Michael Sayers. The former was an acolyte of Yeats who had never quite accepted the twentieth century while Sayers was a full-blown communist who would suffer the horrible effects of McCarthyism following his move to America. Each for Orwell reinforced his suspicion that literary culture was a refuge for self-regard, other-worldliness or hubris. Around the same time he was reacquainted with his old Eton friend, Cyril Connolly, who had reviewed *Burmese Days* favourably. Connolly had become a louche, bacchanalian version of Rees, espousing left-leaning politics more as a fashion accessory than a genuine commitment. Yet Orwell kept in contact with him, and Connolly's clique of writers, thinkers and activists were drawn to this new, somewhat eccentric fellow traveller. Orwell had become something of a social and cultural magnet. After receiving a letter from the social anthropologist Geoffrey Gorer offering unreserved praise for *Burmese Days* he invited Gorer to Parliament Hill and cooked him a supper of liver and bacon. Orwell's guest found the meal hideous but it cemented a life-long friendship and secured for Orwell another contact in the mainstream intelligentsia.

Why did Orwell turn himself inside out in his alter ego Comstock? One thing the author and his invention had in common was temperamental fractiousness, and an inclination to disagree and make trouble just for the sake of it. Heppenstall later presented Orwell as an embroidery of contradictions; 'a curious mind, satirically attached to everything traditionally English, always full of interesting and out-of-the-way information ... but arid, colourless, devoid of poetry, derisive, yet darkly obsessed'. This could be Comstock, except that he internalises his bitterness and detaches himself from the world that provokes it. Orwell settled for a compromise. He disliked what he had become but the opportunities to have sex, make friends and become part of the literary establishment overruled his disquiet. Comstock is his fictionalised act of remorse.

Jack Common wrote articles for the *Adelphi* on his background and a collection of these, *The Freedom of the Streets*, was published in 1938. Common was treated, albeit with respect, as a conscience-salving curiosity by publishers and editors. He was fully aware of this as he was of the presence of another misfit, Orwell. 'He was not as other Bloomsbury souls, they said, he was an outsider, a rebel, a tramp, he lived and wrote in the bottom-most underworld of poverty.' Common saw parallels between them except that he also knew that Orwell aspired to the 'bottom-most underworld of poverty,' while he had been born into it. Nonetheless, he was 'a man to look out for then, a man to meet.' Each of them disliked the system they were part of, that sustained them as writers, but accepted that without it they would not get into print.

Surely things have changed, considerably? In February 2018 Kit de Waal published an article in the *Guardian* called 'Make room for working-class writers'. She intended, in part, to promote her *Common People: An Anthology of Working-Class Writers*, but she included illuminating details on the state of publishing, and literary culture in general, that had become evident to her as she put the anthology together. Contemporary working-class life is still the subject of fiction, she finds, but it is a niche market, something that might bear comparison with the most macabre and morally questionable forms of crime noir. The latter are not read by the kind of people who feature in them; psychopathic serial killers, their victims, and bloodthirsty vigilantes generally make up a small percentage of the reading public. Equally, sink estate residents, drug peddlers and addicts, perpetrators and recipients of domestic violence, let alone those who simply survive on the minimum wage, rarely purchase novels which offer graphic depictions of their lives. Those who do read these novels are from the other side of the tracks, and are tempted to enter another world via a mixture of false empathy and voyeurism. *Trainspotting* is the obvious case. There are no records of how many sadomasochists and lunatics from the Edinburgh lower orders appreciated the book, in comparison with its Scottish and English educated middle-class fans, but one can take a confident guess.

De Waal tells of authors such as Lisa Blower, from a genuinely working-class background in Stoke-on-Trent, who had moved into the 'establishment' by attaining an academic post at Bangor University, but still spent two years trying to find a publisher for her novel *Sitting Ducks*. Editors found it fascinating but were sceptical about the authenticity of the way its characters behaved, perceived themselves, and even the way they talked to each other. Blower was exasperated because she had picked these details from personal experience, while her readers in the prestigious London trade houses had never been to such places let alone grown up in them; they, Blower put it, experienced her depictions 'from the outside looking in'.

Penguin recently launched a project called 'WriteNow', an initiative to find new writers from diverse backgrounds, and emphasis was placed on writers from 'a socio-economically marginalised background', including 'BAME (Black, Asian, Minority Ethnic) or LGBTQ (Lesbian, Gay, Bisexual, Trans, Queer), [and] writers with a disability'. When Orwell became literary editor of the *Tribune* in 1943 he embarked on a similar project, without publicly advertising it, to favour unpublished, usually lower-class, contributors. Many saw their work go into print for the first time and then disappeared without trace. Some were indeed very bad but at least Orwell had allowed them one course from the High Table. Periodically the literary establishment tries to become less of an in-crowd, often to make it feel better about itself, but more often than not the exercise is transient, a token gesture, and normal service is resumed. Penguin also announced that it would waive its previous requirement for an employee to hold a university degree. They did not offer a rationale for this but one must assume that in their view being degreeless ensures a joyless level of deprivation. However, the editorial boards of Penguin/ Random House do not, as far as I am aware, presently include real-life versions of *Trainspotting*'s Renton, Begbie and Sick Boy.

There was a brief period when the working classes communicated directly with the literary establishment and the moderately highbrow reading public, mainly during the late 1950s and early 1960s. The so-called 'angry young men' and 'The Movement' figures of the post-war years (notably Amis, Larkin, Wain, Osborne and Conquest) were largely middle class and Oxbridge educated. The other group, the roughhouse 'kitchen-sinkers', usually came from further north: notably Waterhouse, Braine, Storey, Barstow, Hines and Sillitoe. For the first time in literary history life in the 'bottom-most underworld', as Common put it, had become the raw material for the fiction of writers who'd experienced it. Yet this too was something of an illusion. The majority of these writers had grown up with self-educated working-class parents, some of whom had already crossed the divide between poverty and modest ordinariness, and become teachers, grocers, civil servants and so on. The only exception was Sillitoe, whose father was an illiterate drunk who beat his mother and drove her to occasional prostitution. After this festival of working-class soul-bearing and vituperation things returned to the them-and-us state of 1932–33, with minor variations.

In a paper published in 2016 by Dave O'Brien of Goldsmiths University it was shown that forty-seven per cent of all authors, writers and translators come from middle-class backgrounds – and predominantly have attended private school, Oxbridge or Russell Group universities – while only ten per cent have parents in routine or manual labour (*Cultural Trends*, vol 25, 2016).

Forty-six per cent of positions of significance in the most important publishing houses are held by middle- or upper-class individuals, with the proportion increasing to almost sixty per cent for those editors who make decisions on what should be published or rejected. Ten per cent of those in publishing are from the working classes and for the people who decide on what goes to press the figure drops to four per cent. There has been a change since Comstock/Orwell railed against 'those moneyed young beasts who glide so gracefully from Eton to Cambridge and from Cambridge to the literary reviews,' but only a slight change. Two literary editors of the major broadsheets and weeklies are Old Etonians, and the vast majority of the others are private- and public-school educated, with Oxbridge degrees.

It is interesting that after *Coming Up for Air* Orwell gave up on conventional fiction. He had, and would, write about the working classes and revolution, but only as a commentator. He knew that he could not pretend to belong to, and recreate, the infrastructure of working-class existence. Only those who were part of it could bring it to life in fiction, and the literary world would have to wait until the emergence of Sillitoe *et al* for that. As an inhabitant of the story, he would save his talents as a novelist for two books that were dystopian, politically engaged and gloomily prophetic, but which can never be regarded as documentary realism: *Animal Farm* and *Nineteen Eighty-Four.*

In autumn 1935 Orwell asked his landlady Rosalind Obermeyer if they might co-host a dinner party, given that his bedsitting room was too small for him to offer more than a basic meal to one or two guests. He invited Rees and Heppenstall, and Rosalind asked along a few people with whom she worked and studied. When the evening ended Orwell, nominally the host, accompanied all the guests to the various bus stops, tube and railway stations and on his return announced to Rosalind his fascination with one of her fellow students, Eileen O'Shaughnessy. 'Now *that*,' he said, 'is the kind of girl I would like to marry!' And so he did, less than a year later on 9 June 1936, at St Mary's Church, Wallington, Hertfordshire. Eileen was the daughter of a Collector of Customs in South Shields, near Newcastle, and had won a scholarship to read English at St Hugh's College, Oxford. Since graduating in 1927 she'd had a number of jobs in London and when she met Orwell was reading for a postgraduate qualification in psychology at the University of London, with a view to becoming a social worker. Like him she was alert to the widespread social inequities in Britain in the 1930s but was not, as yet, affiliated to a particular political party or cause. According to accounts by Orwell's friends she was not the most attractive or intelligent of Orwell's girlfriends.

The couple decided to rent a rather run-down cottage in the village of Wallington for no other reason than they hoped the country air would help with Orwell's worsening bouts of bronchitis, and the quietness of the place seemed to offer a suitable environment for his writing. Regarding his health their new residence proved counter-productive. The fireplaces belched smoke, there was no hot water or electricity, only an outside lavatory, and the rusting corrugated iron roof leaked in several places, as well as sending a deafening noise through the cottage when there was heavy rain. Eileen gave up on her projected career, kept house and helped Orwell with his self-sufficiency project: he bought goats and chickens, planted apple trees and converted the overgrown garden into a vegetable patch including areas for potatoes, cabbage, sprouts and carrots. The front room of the house had once been used as the local General Store and Orwell planned to reopen it to sell his own home-grown produce to locals, a profit-free enterprise. When he was paid for articles or an advance was due they would go for drinks in their local, The Plough.

There are only a few anecdotal details regarding Orwell's pre-marital relationship with Eileen, but of its eight months he was absent for nine consecutive weeks. In January 1936, midway between their first meeting and their marriage, Victor Gollancz contacted him and, without asking for a proposal or synopsis, commissioned him to write a book about the condition of the unemployed and the worst-paid manual workers in various parts of Northern England. The advance of £500 was generous indeed and would enable Orwell to convince Eileen that they would have enough to live on as a couple in rural Hertfordshire; the rent for the cottage was seven shillings and six pence per week.

He would spend the two months away from Eileen during February and March 1936 doing research for his Gollancz book. First he took the train to Coventry and after that tried to absorb himself into the lifestyles of working men in Manchester, Wigan, Barnsley, Sheffield, Macclesfield and, briefly, Liverpool. Apart from staying a couple of nights with his sister and brother-in-law, the Dakins, in Leeds, he did his best to repeat aspects of *Down and Out*, at least in terms of his accommodation. His advance would have allowed him to stay in cheap but respectable, and hygienic, bed and breakfasts but instead he went for the rooms that had to be taken by 'bachelor workers' who, as he would make clear in *The Road to Wigan Pier*, suffered more than other working-class men. Without the modest support of family networks that came with marriage, single men were obliged to spend everything they could earn simply on surviving. Jim Hammond, a National Union of Mineworkers official and a communist, was one of many Union and Labour/ILP figures who acted as intermediaries between Orwell and the places and people he intended to write about. He recalled how Orwell chose his accommodation: 'He could have gone to any of a thousand respectable working-class houses and lodged with them or stayed right where he was. But he doesn't do that. He goes to a doss-house, just like he's down and out in Paris still. You see, when they've left the upper class, they've got to go right down into muck and start muckraking ... Did he have a taste for that sort of thing?'

Perhaps, as Hammond suggests, there was a degree of sanctimonious hypocrisy in his insistence on experiencing the worst – he would go back to his modestly paid but secure middle-class environment, while his fellow doss-house dwellers had no prospect for improvement. Yet how else would he be able to report truthfully on the horrible conditions of Northern working-class England? And the reports are extraordinary and horrifying. In one house he encounters 'an old woman with a blackened neck and her hair coming down denouncing her landlord in a Lancashire-Irish accent; and her mother, aged well over ninety, sitting in the background on the barrel that served her as a commode and regarding us blankly with a yellow, cretinous face'. The houses, particularly in Wigan, often took the appearance of three-dimensional surrealist installations, with walls and windows somewhat at odds with what had once been the symmetry of horizontal and vertical alignments. But this was not an anticipation of post-modern post-Bauhaus architecture. The men who lived in these houses were also, inadvertently, destroying them. As the pits drove further into the substructure of the earth so the surface of the land above the mine shafts would experience subsidence. Orwell reports on how a miner returned to his home to find that his front door was jammed in its frame following a shift of a matter of inches while he worked underground. He had to use a sledgehammer to release his family and enter his house. Once the subsidence had caused cracks in the fabric of these already poorly built properties the armies of bugs would move with greater confidence from one room to another.

One of his worst experiences of squalor came during his days as a lodger in the house of the Brookers, who were united in their contempt for their oldest tenant, Mr Hooker, permanently bedridden upstairs. 'Sometimes Mr Brooker would look up from his potato-peeling, catch my eye and jerk his head with a look of inexpressible bitterness towards the ceiling, towards old Hooker's room. "It's a b_____, ain't it?" he would say.' ... 'The Brookers were quite openly pining for him to die. When that happened they could at least draw the insurance money.'

Orwell is particularly appalled by the Brookers' seemingly gratuitous attachment to the unhygienic. 'However tactfully I tried, I could never induce Mr Brooker to let me cut my own bread-and-butter; he *would* hand it to me slice by slice, each slice gripped firmly under that broad black thumb.' At breakfast slices of bread and butter laid out from the night before always carried conspicuous thumb-marks, as if to remind lodgers that the tactile presence of the Brookers was a consistent feature of all food consumed in the house. Mrs Brooker was equally unsavoury and:

> … had a habit of constantly wiping her mouth on one of her blankets. Towards the end of my stay she took to tearing off strips of newspaper for this purpose, and in the morning the floor was often littered with crumpled-up balls of slimy paper which lay there for hours. The smell of the kitchen was dreadful, but, as with that of the bedroom, you ceased to notice it after a while.

Orwell decided that he could no longer endure lodging with the Brookers after he found a full chamber pot under the breakfast table. For anyone who has read *Down and Out* the implication is that the English working classes are capable of treating their own with contempt while the French, in the hotel in which he worked, reserved special portions of phlegm, spit and hair oil only for diners who could afford extortionately priced meals. Is he disgruntled by the behaviour of his native dispossessed? The thought occurs to him:

> Of course the squalor of these people's houses is sometimes their own fault. Even if you live in a back to back house and have four children and a total income of thirty-two and sixpence a week from the PAC, there is no *need* to have unemptied chamber-pots standing about in your living room. But it is equally certain that their circumstances do not encourage self-respect.

The Parisians with whom Orwell mixed were poverty-stricken opportunists, constantly shifting from one job to another and making the best of whatever was available. The working classes in Northern England, particularly the unemployed with families, were stuck in a downward spiral which incessantly stripped them of anything resembling pride or dignity.

In the mining towns pitmen who had managed to stay in work survived as well as they could in overcrowded terraces, but those who had lost their jobs following the General Strike in 1926 had become the equivalent of tramps, but tramps with wives, children and sometimes mothers and fathers. When the dole was no longer sufficient to cover their rent they joined what Orwell refers to as 'caravan-colonies'; but he guards the reader against forming a picture of 'a cosy gypsy-encampment'. Most of the 'caravans' in Wigan were rusting single-decker buses, minus their wheels and propped on planks of wood. Others were railway wagons with canvas roofs precariously supported by any pieces of timber that could be scavenged from the waste ground 'on which the caravans have been dumped like rubbish shot out of a bucket'. All of these crude habitations were permanently damp from the bog-like ground on which they were propped, close to 'Wigan's miry canal', with mattresses often still wringing wet at eleven in the morning. The only heat came from crude 'kitcheners', often disused barrels or dustbins, which burned anything free and flammable, usually coal that could be picked from slag heaps. Water was shared by all caravaners – there were more than 1,000 at Orwell's estimation – from a single hydrant. Each family built a hut which served as their lavatory and every few days dug a hole nearby to bury their buckets of faeces. He finds it impossible to describe the dirt, congestion and smell of the colony; it reminds him of the worst he had seen in Burma. 'But, as a matter of fact, nothing in the East could ever be quite as bad, for in the East you haven't our clammy, penetrating cold to contend with, and the sun is a disinfectant.' The local council might have found a clause related to standards of hygiene or public decency in the 1824 Vagrancy Act as a means of closing down the colonies, but they probably chose not to because there was nowhere else for these people to go. Today (see the *Guardian*, 18 June 2019) local authorities across Britain are involved in a purge of 'encampments', usually made up of tents but sometimes involving sheds. The most assiduous purgers are Peterborough, Bristol, Milton Keynes, Cardiff, Manchester, Leeds and, of course, London. These modern versions of Orwell's caravan-colonies have been set up on waste land or church property to avoid the attention of police who patrol city centre pavements – the C of E being generally more indulgent than local government. Nonetheless local authorities tend to opt for a literal interpretation of the Vagrancy Act, which includes prosecution for 'lodging … in the open air, or under a tent, or in any cart or wagon'. In Brighton the council seizes the tents of encampment rough sleepers on a regular basis, charging them £25 for the return of the tent in each instance. In East Dorset the fee is £50. Despite the filth in which they lived, Orwell's caravaners did not need to fear that their 'cart or wagon' would be taken from them by local authorities.

For those in employment, the miners, Orwell offers a minutely detailed account of their working life. The route to the coalface involves something close to voluntary torture. For much of the journey they might be on all fours and for the rest the best headroom they can hope for is four feet, punctuated by beams, 'and sometimes you forget to duck'. The atmosphere was stifling, in terms of the heat, and asphyxiating and blinding because of the dust. Every miner was stripped to the waist and each carried a badge of service known as 'buttons down the back', a scab on each vertebra caused by being permanently bent and colliding routinely with rock, timber or steel in spaces so confined that it was sometimes impossible to turn around. 'Travelling' from the surface to the coalface is, as Orwell points out, at least as frightening and exhausting as turning the coal or servicing machinery, but the miners are not paid for the time taken. In the pit he goes to, the distance from the pit-bottom, where the cage lifts and descends, is around one mile, but this is mercifully short compared with others in the locality where men are expected to walk or crawl up to five miles before and after earning their hourly pay. 'I had not realised that before he even gets to his work he may have to creep through passages as long as from London Bridge to Oxford Circus.'

Orwell writes that 'the miner's job would be as much beyond my power as it would be to perform on the flying trapeze or to win the Grand National'. This was not false modesty or hyperbole. Despite his bouts of bronchitis he had a wiry athletic physique, and the account given much later by the man who was his principal guide underlines Orwell's claim that miners were subjected to conditions that even the fittest would find inhumane. Orwell himself edited out of *The Road to Wigan Pier* details of the physical effects that even a brief period underground had on him. His guide, Jerry Kennan, was an electrician and an ILP member and he adds anecdotal evidence to Orwell's comment that 'sometimes [they] forget to duck' the beams. Orwell had a good six inches on the tallest of the underground workers. 'Well we rigged him out in a helmet and a lamp, and trammelling down the main road which ... I could comfortably stand up in ... we hadn't gone more than 300 yards when Orwell just didn't duck his head quick enough. It didn't knock the helmet off; it knocked him down. He was flat out.' However, once they revived him conditions became even worse: 'I think ... we travelled the best part of three quarters of a mile, bent absolutely double.' There had been a heavy rock fall and after a detour they reached the face. 'And the working face was, I think, 26 inches.' Before they got to the surface again Orwell passed out several times, as Kennan recalls, '... there were three occasions altogether in which he was completely out'. Orwell had faced the stark horrors of what went on underground for men who enabled life on the surface to continue.

Practically everything we do, from eating an ice to crossing the Atlantic, and from baking a loaf to writing a novel, involves the use of coal, directly or indirectly. For all the arts of peace coal is needed; if war breaks out it is needed all the more. In time of revolution the miner must go on working or the revolution must stop, for revolution as much as reaction needs coal. Whatever may be happening on the surface, the hacking and shovelling have got to continue without a pause ... In order that Hitler may march the goose-step, that the Pope may denounce Bolshevism, that the cricket crowds may assemble at Lords, that the Nancy poets may scratch one another's backs, coal has to be forthcoming. But on the whole we are not aware of it ...

During the 1950s and 1960s coal was still the main source of energy in the UK, carbon fuel being the primary means of producing electricity. Its competitors were nuclear power, with the first reactor opening in 1956, followed by North Sea gas and oil. In 2018 renewables, such as wind farms, supplied a record share of UK electricity generation. In 2017, to demonstrate its growing independence from coal the National Grid ceased burning fossil fuels for fifty-five consecutive hours, though whether this was a token gesture of its green commitment remains to be seen. A cynic might comment that while we could survive for just three days without coal-fired power stations the cooling towers would need to be reopened for the other 362.

Orwell's vision of all aspects of the advanced world coming to a halt without coal is no longer valid, at least for nations such as the UK, but we still import an enormous amount of it, and his presentation of what occurs on the surface as entirely dependent on 'hacking and shovelling' beneath it perfectly encapsulates the state of the world's fastest-growing economy, China.

Let us not deceive ourselves that the decline in coal mining in the UK was due to the green conscience of the nation and its politicians. The latter, specifically Mrs Thatcher's Conservative government, embarked on a policy of systematically closing down Britain's mines long before green-awareness became a force for change. In the early

1980s, when Arthur Scargill's National Union of Mineworkers went into a head-to-head battle with the government, irrespective of its negotiations with the National Coal Board, Orwell's vision of coal as vital to the lifeblood of the economy still held true. This was Scargill's – and the extreme left's – weapon against Thatcherism, and Thatcher and her Cabinet knew that if they could defeat the NUM they would undermine the power of all major trade unions. Ten years after the miners' strike deep mining in Britain had all but disappeared, and whole communities which had been created by coal and sustained by it for a century and a half were left without any sense of focus or purpose.

James Bloodworth in Part III of *Hired* comes closest to invoking Orwell's experiences with the miners. He drives to South Wales to work for Admiral Insurance, but the most evocative passage involves his experiences with people in the Glamorgan and Swansea regions who appear to exist in a state of involuntary torpor. Most had been miners. He meets 'Flash' who helps run a museum preserving memories of mining in South Wales. Flash and others are not nostalgic about life underground; it was rough and dangerous. But the aftermath of having the soul of their communities torn from them is much worse. Bloodworth sums up Flash's recollections:

> Life underground, where death was omnipresent, potentially lurking in the next roof cavity or pit shaft, had the power to bind men together like the braiding of a copper cable. Selwyn [Flash's real name] told me emphatically that given the chance he would 'go back tomorrow' because 'everybody stuck together, no matter what'.
>
> ...
>
> 'The comradeship, the laughter. Sad times, mind, but good days. It was a good, good comradeship. You wouldn't get better than that, I think, because you didn't know if you turn your back you're dead. So you just as well say we lived for today, or we lived for the moment.'

In this respect little had changed in the pits since 1936. Orwell too found that men forced to work in horrible life-threatening conditions formed special bonds. The account by Jerry Kennan testifies to the authenticity of Orwell's and Bloodworth's view of mining as creating a unique fellowship. Kennan is honest about their sense of Orwell as a faintly bizarre stranger with an accent that they'd only previously come across on the wireless; but once he was down the pit, and injured, he became one of their own.

In the second part of *The Road to Wigan Pier* Orwell reflects on what can and should be done about the appalling conditions in which the working classes of the North were obliged to live. He considers the contradictions and anomalies of socialism, at least as he perceives it. He regards the ideology as synonymous with the replacement of human effort with the machine. Work, as a tedious obligation to satisfy the greed of employers and industrialists, would no longer exist. But what would replace it?

> But what is work and what is not work? Is it work to dig, to carpenter, to plant trees, to fell trees, to ride, to fish, to hunt, to feed chickens, to play the piano, to take photographs, to build a house, to cook, to sew, to trim hats, to mend motor bicycles? All of these things are work to somebody and all of them are play to somebody. There are in fact very few activities that cannot be classed either as work or play according as you choose to regard them ... The truth is that when a human being is not eating, drinking, sleeping, making love, talking, playing games or merely lounging about – and these things will not fill up a lifetime – he needs work and usually looks for it ...

Marxists of various stripes would probably quarrel with Orwell's vision of the socialist utopia as a numbing state of pointlessness, something that goes against the vital human instinct to tackle and endure things. But what is most interesting about *The Road to Wigan Pier* is that in the first part of the book he offers us a description of almost exactly this same condition of involuntary apathy, except this time its cause is unemployment, brought about by capitalism:

> I remember the shock of astonishment it gave me, when I first mingled with tramps and beggars, to find that a fair proportion, perhaps a quarter, of these beings whom I had been taught to regard as cynical parasites, were decent young miners and cotton-workers gazing at their destiny with the same sort of dumb amazement as an animal in a trap.

He goes on to describe how unemployment affects not just individuals but entire communities, which become infected with feelings of impotence and despair. There is, he observes, a spiralling descent propelled by guilt, as if they are in some way blaming themselves for their condition, and an equally degrading inability to be able to do anything about it:

> Everyone who saw Greenwood's play *Love on the Dole* must remember that dreadful moment when the … working man beats the table and cries out 'O God, send me some work!' This was not dramatic exaggeration, it was a touch from life. That cry must have been uttered, in almost those words, in tens of thousands, perhaps hundreds of thousands of English homes, during the past fifteen years.

Across Lancashire and Yorkshire, Orwell diagnoses a 'something to live for' trend towards cheap clothes that look like they've been 'tailored in Savile Row', two-pound bags of sweets bought for the same price as one square meal, the Football Pools, any other form of gambling, 'fantastically cheap' cinemas, and the wireless. 'Twenty million people underfed but literally everyone in England has access to a radio.' He is certainly not being preachy or sanctimonious – he confesses that in the same circumstances he too would opt for escapism as a compensation for ineluctable futility. What enrages him is the middle-class consensus that anyone unemployed who even appears to be indulging a daydream is sufficient proof that the working classes are endemically lazy and certainly not victims: 'My dear, … only last week we wanted a man to weed the garden, and we simply couldn't get one. They don't *want* to work, that's all it is!'

In Bloodworth's experience, in South Wales, the prejudices of Orwell's middle-class stereotype have shifted down the social scale:

'I reckon there's jobs out there for people and they don't wanna work,' one retired drinker told me in the bar in Wetherspoons, 'they're quite happy, they're living with the parents, they're getting the dole money once a fortnight, giving their mam a couple of bob, and the rest is theirs.'

Bloodworth asks him what he would do about these people and the man replies that the government should take away their social security and 'make them fucking work':

'Do something, painting fences, anywhere. Don't let them sit in the house with their feet up watching telly … I left school in 1961 and I worked all my life. I worked all my life. And I had some stinking jobs.'

In 2020 the notion of a quintessentially working-class person or outlook has become more sphinx-like than ever. Bloodworth's drinking partner echoes Norman Tebbit's famous recollection of his unemployed father: 'He got on his bike and looked for work, and he kept looking till he found it.' The men Orwell encountered would need to cycle a very long way to find work and then compete with other cyclists for the same job. The 'authentic' beer-swilling, faintly anarchic presence of Sillitoe's Arthur Seaton is still curated by left-leaning liberals in their museum of the common man but Flash seems to confirm that this notion of comradeship and angry anti-establishmentism is, for those still at the bottom, just a mirage. The real-life Seatons of the 2016 Referendum certainly dispelled the myths regarding the East Midlands or Northern working classes that might have endured among the metropolitan left.

In January 1936 Orwell attended a meeting hosted by Oswald Mosley in Barnsley Town Hall. Mosley was the leader of the British Union of Fascists (BUF), a group modelled on Hitler's Nazis and Mussolini's National Fascist Party. About 700 were present; a small number booed and others were ejected for protesting, but Mosley 'to my dismay seemed to have the meeting mainly with him'. Orwell left any reference to this out of *The Road to Wigan Pier*. Did he feel the apparent support for Mosley disclosed unedifying features of the common people of the North? Looking back some might see it as a straw in the wind. In April 1968 Enoch Powell's 'Rivers of Blood' speech received its most vibrant public support in a march by London dockers. Today many Labour MPs who might be horrified by the economic and social prospects of Brexit are reluctant to voice their opinions let alone vote against the implementation of withdrawal. Their 'safe' Labour constituencies polled overwhelmingly to leave. It would be wrong to generalise about the reasons for this demographic trend but the glorification of xenophobic nationalism, the systematic stereotyping of Brussels as a 'threat' to our independence, and the swamping of our land by foreign immigrants probably played a part. Orwell wrote in his *Diary*:

M. [Mosley] is a very good speaker. His speech was the usual claptrap – Empire free trade, down with the Jew and the foreigner, higher wages and shorter hours all round etc. etc. … the (mainly) working-class audience was easily bamboozled by M. … condemning the treachery of successive governments towards the workers. The blame for everything was put upon mysterious international gangs … it struck me how easy it is to bamboozle an uneducated audience if you have prepared beforehand a set of repartees with which to evade awkward questions …

In Mosley's speech the instigators of the various threats to the integrity of Britain are mainly Jews, but shift the emphasis towards the ghastly agents of the EU or the 'foreigner' (the immigrant) stealing our jobs, hospital beds and welfare benefits, and the speaker could be Nigel Farage MEP, or any other senior member of UKIP, the Brexit Party or the Tory European Research Group (ERG). Add to this the 'bamboozling' promises of guaranteed higher prosperity, then figures such as Boris Johnson come to mind, standing beside the bus which brandished the eye-watering claim that 'Leave' will save us £350 million a week.

Mosley's decision to leave bipartite politics and found a party of his own mirrors a number of developments at the extremes of our own left/right cartel, particularly the far right of the Tory party and its uninvited right-wing nationalist guest, the Brexit Party. When he was a Labour MP Mosley advocated protectionist economics as a means of securing Britain against the global shifts and, potentially, further crises. He argued that an export-based policy should be replaced by an 'insulated' UK-focused market, the success of which would be guaranteed by our trading relationship with the Empire, an expanded version of protectionism. On 13 May 2019 Featherstone Working Men's Club was packed with men – and women; we've changed since the 1930s – who greeted Farage with a thunderous round of applause. Farage did not offer a detailed account of how a no-deal exit would improve our lives, but his Trumpish recipe of making the nation great again, humiliation by foreigners and betrayal by the political establishment did the trick. He was acclaimed as Britain's saviour (*Guardian*, 18 May 2019). A hero's welcome was also proffered to his newest recruit to Brexit, Ann Widdecombe, dedicated acolyte of Thatcher, who a week later would announce that gays could be 'cured'. Less than two miles from the club is a small business park, largely funded by the EU, which is the only serious source of employment opportunities in a mining area where work has been in short supply since the pits closed.

Labour and the Conservatives were united in their rejection of Mosley's policies, but he took them forward to the manifesto of his 'New Party' which would soon mutate into the BUF. Rather than bore his target electorate – those worst affected by the Depression – with the complexities of radical Keynesianism, he boiled down his theses into a formula which placed the blame for recent events on international conglomerates of economies and offered a vision of the future involving the promise of independence and renewal for all Britons, especially those in the Midlands and the North. He transformed an elaborate economic plan and projection – flawed but as intellectually robust as Roosevelt's policies in the US – into the more simplistic fantasy where Britain would be unshackled from nations outside the Empire which had dragged it into the Depression and launch itself into the sunlit uplands of independence and prosperity. Anyone who does not see parallels between this and the rise of UKIP, the extreme Leave faction of the Conservatives, and the new Brexit Party has probably been asleep for some time.

Have the British working classes turned right? Some of them, probably, but with the assistance of toxic populism brewed first by Kelvin Mackenzie's *Sun* in the 1980s and evident today in the mantras of Michael Gove, who advised people to ignore the advice of 'experts' (i.e. academics, economists, industrialists *et al*) on the effects of Brexit. The implication being: trust instead your most rabid, feral (and probably xenophobic, racist) instincts. The shift was also brought about by the effects and after-effects of Thatcherism. De-industrialisation involved the fragmentation of any sense of workers since the 1980s as being part of a community or of a union, at least for those at the bottom.

Amazon warehouses, call centres and various types of service labour – primarily supermarkets and budget hotels – incubated a system of zero-hours contracts, threats and bullying, which is if not worse, then at least more dehumanising than the working conditions of Orwell's miners. The 'them' who make your life miserable are no longer private mine-owners but something more insidious and intangible, and thus the Leave/UKIP/ERG/Brexit Parties have been able to 'bamboozle' the voter in projecting populist blame across the Channel towards those nasty people in Brussels.

When he went north Orwell hadn't quite committed himself to a political cause. But he was eyeing up the various policies laid out by left-wing groups from Labour and the ILP to the Communist Party of Great Britain (CPGB), with various marginal radical groups in between. He would soon ally himself with the ILP.

8

SPAIN AND SERIOUS POLITICS

Geoffrey Gorer, who got to know Orwell in 1936, described his first year in the cottage in Wallington, during which he married Eileen and travelled in the North, as 'the happiest of his life'. He began work on *The Road to Wigan Pier* in May 1936 and little more than a month later he and Eileen were married in Wallington parish church, a day that could have served as a pilot episode for an Ealing Comedy. Early that morning he drafted a letter to his Etonian acquaintance in London, Denys King-Farlow, regretting that he could not attend a party in the city in two days' time. 'I am getting married this very morning – in fact I am writing this with one eye on the clock & the other on the Prayer Book, which I have been studying for some days past in hopes of steeling myself against the obscenities of the wedding service.' Eileen was an agnostic and Orwell loathed all forms of organised religion but they had agreed to go through the motions for the sake of their respective families and some of their friends. They walked together unaccompanied down the lane from the cottage to the church and he vaulted over the churchyard wall to be waiting for her as she passed through the lychgate. Picking her up he carried her to the church door. The 'reception' was a beer-and-sandwiches event held in The Plough, a few yards from their cottage, before they returned home with a select number of guests. Orwell's mother and sister took Eileen, whom they'd met only once before, upstairs and said they were very sorry for her, that they were painfully aware of what she had taken on. She agreed and said that she didn't mind. One of their presents was a pot of homemade marmalade which next day Eileen opened and placed at the centre of their rickety kitchen table. Orwell's insistence that it should properly be decanted into a jam dish caused her to laugh, and she pointed out that his working-class friends, up north, had probably never heard of such bourgeois practices. He laughed, and they ate it straight from the pot.

Each morning Eileen insisted on preparing for Orwell what is known today as the 'full English breakfast'. She wanted to fatten him up – he carried no spare flesh to fuel his endurances – and without refusing her bacon and eggs he generally accompanied them with diatribes on how local people, mostly farm labourers, were prevented from keeping their own chickens and pigs.

The most vivid portrait of Orwell in his Wallington years comes from Jack Common, who rented a *Good Life*-style farmhouse in a village about four miles away. Orwell, who had kept in touch with him since their first encounters as contributors to the *Adelphi*, sought his advice on how to keep basic livestock, notably chickens and goats, and make use of home-grown vegetables. Common's account of Orwell's visit to him is revealing and touching. Common liked Orwell when they first met without quite making up his mind if he was an upper-class role-player or a committed radical, but in Hertfordshire he became less of an enigma. His recollection, verbal not written, reveals that his feel for the enchanting simplicity of language matched that of his friend:

> I leaned against a three-armed signpost which read To Knebworth, Woolmer Green; To Datchworth Green; To Bragbury End. From that last direction and very much downhill, there presently appeared a solitary cyclist, a tall man on a tall bike. He could have got off and walked at the worst gradient. Not he. This Don Quixote weaved and wandered this side, that side, defeating windmills of gravity till he grew tall on the hillbrow and tall too that *Rosinante* of a bicycle, an ancient Triumph that could have belonged to his father.

Fellow-countryman, men of Herts, we made greetings. It was an odd vision, seeing him in these country circumstances. He might have been a seedy Empire-builder, the reality of some character read about in boys' adventure stories, a broken-down ex-officer. Whatever it was I saw that morning, I am sure I had a fuller appreciation of my friend Eric.

(Extract from Common's interview with Crick)

They talked of Common's experience in creating a garden out of bare meadow. Orwell was planning to do the same by renting a piece of rough land opposite the cottage where he would also keep hens and sell the eggs and vegetables from his own 'Store'. After that they went to the pub where the landlord, 'a cheerful drunkard ex-navy rating' insisted on addressing Orwell as 'sire'. Commendably he never tried to pretend that his accent was anything other than the one he was stuck with. Over pints they talked of politics, particularly the ILP, an organisation as sphinx-like in its political outlook as Orwell himself. Some saw it as the radical, purist branch of the parliamentary Labour Party, others as its quixotic, unfocused relative.

In 1937 Richard Rees drove to Wallington to introduce Orwell to his latest proletarian curiosity, Mark Benney. Benney had recently published *Low Company*, a story of his life as an uneducated Londoner who opted for burglary as a profession and spent most of his early years in prison. With the same amused fascination as Common, Benney tells of how he and Rees had interrupted Orwell's struggle with the chimney. The door 'was opened by a tall figure, face and clothes covered with coal smuts, who peered at us through a billowing cloud of smoke'. Stones had become dislodged from the back of the fireplace and further up the chimney, and Orwell asked Rees and Benney if they'd help him by bringing in decent-sized pieces of granite from the back garden. They found some suitable blocks but when they showed them to Orwell he explained that he didn't feel right using them as they were fragments of old tombstones from the church. Benney wrote:

> I was later to become more familiar with Eric Blair's reverence for traditional things; at the time I simply wrote it off as slightly loony. But later, as we drove back to town, Richard was positively ebullient: he seemed to feel that we had witnessed an impressive demonstration in how to be painfully scrupulous while painfully uncomfortable.

By early autumn 1936 Orwell had completed the documentary chapters of *The Road to Wigan Pier*, Part I, and was working on the second half of the book, involving political speculations and hypotheses. He was also paying close attention to events taking place abroad which within months would bring what Gorer called his 'happiest year' to an abrupt close.

The Spanish Civil War began officially on 17 July, when a group of anti-government conservatives, including the most senior generals in the army, brought about a number of military uprisings designed to overthrow the democratically elected coalition of predominately liberal and left-wing parties. The original, nominal leader of the so-called Nationalists was General José Sanjurjo, but within months General Francisco Franco took over. Franco would lead the Nationalists, or more accurately the Fascists or Falangists, to victory in 1939, and he would rule Spain as an unelected dictator until his death in November 1975. The nexus of the rising was Morocco, a Spanish protectorate, which the Fascists seized in a matter of days and then used as a base for ferrying regiments of the largely Moorish African army to the Spanish mainland. They expected to take Madrid within a matter of weeks, given that the vast majority of the permanent army, inside and outside the capital, was under the command of the generals. The government was forced to arm largely untrained factory workers and anyone else prepared to serve, and to the astonishment of the Fascists and indeed the global audience the rebels were checked and Madrid remained in the government's hands. Across Spain a number of similar anti-Fascist militias succeeded in holding out against the army and by August the only major city controlled by the rebels was Seville.

As early as July, Nazi Germany was openly sending arms and military advisors to assist the Fascists but, fearing a backlash by other nominally non-interventionist states, Hitler disguised his active involvement in the war by creating the Condor Legion, made up supposedly of volunteers, though how exactly these 'voluntary' legionnaires managed to take with them Stuka dive bombers and light tanks was not explained. Mussolini's Italy was more openly supportive, and provided Franco with over 50,000 soldiers and airmen, as well as using its Mediterranean fleet to blockade supplies to the government forces. Like Germany, Salazar's Portugal hid behind an allegedly volunteer force of 20,000 men, the *Viriatos*, and discreetly moved arms and equipment across the border for Franco's use.

Stalin was the most powerful supporter of the government forces and factions. Despite signing the Non-Intervention Agreement he immediately began disguising merchant ships with false decks for transporting arms and equipment and trimmed the vessels with false flags. Around 500 Soviet troops saw frontline service but far more significant was the arrival of 2,000–3,000 so-called 'military advisors', most of whom were members of or under orders from the NKVD, the forerunner of the KGB.

King-Farlow visited Wallington in September and later recalled that Orwell was devoting almost as much time to following events in Spain as he was to completing his book. He read every newspaper report available and would no doubt have been aware that the political allegiances of the various press outlets often distorted authenticity. Claud Cockburn, who provided a regular column for the *Daily Worker*, the mouthpiece of the Communist Party, later admitted to making up stories about Republican successes when he had no knowledge of the actual events. Papers such as the solidly conservative *Daily Mail* carried regular reports of the mass murder of landowners and clergy conducted by communist and anarchist militia. In *The Road to Wigan Pier* Orwell wrote: 'If you want some unmistakable illustrations of the growth of Fascist feeling in England, have a look at some of the innumerable letters that were written to the Press during the Abyssinian war, approving the Italian action, and the howl of glee that went up from both Catholic and Anglican pulpits (see the *Daily Mail* of 17 August 1936) over the Fascist rising in Spain.' The Labour Party was guardedly supportive of the Republicans but reluctant to ally themselves officially in fear of alienating Catholics in their northern constituencies, especially Liverpool, and in Scotland. The ILP was less restrained, committing itself unapologetically to the armed struggle against the Fascists.

In July, shortly after the Spanish war began, there was an ILP summer school in Letchworth. There is no proof that Orwell attended but it is likely that he did given his regular contacts with Common, who was present. In Part II of *The Road to Wigan Pier* he tells of his experience on a bus in Letchworth. The vehicle is boarded by two 'dreadful-looking old men' in 'pistachio-coloured shirts and khaki shorts' who in his view encapsulate the worst aspects of socialism and communism as a magnet for 'every fruit-juice drinker, nudist, sandal-wearer, sex maniac, Quaker, "Nature Cure" quack, pacifist and feminist in England'. The current leader of Her Majesty's Opposition on his way to his allotment sporting a shiny tracksuit is brought to mind. Why was Orwell on this bus if he had not, like the dreadful-looking men, been to the ILP event? He was dismayed by the group's growing reputation as a politically spent force – it no longer had any MPs of its own – and as a home of cranks. Yet it and the CPGB were the only organisations who were willing to take an unreserved stand against the Spanish Fascists.

The second part of *The Road to Wigan Pier* has been treated by Orwell's biographers as proof that he had, at best, only a second-hand understanding of the essentials of Marxism, socialism, communism and their various permutations. I'd prefer to see it as the commendably honest reflections of a man witnessing a country, a continent, in a state of turmoil that could not be explained by a particular ideological code or formula. He was certain that Fascism was intrinsically, fundamentally, evil, but he was unsure about why so many were drawn to it and what its alternative would provide and guarantee.

He tells of how at Eton his class was asked to name, in their opinion, the ten greatest figures in history, and of his sixteen peers fifteen included Lenin in their list. Extreme socialism, or preferably communism, had since the Russian Revolution become a fashion accessory of his, Orwell's, class:

> Look at Comrade X, member of CPGB and author of *Marxism for Infants*. Comrade X, it so happens, is an Old Etonian. He would be ready to die on the barricades, in theory anyway, but you notice that he still leaves his bottom waistcoat button undone. He idealises the proletariat, but it is remarkable how little his habits resemble theirs.

Some things seem to endure, such as Orwell's stereotypical far-left activist. A generation ago we had Tony Benn (Westminster and Oxford), and these days the brains behind the rise of Corbynism is Seumas Milne (Winchester and Oxford), at the last count drawing a salary of £110,000 from Labour.

In Orwell's view the jargon of the hard left ('class consciousness', 'expropriation of the expropriators', 'bourgeois ideology', 'proletarian solidarity') alienates the kind of people whose lives Marxists promise to transform. He believes socialism must involve a simple formula whereby 'all people with small, insecure incomes are in the same boat and ought to be fighting on the same side' against financial inequalities, and that 'the "proletariat" includes the village grocer, the clerk ... the schoolmaster, the half-starved journalist, the jobless Cambridge graduate and the lower grade civil servant as much as the navvy, the factory-hand and the miner'.

Also he feels that his simple brand of socialism will be the last bastion against a threat facing the peoples of Europe that is just as horrifying as the aftermath of the Great Depression. And here his concern with events in Spain is evident:

> In the next few years we shall either get that effective Socialist party that we need, or we shall not get it. If we do not get it, then Fascism is coming; probably a slimy Anglicanised form of Fascism, with cultured policemen instead of Nazi gorillas and the lion and the unicorn instead of the swastika.

Clearly he did not envisage a Nazi invasion of Britain. Rather, the passage is inspired by what he had witnessed at Mosley's rally in Barnsley. What he feared was the attraction of Fascism as a roughhouse-brand of socialism mixed in with xenophobia and mob-rule patriotism, something which appealed to the crowd in Barnsley who felt let down by the official Labour Party.

Mosley (Winchester) was the archetypal 'cultured policeman', an aristocrat and orator who the *Westminster Gazette* described as 'the most polished literary speaker in the Commons', a man who could turn his 'graceful, epigrammatic phrases' downmarket to the rapturous applause of more than 700 Lancashire manual workers.

Tommy Degnan was a miner and activist who had visited Germany in 1930 and seen how Hitler had succeeded in persuading strikers in the Ruhr coalfields that his form of National Socialism would offer them a better future than that promised by the Communists or the Social Democrats. Orwell met him in Barnsley and Degnan put it to him that Mosley could succeed in Britain just as Hitler had in Germany. A few days after the Mosley meeting Degnan spoke at a CPGB rally in Barnsley which, as Orwell recorded in his *Diary*, attracted only 150 people, who listened to Degnan with 'entirely expressionless faces'. This too was left out of *The Road to Wigan Pier*. Much later Degnan told Crick that he'd failed to convince Orwell that Mosley could turn Fascism in Britain into a mass movement. By the time he wrote up the second part of *The Road to Wigan Pier* Orwell appeared to have changed his mind.

Orwell circa mid-1930s

Group photo of the police training school, Burma

Orwell feeding a goat

Orwell in Morocco

Eileen Blair

Sonia Blair (née Brownell),
bottom left, in the *Horizon*
office, 1949

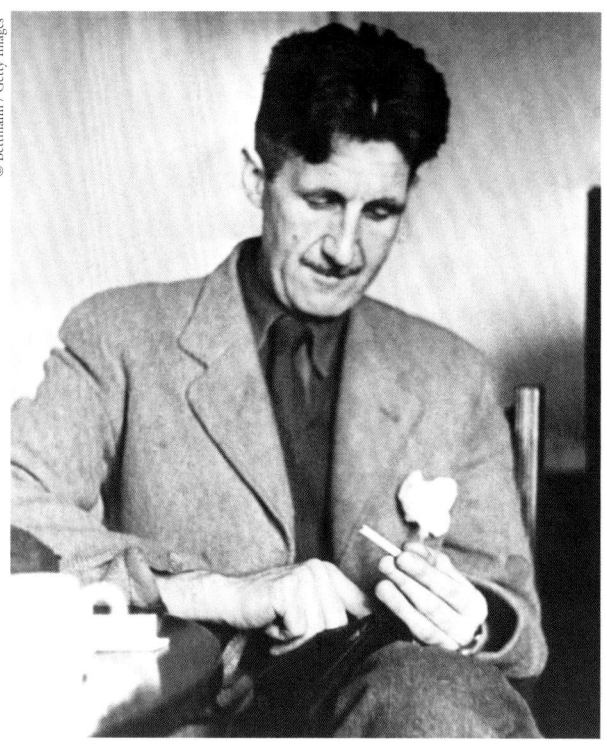

Orwell with cigarette,
circa early 1940s

Orwell at the BBC in 1941

Statue of Orwell outside BBC Broadcasting House, London

Sign in the square dedicated to Orwell in Barcelona, Catalonia

Montague House, Southwold, home of the Blair family in the 20s and 30s

House in Notting Hill where Orwell lodged in the late 1920s

© Robert Evans / Alamy Stock Photo

© Kevin George / Alamy Stock Photo

The 'Stores', Wallington, today. Orwell and Eileen lived here in the late 30s

Canonbury Square, London. Orwell and Eileen lived in 27b during the war. The building is on the right, marked with a green plaque

Church of St Mary, Wallington, where Orwell and Eileen were married

Barnhill, Jura, today. Orwell wrote *Nineteen Eighty Four* here

2018 cartoon depicting Trump as Napoleon of *Animal Farm*

Senate House, University of London. The inspiration for the Ministry of Truth in *Nineteen Eighty Four*

Peter Cushing as Winston Smith and Yvonne Mitchell as Julia in the first television adaptation of *Nineteen Eighty Four* (1954)

Edmond O'Brien as Winston Smith and Jan Sterling as Julia in the first film adaptation of *Nineteen Eighty Four* (1955)

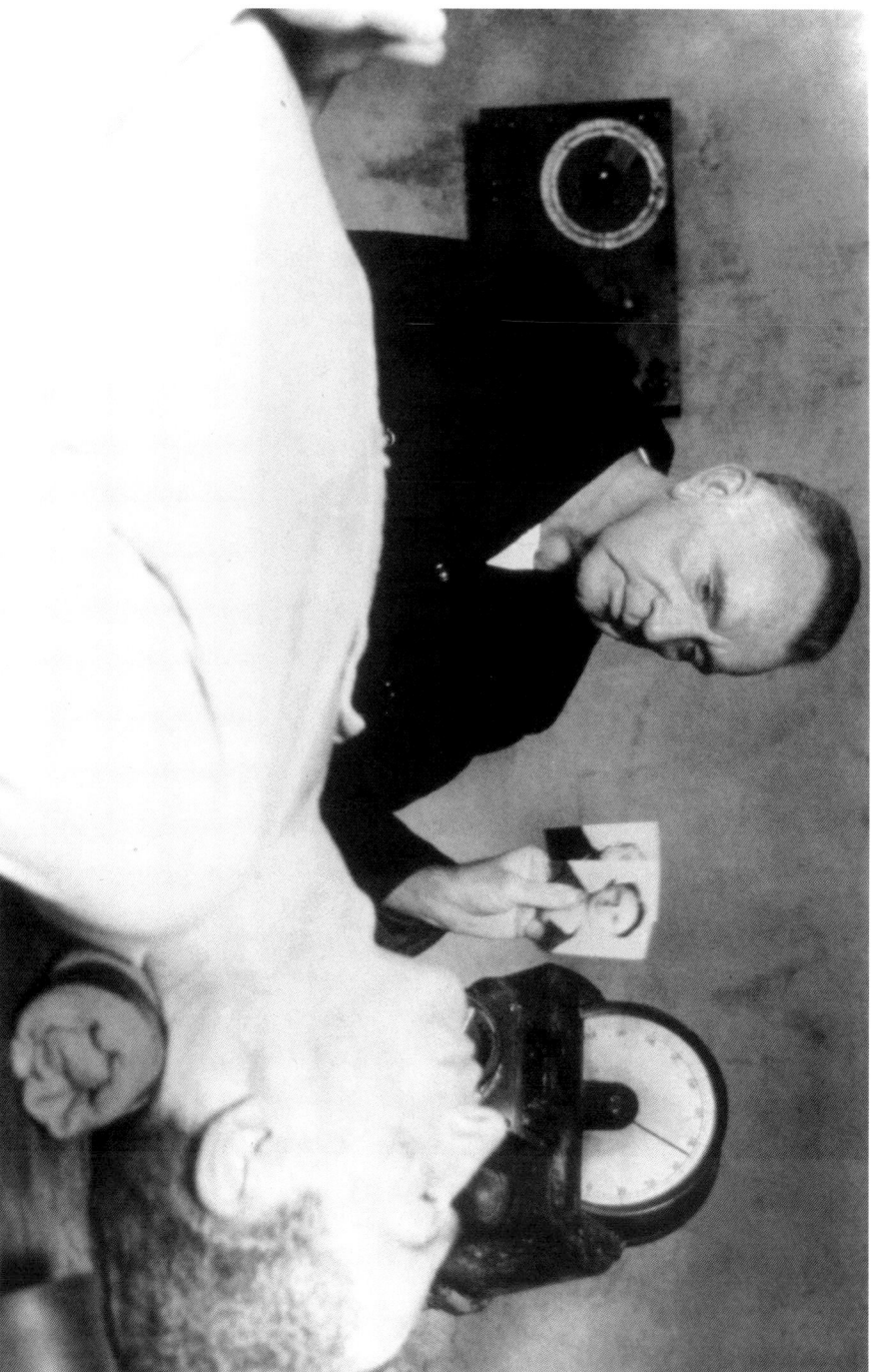

Richard Burton and John Hurt in the 1984 film adaptation of *Nineteen Eighty Four*

Orwell in Wallington churchyard

Orwell's gravestone in Sutton Courtenay churchyard

Whether speaking to the Commons or touching the nerve strings of the workers ('If you love our country you are national, and if you love our people you are socialist' was his most repeated mantra), Mosley was the precursor of what we now refer to as our 'post-truth' era (the Oxford English Dictionary anointed the term as its 'word of the year' in 2016). But unlike many of our most prominent politicians, including the current prime minister, Mosley rarely told outright lies. Instead he clouded verifiable facts with spellbinding eloquence. It shows how far we have fallen when the habitually mendacious president of the US can brainwash his electorate just as effectively with quasi-literate banalities.

The BUF reached the peak of its popularity in 1936 when Orwell witnessed events such as the one in Barnsley. Later that year the Battle of Cable Street caused many in the working classes to recognise the nastier elements of Mosley's politics and see parallels with what was happening in Germany, Italy and most recently Spain. Support for his British Fascists went into rapid decline thereafter and Orwell's fears of some grotesquely Anglocentric brand of Fascism becoming a major political force proved unwarranted.

The most enduring similarity between then and now involves the ability of politicians to present lies as discernible facts, and the willingness of the electorate to accept falsehood as truth, even though both know that they are deceiving themselves. It would be twelve years before Orwell created the dystopian vision of a society in which individuals accepted that '2 + 2 = 5', even though they knew it does not, but his experience of the audience being 'easily bamboozled' by Mosley's 'claptrap' must have sown the seeds for it: sell people a fantasy they hunger for, however ludicrous, and they'll convince themselves that it is possible. I do not know what will happen on 31 January 2020, but I will not revise this sentence once I do because as I write this country is undergoing a bout of '2 + 2 = 5' that outdoes Mosley's bamboozling and the enforced self-delusions of *Nineteen Eighty-Four*. Theresa May held to the mantra that 'No deal is better than a bad deal' for almost three years, and the majority of her extreme Brexit supporters offered her unreserved support in this. Virtually everyone else, from the NHS to the CBI, held that no deal was, demonstrably, an act of economic and political suicide. Quite suddenly Mrs May accepted that she was lying (without quite using that word); however, her successor Boris Johnson has embraced no deal as a noble alternative to further delays. Recently, a YouGov poll indicated that in the country as a whole support for no deal has risen from thirty-five to more than forty per cent in two weeks. As Mosley and *Nineteen Eighty-Four* demonstrated, lies and self-deluding madness can sometimes become addictive.

On 21 December 1936 Orwell left Wallington for London, only six days after posting the draft of *The Road to Wigan Pier* to Gollancz, in search of an organisation that would endorse his journey to Spain. He first went to the headquarters of the CPGB in King Street, where the General Secretary, Harry Pollitt, agreed to meet him, probably after consulting Victor Gollancz. Pollitt was suspicious of Orwell's apparent reluctance to affiliate himself to any political group, let alone the Communists, and despite his refusal to offer him any official support advised him to visit the Spanish Embassy in Paris, which still represented the elected government, and to declare his support for their cause. The only other party which had aligned itself with the Republicans was the ILP, so the following day Orwell met their leader, Fenner Brockway. Brockway provided him with letters of recommendation for the ILP representative in Barcelona. While there is no record from these meetings that he expressed an intention to fight, it was evident to all that he would do more than produce articles and later a book. Jack Common later recalled that shortly before he left Wallington Orwell told him that if everyone who went to Spain killed a Fascist then there wouldn't be many left.

On 23 December, a day after his meeting with Brockway, he set out for Paris. A few months earlier he had corresponded with Henry Miller on the subject of the latter's second novel, *Black Spring*, and on his arrival in the French capital he called on Miller in his Montparnasse studio. It would be difficult to envisage an exchange between two figures so antithetically opposed on the role of the writer. Miller treated literature as a branch of *schadenfreude* and its practitioners as those who should contemplate and speculate on the state of their world – including its most vile inhabitants – but never attempt to intervene. He agreed with Orwell on the threat posed to civilisation by Fascism but opted for disinterest when their conversation turned to events taking place across the Pyrenees. Miller's friend Alfred Perlès recalled that he treated Orwell with amused tact, as a figure 'tough, resilient and politically minded, ever striving in his bid to improve the world' but, with a smile forming, Miller asked him if he wouldn't be of better use in doing so 'alive than dead' in Spain. Their conversation should dispel any suspicions that Orwell was undecided about what he intended to do when he set off from his house a few days earlier: he most certainly intended to fight Fascism.

There is a passage in *The Road to Wigan Pier* where he records his utterly depressing impression of the outskirts of Wigan as the train bears him away from the town. He tells of the 'monstrous scenery of slag-heaps, chimneys, piled scrap-iron, foul canals, paths of cindery mud criss-crossed by the prints of clogs', and then a particular image of human misery fixes his attention:

> At the back of one of the houses a young woman was kneeling on the stones, poking a stick up the leaden waste-pipe which ran from the sink inside and which I suppose was blocked. I had time to see everything about her – her sacking apron, her clumsy clogs, her arms reddened by the cold. She looked up as the train passed, and I was almost near enough to catch her eye. She had a round pale face, the usual exhausted face of the slum girl who is twenty-five and looks forty, thanks to miscarriages and drudgery; and it wore, for the second in which I saw it, the most desolate, hopeless expression I have ever seen ... She knew well enough what was happening to her – understood as well as I did how dreadful a destiny it was to be kneeling there in the bitter cold, on the slimy stones of a slum backyard, poking a stick up a foul drain-pipe.

Despair. Orwell implies that the woman and most of her like are resigned to a life of grim deprivation with no evident hope for change; apart from a few figures such as Degnan the working classes seemed willing to put up with their fate as a kind of hell before death. Compare this with his record of another train journey, nine months later, from Paris through Southwest France to the Spanish border:

> But that night I left for Spain. The train, a slow one, was packed with Czechs, Germans, Frenchmen, all bound on the same mission … the train was practically a troop train, and the countryside knew it. In the morning, as we crawled across southern France, every peasant working in the field turned round, stood solemnly upright and gave the anti-Fascist salute. They were like a guard of honour, greeting the train mile after mile.

The peasants of Southwest France and, as he would find, the manual workers and farm labourers of Catalonia were prepared to make a stand, even if only via an arm gesture, against Fascism and political conservatism. But most of their counterparts in Northern England appeared gloomily reconciled to victimhood.

Many writers have made use of active service experiences in their work and the vast majority of these fought for their own country as conscripts or volunteers. Only a tiny number have taken up arms abroad because of some ostensible ideal and for most of these their true motives were self-aggrandisement and egotism (see Byron and Hemingway). Only one was genuinely committed to his cause and prepared to die for it, irrespective of the creation of some legend: George Orwell.

He crossed the border into Spain without incident, and once in Barcelona went first to the office of the ILP's representative John McNair, a working-class Tynesider, who recalled the sentry announcing that 'a great big Englishman … wants to see you'. The tall stranger entered and 'drawled in a distinctly bourgeois accent, "I'm looking for a chap named McNair …" I curtly replied

"I'am the lad ye're looking for.'" Orwell handed him the letters from Brockway and when McNair asked him why he had come to Spain he replied, 'I have come to … join the militia to fight against Fascism.' Only after reading the letters did McNair realise that this man was the author of a work on the plight of the British poor, a book he greatly admired. Orwell insisted that he was well trained as a rifleman, from his service in the Colonial Police, and McNair escorted him to the POUM (Workers' Party of Marxist Unification) barracks where he signed up as a member of the militia.

When he spoke with Pollitt in London Orwell was reasonably knowledgeable about the alliance between the International Brigades and the communists, which caused him to prevaricate on joining the former. It is unlikely that he realised quite what was happening in Barcelona, and Catalonia as a whole, at least before he arrived. Once there he became enraptured by the chaotic revolution that had enveloped the region. He became part of the armed branch of the POUM because of its association with the ILP but without properly understanding what the Spanish party represented. In truth, even those involved with the POUM were not certain about what it was. It endorsed socialism and various aspects of communism while alienating itself from the Soviet-sponsored mainstream communists. Instead it formed an alliance with anarchist and anarcho-syndicalist groups that thrived in Catalonia, the CNT (Confederación Nacional del Trabajo) and FAI (Federación Anarquista Ibérica). Irrespective of their differences the three groups were united in their support for an anti-authoritarian revolution. They wanted to overthrow the orthodoxies that until the 1930s had caused Spain to remain hidebound as a pseudo-feudal state, primarily the nobility, the landowning upper classes, the military and the Catholic Church. They certainly did not intend to replace one brand of absolutism with another, which is why they set themselves against the communists, a policy that would lead to their obliteration at the hands of the latter.

If the POUM-anarchist manifesto was a little vague in the abstract its practical implementation soon became evident to Orwell. Many

of Barcelona's churches had been ransacked and all of the priests
and nuns seemed to have gone into hiding. The dining rooms and
bars of the city's best hotels were now canteens for members of the
militia and civilians working to keep the urban infrastructure intact.
No one tipped those who served them in bars, restaurants or shops.
Ties and hats – signs of bourgeois seniority – had disappeared and
all brothels and nightclubs had been shut down. The latter might
carry a whiff of Puritanism but in effect it was feminism in action.
Women were no longer expected to be hostesses, let alone descend
to prostitution. Some women were now trained, armed and serving
in the militia. Basic resources, food included, were in short supply,
but without any orders being issued from an official body it became
the convention either to barter something owned for something
needed – a decent bottle of wine for a loaf and some cheese for
example – or for those serving in the random impromptu cafeterias,
butchers or general stores to give things away if it was evident that
the 'customer' was in sufficient need but without the means to pay.
In other circumstances this unchecked system might have provided
an opportunity for bouts of fraud and racketeering, but all citizens
seemed to treat each other with trust and mutual respect. Jason
Gurney, another English volunteer, recalled that 'what was exciting
was the glorious feeling of optimism; the conviction that anything
that was not right with society would assuredly be put right in the
new world of universal equality and freedom which lay ahead'.

Joaquín Maurín and Andreu Nin were the co-leaders of the POUM
but neither attempted to establish themselves in positions of political
authority in Barcelona and nor did they or their POUM/anarchist
compatriots try to install anything that resembled an administration.
The city and much of Catalonia seemed to be running itself whilst
not descending into chaos or criminality. Even money, as a means of
exchange, appeared almost obsolete. It was the only time in history
that a region, a people, came close to the practical implementation
of the anarchist idyll dreamt of by figures such as Proudhon, Godwin
and Bakunin. It would last no more than a year.

Many of Orwell's non-fiction works have been treated with scepticism as literal, authentic accounts of the experiences and events they claim to record. *Homage to Catalonia*, despite being loathed by figures on the left from London to Moscow, can be regarded as the absolute truth for the simple reason that those who served alongside Orwell and survived to tell the tale went on to confirm all the main incidents he describes. Some, McNair in particular, lend a sardonic, affectionate colouring to the episodes in the book:

> Gone was the drawling ex-Etonian, in his place was an ardent young man of action ... George was forcing about fifty young, enthusiastic but undisciplined Catalonians to learn the rudiments of military drill. He made them run and jump, taught them to form threes, showed them how to use the only rifle available, an old Mauser, by taking it to pieces and explaining it.

The Mausers dated from the 1880s and were deemed unfit for service by the German military before the beginning of the First World War. Some were rusty but Orwell, always practical and a shooting enthusiast, instructed his recruits on how to clean and repair their antique weapons. He trained and commanded fifty men but held only the rank of full corporal, without wearing two stripes on his arm. Indications of seniority were difficult without uniforms. Orwell sported the corduroy trousers and leather jacket given to him by Miller in Paris plus a heavy woollen scarf. Catalonia in January could be cold.

McNair, thirty-five years later, recounted verbatim Orwell's story to him of how the young recruits had tried to get him drunk. 'They did not know that I had worked for a year and a half in Paris in hotels and pubs and knew all about cheap red wine.' He out-drank them, got up first the next morning and dragged them out of their beds. 'Now young fellows, we had a jolly good night but we're not here to booze, we're here to smash the Fascists. You will now all drill under my orders and follow what I do.' Thereafter, he told McNair, 'they treated me with comradeship and respect'.

After only a week training members of the militia Orwell was despatched to Alcubierre on the Aragon front, north-west of the Catalonian border with Spain. He was second in command of what amounted to a small platoon of twelve men and would serve there for five months. The revolutionary energy of Barcelona was, for the young militia men, dissipated by what was effectively a rerun of the Western Front of the First World War. It was an attritional conflict fought across a largely treeless hilly landscape with both sides dug into trenches roughly 700 metres apart.

Even skilled snipers with good rifles had difficulties picking out targets. As with the trenches of the previous war, sanitation was foul and feelings of lethargy and pointlessness began to sap the enthusiasm that Orwell had tried to instil into his recruits in Barcelona, though he managed to initiate one of the more memorable exchanges of fire, albeit accidently. Throughout his life he feared and loathed the presence of rats (c.f. the torture of Smith in *Nineteen Eighty-Four*), and they were running wild and fast among the excrement and rotting food of the trenches. He had on one occasion punched one to death, and later when a particularly well-fed 'beast' had faced him down he blew it to pieces with his revolver. The shot echoed across the valley and the subsequent minor battle left the Republican cookhouse riddled with machine-gun bullets and two of its buses all but destroyed. Orwell would shave using wine, which was more plentiful than water, and suffered terrible bouts of bronchitis in the cold, dry environment of the Aragon hills. The platoon was led by Bob Edwards, an English militiaman and later a Labour MP, and he describes him vividly for Crick:

> He came striding towards me – all six foot three of him – dressed in a grotesque mixture of clothing – corduroy riding breeches, khaki puttees and huge boots caked with mud, a yellow pigskin jerkin, a chocolate-coloured balaclava helmet with a knitted

khaki scarf of immeasurable length wrapped round and round his neck and face up to his ears, an old-fashioned German rifle over his shoulder and two hand-grenades hanging from his belt.

Edwards added that as a soldier 'he was absolutely fearless' and tells of how about three times a week Orwell would announce that 'I'm out for potatoes.' Within thirty or forty yards of the nearest Fascist machine-gun post was a small field of potatoes and Orwell would crawl out to it and fill a sack. Edwards implored him to avoid what seemed to be acts of near-suicidal madness; every time he went out the machine gunners opened up on him. Orwell smiled. 'They can't hit me, I've already proved it.' Orwell had worked out that while the gunners could easily elevate or swing the barrel right or left, tilting it downwards to a target close to and slightly lower than the sandbags was extremely difficult. But, as he and Edwards knew, it was difficult but not impossible.

In *Homage to Catalonia* Orwell gives an honest account of the brief periods when he and the other militiamen left their trenches and engaged the enemy directly, often involving hand-to-hand combat with bayonets and grenades. Many who served with him, including his commander Georges Kopp, who soon become a friend, later confirmed the authenticity of the book. One is struck, however, by what Orwell left out. The ILP journal, the *New Leader*, printed a story in April, gleaned from letters and reports from its members, not including Orwell:

> 'Charge!' shouted Blair ... In front of the parapet was Eric Blair's tall figure coolly strolling forward through the storm of fire. He leapt at the parapet, then stumbled. Hell, had they got him? No, he was over ...

There were other stories told later by Orwell's comrades, notably John ('Paddy') Donovan and Stafford Cottman, then a teenager, of how Orwell always seemed to lead the charge. Despite having instructed recruits in Barcelona in the British technique of 'run-hit-the-ground, run-hit-the-ground, then aim-and-fire, and repeat the exercise', Orwell in action ignored his own advice and went straight towards the enemy lines drawn up to his full height of six foot three, firing as he strolled.

He became the talisman of the unit as much for his being a misfit as for his heroism. Edwards described the 'bloody scribbler' spending his spare time in the trench filling in page after page of his notebook. Cottman was at first uncertain of how to deal with a man whose accent indicated a background in the minor gentry but later found him 'ordinary and decent' and 'ready to muck in'. Those nearest to him in the dug-out were almost choked by his use of black shag pipe tobacco for roll-up cigarettes, which he smoked incessantly, and were astonished that a man plagued with bronchitis seemed intent on worsening his condition.

Bob Edwards returned to England at the end of March to attend the ILP annual conference and, in accord with ILP/POUM pluralism, his successor as leader of the militia unit was decided through election by volunteers. Orwell was their unanimous choice. His command lasted about three weeks.

In February Eileen had arrived in Barcelona to work as a secretary and general assistant for the ILP and it was to her that Orwell sent, when he could, the longhand drafts composed in the trenches, for her to type up. We will never know whether this work was the prototype for *Homage to Catalonia* or something else – the material was seized by the NKVD after the Orwells had fled from Barcelona and it is alleged to be stored in an archive in Moscow. At the end of April Orwell joined Eileen in the city, on leave, 'completely ragged, almost barefoot, a little lousy, dark brown & looking really very well,' as she wrote to her brother.

Three days later units of the Civil Guards, the official instruments of the Madrid-based Republican government, attempted to seize control of Barcelona from the POUM and the anarchists. Even today the exact nature of the 'coup' and the ensuing conflict is a matter

for dispute among historians and political commentators. There are
no reliable records of who in Madrid ordered the Civil Guards to
act and to what end, but the opinion that prevailed in the Spanish
capital during and after the battles between government forces and
POUM/anarchist militiamen was that the latter had been infiltrated
by Fascist *agents provocateurs*, that the ungoverned and ungovernable
condition of Barcelona and Catalonia had nothing to do with a
popular anti-authoritarian consensus; rather it was brought about
to weaken the north-west of Spain against Franco's forces. This
narrative was created exclusively by propagandists working for the
Soviet-backed communists.

The centre of the early conflict was the telephone exchange, held
by the anarchists, which the Civil Guards attempted to seize on 3
May, but exchanges of fire between small units soon spread across
the city as a whole. The telephone exchange was on the Ramblas,
one of the main thoroughfares, close to the Hotel Continental
where Eileen was staying. Orwell found himself sheltering from
fire at the other end of the street in the Hotel Falcón, which had
quickly become an outpost for POUM and ILP militiamen, most
of whom were in the city on leave. John McNair arrived with
supplies of cigarettes and Catalan volunteers followed him with
rifles and ammunition. Orwell armed himself and on 4 May made
his way to the Continental to find his new friend Georges Kopp
sharing a bottle of wine with Eileen as he tried to chat her up.
She, amused and flattered, kept her distance and Orwell took
no offence.

During the next few days events took on an air of exhilaration
and lunacy. Also close to the Continental was the POUM headquarters and next door to that was the Café Moka. Around thirty
Civil Guards had barricaded themselves into the café, but it was
not clear if they were preparing for another assault on the telephone exchange or had just gone into hiding. A unit of the so-called
POUM 'shock troopers' besieged the place, firing randomly at the
windows and rolling grenades down the pavement towards the

front doors. The troopers – bizarrely, given ongoing and imminent events – were all German volunteers. They were ordered
to cease firing by Kopp who then, with mannered insouciance,
walked to the door of the café. Everyone expected he would be
shot, but within minutes he had opened a conversation with the
Guards and summoned one of his men to bring forward a crate
of beer. A ceasefire was agreed and the Guards dispersed, some
deciding to join up with the POUM. Orwell could never decide on
whether Kopp was a superman or a confidence trickster. He later
found that he had persistently lied about his past and heritage.
Yet there was something about him, a blend of irresponsibility
and heroic commitment, that seemed to encapsulate the mood
of Catalonia, at least before the communists gained control. He
ordered Orwell to take a rifle up to the rooftop conservatory of
the Poliorama cinema, telling him to open fire on any government forces approaching the POUM headquarters on the other
side of the road. He fired one shot before he went up on the roof,
to destroy an unexploded grenade thrown earlier by the German
POUM storm troopers. He missed.

Hostilities in the city ceased, for a while, and on 10 May Orwell
returned to his POUM unit in Aragon, now its acting head and
promoted to the rank of second lieutenant. He had, briefly, thought
of volunteering in the International Brigades to become involved in
the fierce, probably decisive, battles for the survival of Madrid. He
decided against this course of action however, because during his
ten days in Barcelona it became clear to him that the communists
were intent on stifling the spirit of the Catalan revolution; and the
Brigades were run by the communists.

At 5 a.m. on 20 May Frank Frankford was talking to Orwell
about Paris, where they'd both lived. They were just above the
parapet 'and all of a sudden, down [Orwell] goes, shot through
the throat'. A sniper's bullet had gone straight through his neck,
miraculously missing his carotid artery and his spinal column, but
damaging his vocal cord. In the field station it was assumed he

was fatally wounded, but against the odds he survived, and after spending time in hospitals in Lérida and Tarragona he found Eileen and Kopp seated either side of his bed in the Sanatorium Maurín on the outskirts of Barcelona. His war was over.

Despite being informed earlier that he would never speak properly again Orwell's voice gradually returned after electrotherapy, but thereafter his manner would be predominantly flat and toneless. He and Eileen were to leave Spain at the beginning of July but the five-week interim period between his injury and their departure would have a pivotal effect on everything Orwell thought, said and wrote for the remainder of his life.

While he was in the sanatorium the de facto ceasefire between the local militias and the various government forces, including the Civil Guards and the police, began to break down. The communists had taken advantage of the power vacuum in the region, become dominant in the Catalan administration and pursued a campaign of 'official' propaganda which presented the POUM and anarchists as Trotskyites co-operating with the Falangists to undermine the Soviet Union's support for the Republicans.

Another civil war had begun in Catalonia with government forces following orders from the communists to eliminate the POUM and the anarchists. NKVD agents were directly involved in a campaign involving the imprisonment without trial, torture and judicial murder of POUM figures and individuals associated with the group. Bob Smillie (grandson of the Scottish miners' leader and member of the ILP/POUM contingent) was arrested and died soon afterwards in a Valencia jail; acute appendicitis was the government explanation, but he was probably murdered. Georges Kopp was imprisoned and tortured regularly for eighteen months and, after access to him by friends was denied, it was assumed he was dead. Andreu Nin was kidnapped by the NKVD and shot.

In the hospital Orwell and three of his injured colleagues from the Aragon front – Cottman, Robert Williams and Arthur Clinton – set about destroying all documents relating to ILP policy, the operations of the militia, maps included, and its connections with the POUM. They had been warned of the purge taking place in Barcelona and spreading across Catalonia.

Orwell applied for a medical discharge from service which was granted on 14 June and five days later he joined Eileen in Barcelona. She was waiting in the foyer of the Hotel Continental and insisted that they should leave the building immediately. The POUM and allied organisations were now officially illegal and any suspicion of association with them would lead to immediate arrest by the police or Civil Guards or, even worse, detention by the NKVD. For the next ten days they went on the run, hiding, sometimes sleeping, in ruined churches or seeking shelter in safe houses with the help of John McNair who was also a fugitive. Unknown to him, Orwell had earned the dubious distinction of being put on a Moscow hit list following the publication of *The Road to Wigan Pier* on 8 March. Had the NKVD kidnapped him he would undoubtedly have suffered the same fate as Nin.

In an act of outstanding courage, verging on madness, Orwell and Eileen managed to arrange a visit to Kopp in prison. Kopp told them that after his arrest a letter he was due to send to a colonel in the Corps of Engineers had been confiscated by the police and if there was any hope at all for the survival of the militia its retrieval was vital. Orwell went straight to the colonel's office in central Barcelona, found that the officer was not yet in custody and told him that the letter to him from Kopp had been taken. The colonel drove to the headquarters of the Chief of Police and, via force of personality, demanded the return of the letter which eventually the Chief gave up to him. The tactical value of the document was negligible given that at this point the military arm of the POUM had been overwhelmed by its erstwhile allies. But Orwell had risked his life by involving himself in Kopp's knowingly futile attempt to keep alive the flame of a cause they had both believed in as surpassingly just.

The day before this episode the Orwells had joined McNair and Cottman at the British Consulate to ensure that whatever identification papers they had would be sufficient to enable them to cross the border into France. The advice they received was neither reassuring nor particularly ominous. The diplomats were honest in their uncertainty about the fluidity of the situation; government officers were nominally in charge of Catalonia but a pervasive threat continued to come from the Soviet communists who were intent on rounding up POUM or anarchist supporters, even if all the latter intended to do was leave the country. The four fugitives went to the railway station the next day only to find that the train for France had departed early. They spent three further days and nights in bars and cafés in the daytime, and at night slept rough in ruined buildings. Eventually they boarded a train for the border, making a point of taking seats in the restaurant carriage where they could blend in with political observers, tourists and journalists. They crossed without being questioned. In Perpignan they found lodgings and met up with Fenner Brockway who was heading in the other direction in an attempt to rescue ILP members who had been found guilty-by-association with the POUM. The five of them talked all night, mostly about how difficult it would be to convince left-wing sympathisers in Britain that the communists in Spain were, as much as the Falangists, set upon merciless authoritarianism. Orwell was already aware that the book for which he had taken notes and would write once he returned to England would be rejected by Victor Gollancz. It would be, he explained to Brockway, more than a report on his experiences during the Civil War. It would also show that Stalin's communists had systematically ruined the Republican cause. Brockway later reported that, from this, he had 'found him far more mature as a socialist'. He meant that Orwell now treated socialism as a commitment to improving the condition of the impoverished and the oppressed, while disavowing itself from any inflexible ideology or doctrine. Three weeks after George and Eileen had crossed the border a document was submitted to the Tribunal for Espionage and Treason in Valencia. They were, it declared, 'confirmed Trotskyists' and that 'ERIC B took part in the events of MAY [1937]' in an attempt to undermine the Republican cause on behalf of Franco's forces. The Tribunal was an instrument of the NKVD and the Orwells had been found guilty in their absence. The sentence would have been death.

Orwell would later state that 'this book was first thought of, so far as the central idea goes, in 1937 ...' He was referring not to *Homage to Catalonia* but to *Animal Farm*. The novel did not begin to take shape until 1943, when the British were in deference to their new Soviet allies, conveniently forgetting the recent Molotov–Ribbentrop Pact, the subsequent Russian invasion of Poland and the open secret that Soviet Russia was a totalitarian state. But by the time he reached Perpignan and set off for Wallington the seeds for the book were sown. Two incidents, which he left out of *Homage to Catalonia*, are salient here. In action he once sighted a Falangist soldier running along the brink of his trench and offering himself as an easy target for any riflemen of average competence. Orwell aimed but could not pull the trigger. The man had lost his belt and was running unsteadily, holding up his trousers, and he had, Orwell reflected, become something other than a Fascist: a rather comic, vulnerable human being. Orwell held his fire, as he did when he entered a Falangist trench and pressed his bayonet against the chest of a disarmed unguarded soldier. Why kill another man, just for the sake of it? *Animal Farm* is about the narrow line between idealism and blind inhumanity. In 1938 Orwell wrote to Frank Jellinek, who had also been in Spain, about what the experience had meant to him. 'I am not a Marxist and I don't hold with all this stuff that boils down to saying "Anything is right which advances the cause of the party".' *Animal Farm* is about what happens when individuals cease to act according either to their conscience or their notions of right or wrong, and in this respect the Party-hardened communists were, for Orwell, as bad as the Fascists.

The Spanish Civil War has long been regarded as unique. Never since has such a conflict drawn 40,000 volunteers to fight for a democratically elected government against a tyrannical military coup. However, the attraction of Islamic State for foreign-born jihadists, many from countries such as France, the UK, Germany and the Netherlands, drew commentators to ISIS/Spain comparisons like dim-witted moths to a flame. George Monbiot (*Guardian*, 10 February 2014) entitled his piece 'Orwell was hailed a hero for fighting in Spain. Today he'd be guilty of terrorism.' Orwell features prominently in all of the articles on this topic. Monbiot focuses on the Blair government's 2006 Terrorism Act in which anyone proved to have been involved in military action abroad with a 'political, ideological, religious or racial motive' can be jailed, potentially for life. His article is founded upon the relativistic stance of the new liberal left, in which the old-fashioned notions of right and wrong, good and evil, are seen as simplistic polarities which cloud the nuanced biases, prejudices and subterfuge of public discourse. Monbiot argues that the former foreign secretary Sir Malcolm Rifkind might be open to prosecution if 'finance' had been included as one of the motives; he had been chairman of an arms manufacturer which exported their products to very suspect regimes. Eric Blair's namesake, Tony, could, he contends, be subject to prosecution given that he had had, without democratic sanction, participated in the invasion of Iraq; but he, and his Cabinet, were protected by crown immunity.

Monbiot leaves open to question the difference between the jihadists who went abroad to risk and sometimes lose their lives for a cause and members of the International Brigades and militias. From the other end of the political spectrum the *Daily Mail* (5 December 2015) took against recent pronouncements by the 'Stop the War' group which, as they jubilantly pointed out, had once been led by the Labour leader Jeremy Corbyn. Hilary Benn had defended his party's support for the Cameron government's decision to mount air attacks against ISIS, by invoking the spirit of the International Brigades. The RAF, he contended, were defending the more liberal anti-Assad fighters against ISIS. His perversion of history and political allegiance is odd to say the least but nowhere near as bizarre as the response by Stop the War:

> Benn does not even seem to realise that the jihadist movement that ultimately spawned Daesh [IS] is far closer to the spirit of internationalism and solidarity that drove the International Brigades than Cameron's bombing campaign – except that the international jihad takes the form of solidarity with oppressed Muslims, rather than the working class or the socialist revolution.

In the *Daily Telegraph* (21 May 2014) Dr Usama Hasan, an academic and expert in Middle Eastern politics who had given evidence at trials of ISIS returnees, stated that Monbiot's article was 'an unhelpful observation' and that: 'We would do well not to propagate the myth that these men are freedom fighters or that they should be compared to Britons who fought in the Spanish Civil War; both legally and politically, times have changed since 1939.' Hasan's codicil indicates that he and Monbiot, despite their apparent differences, share certain preconceptions. Specifically, deeds and motives must be treated as products of historical change and circumstance, and notions of good and evil as enduring absolutes are illusions.

Let us be clear about something that each of these commentators, including the Tory *Daily Mail*, has in common. None is willing to point out that the jihadists are brainless, murderous ideologues while the Civil War volunteers were courageous agents for a Europe rooted in democracy and freedom of speech. Their inability or unwillingness to do so is probably due to the ongoing ordinance that we must not dare to insult violent idealists for fear of offending supposedly non-belligerent figures who share their beliefs. The men, and women, who went to defend the democratically elected government of Spain were largely left-leaning but they were not morally or ideologically purblind. Orwell's refusal to shoot and bayonet almost comically compromised Falangists – such as the one fleeing while trying to hold up his trousers – testifies to this; they were on the wrong side but they were fellow humans. The elected Spanish government was a disparate entity but it was united in its determination to drag the country into a post-Enlightenment condition enjoyed by much of western Europe. At the beginning of the twentieth century, Spain was a relic of its feudal past, run by the Church, the landowning classes and the aristocracy. Franco wanted to refashion this as ultra-nationalist Fascism, and the foreign volunteers who fought against him did so to offer their Iberian compatriots a future involving freedom of speech and democracy. ISIS volunteers are committed to the opposite, a return to a past in which thought is surrendered to zealous religious fanaticism. It is difficult to imagine an Islamist who would, as Orwell did, refrain from pressing the trigger or using their bayonet. They regard their cause as the licence for foul one-on-one cruelty; they enjoy murder and mutilation in the name of Allah. Many of those who went to fight for the Spanish government were middle class but far more were from the self-educated working classes, people who regarded the First World War as the last gasp of European imperialism and the future as excitingly fluid, an improvement on what had gone before but involving humanist conversations between those who would shape it. Fascism was their worst, most obvious, enemy, but even for those who served in the communist-dominated International Brigades Soviet totalitarianism was seen as an equal threat, at least after Franco had triumphed. How did these men and women differ from ISIS volunteers? The latter are incapable of thinking; they are enslaved to an implacable, fundamentalist creed. They do not volunteer to enable people to live as they choose to live; they want to enforce a cretinous religiosity upon them. There are no parallels between Republican volunteers and ISIS terrorists. They are absolute opposites.

9

BETWEEN WARS

By the beginning of July 1937 the Orwells were back in the Wallington cottage. Jack Common had looked after the building in their absence and had tended to the chickens and animals that Eileen left behind when she set out for Barcelona. The first sign that *Homage to Catalonia* would be treated with scorn by the orthodox left in Britain came when Orwell was asked by the *New Statesman and Nation* to review Franz Borkenau's *Spanish Cockpit*. Borkenau had worked for the Comintern in Moscow and had been an enthusiastic communist, until Spain. There, in Catalonia, he had witnessed a version of Stalin's show trials and totalitarian policies: if you did not follow the party line you were tried without defence, or simply 'disappeared'. He made this clear in his book and Orwell, as reviewer and fellow volunteer in Catalonia, enthusiastically upheld Borkenau's testimony. The editor, Kingsley Martin, wrote to him that it was 'not possible' for the magazine to publish the review because it 'too far controverts the political policy of the paper' (29 July 1937). Martin did not claim that Borkenau and Orwell were not telling the truth; simply that he, his fellow editors and their readers did not wish to read what they had to say.

Most of the reviews of *The Road to Wigan Pier* appeared in March but Orwell had heard very little of them in Spain. When he arrived home they awaited him as the beginning of a firestorm of political controversy. The ILP's *New Leader* felt it was 'a great pity ... he did not confine himself to facts and figures', implying that they did not welcome his political opinions. Arthur Calder-Marshall in

Time and Tide offered a measured estimation while suspecting that he had exaggerated the levels of degradation he encountered in boarding houses and elsewhere. Harry Pollitt, General Secretary of the CPGB, insisted on doing the review for the *Daily Worker* himself, in which he accuses 'a disillusioned little middle-class boy' of 'snobbery' and an innate aversion to the working classes whose cause he avows to support.

On 28 July Orwell wrote a long letter to Victor Gollancz implying that the orthodox left, including the official Labour Party and the communists, were colluding in a conspiracy against him. Pollitt had claimed that in *Wigan Pier* his persistent references to the 'smell' of the homes, clothes and people he encountered testified to his regard for them as irrevocably inferior, and a number of other reviews and articles on the book had also made a point of Orwell's alleged revulsion to the lower orders, as evidenced in his charge that they 'smell'. He points out to Gollancz that he uses the term infrequently and even then in relation to ineradicable problems with hygiene that are caused by poverty. More significantly, he makes it clear that it was not accidental that such exercises in character assassination properly began when news reached the UK that he was involved with the POUM militia. He points out that as early as March, when his book came out, the CPGB and Soviet communists in Spain were alleging that the POUM was both Trotskyist in its politics and working as a fifth column for the Falangists. Next he moves on to 'a more serious matter' involving a 'campaign of organised libel' against a number of his close comrades, including 'a boy of eighteen whom I knew in the line'. Shortly before drafting the letter he had travelled to Bristol to defend the 'boy', Stafford Cottman, at a meeting of the local CPGB. Cottman had been expelled from the Young Communist League and the house where he lived with his parents was picketed by enraged Party members. All because he, like Orwell, was associated with the POUM. Cottman had received an official letter from the Party describing him as 'in the pay of Franco', and Orwell pointed out to those Party members who were prepared to meet him that while Stalin might mount show trials of this kind in Russia, Britain was, for the time being, still a free country where such baseless accusations could be treated as libellous. He also pointed out that his righteous CPGB accusers were not veterans of the Civil War. Orwell, in the letter to Gollancz, stated that he too had, in print, faced the same allegation – being 'in Fascist pay' – and that he did not '"pull [his] weight" in the fight against the Fascists,' specifically that he had allowed Falangist forces to achieve easy victories. He enclosed the article in which these claims were made and underlined the passages for Gollancz's attention. Why did he write to Gollancz? At the close he apologises, a little disingenuously, for putting 'this kind of thing upon you' but explains that as his publisher 'your good name is to some extent involved with mine'. His apology and explanation were spurious. Earlier in July he had met with Norman Collins, Gollancz's junior editor, and informed him of what he intended to do in *Homage to Catalonia* and Collins, knowing his boss, thought it more than 'probable' that Gollancz would refuse to publish. The letter was his goodbye note to his publisher and, by implication, a statement to those within the orthodox-left colloquy for which he assumed that Gollancz, as a fellow member, would act as messenger, and he was right. A few days later Gollancz forwarded a copy of the letter to Harry Pollitt.

When he was in Spain Orwell was asked by the Moscow-based *International Literature* for a review copy of *Wigan Pier* and an article on his experiences with the working classes of the North. He replied that he would ask his publisher to forward the book but that he would at present be unable to do a piece for them, given that he was recovering from his injury. Naively he also mentioned that he had been shot when serving with the POUM militia. He did not receive a reply from Moscow until August, after he had returned to Wallington. 'Our magazine,' he was informed, 'has nothing to do with POUM members; this organisation … is part of Franco's "fifth column".'

Despite his continuing insistence that Europe faced a threat from the growing number of nations espousing Fascism Orwell also felt that he was being turned into a 'non-person' by virtually all elements of the left.

All of this occurred when he was preparing the first draft of *Homage to Catalonia*, mostly in Wallington and sometimes, for the sake of his health, in the O'Shaughnessy house in London. It was in these early days too that he fixed upon a title. The book was about Spain, but Catalonia seemed, to him, to have encapsulated the uniqueness of what had occurred, albeit briefly, in 1936 and 1937. This region of Spain had become a state-within-a-state, a collage of radical factions, none of which quite agreed on their overall objective but co-operated as a mixture of rebellious energies. Even today Catalonia is regarded by the rest of Spain as the renegade province. Why else would its nationalist leaders remain in prison without charge? Many still see Nin as the province's chief martyr, a man as much dedicated to the uniqueness of the region as to an ideology. There is a square dedicated to him in Barcelona, and about a kilometre away you'll find Plaça de George Orwell.

Orwell finished *Homage to Catalonia* during the closing days of 1937, a remarkable feat given the continuing pain from his throat wound and worsening problems with breathing. He was spared having it formally rejected by Gollancz when Secker & Warburg wrote to him early in 1938 asking if they could see the draft. They decided, without hesitation, that it was for them. During the second half of 1937 Orwell attended an ILP summer school, mostly to seek out friends from Spain – notably McNair, Cottman and Fenner – rather than to commit himself to the group. He is also remembered for his kindness at another camp, again organised by the ILP, for refugee Basque children, few of whom could speak English. Most were suffering from what we now call PTSD. Those who spoke to Crick, decades later, recalled Orwell as a gentle father-like man.

Figures from the International Anti-Fascist Solidarity Committee – a front organisation for anarchists – also tried to woo Orwell.

In *Homage to Catalonia* he wrote that in Spain 'as far as my purely personal preferences went I would have liked to join the Anarchists.' They were, he explained, 'the main revolutionary force' and he implies that their somewhat irregular, almost dissolute ideology suited him better than the unbending mantras of other groups, especially the communists. But for the time being he chose not to join anything, and only in 1938 did he decide to become a member of the ILP, which he regarded as a British version of the POUM – loosely affiliated to Marxism and socialism yet open to ideas on what either might ultimately involve.

In early March 1938 Orwell's left lung suddenly began to bleed badly. This was quickly diagnosed as a tuberculous lesion. Eileen's brother Laurence was a doctor with highly placed contacts in the medical profession and he secured a place for him in Preston Hall Sanatorium in Kent, a prestigious institution. Orwell's condition was so serious that he remained there for six months and as a diversion from the tiresome process of trying to breathe again Orwell caught up on the accusations in print from various quarters on his ideological treachery.

Homage to Catalonia was published in April, only six weeks after his confinement, and some of the early reviews, particularly in the *Manchester Guardian* and the *TLS*, were respectful regarding its documentary account of the war but sniffily doubtful on its political import. The anonymous *Listener* reviewer stated that Orwell was part of the 'Trotskyist ... Fifth Column of whom General Franco has so constantly boasted'. the *Daily Worker* printed a brief perfunctory notice, repeating the charge that the book was written by a Trotskyite who had colluded with Falangists, an accusation repeated in four other left-wing journals and weeklies.

Outside the public media Orwell received reassuring letters from others who knew that he was telling the truth, notably Borkenau whose book on Spain he'd reviewed; the rejection of the review by the *New Statesman and Nation* testified to the two men being comrades in arms. Borkenau visited him in the sanatorium. The noted left-wing writers Naomi Mitchison and Herbert Read wrote to him praising his honesty and his courageous resistance against the solidly right-wing pro-Franco stance of most mainstream British newspapers and the unyielding acceptance of the Soviet communist narrative adopted by all parties of the British left, with the exception of the ILP. The book caused public controversy but sold very few copies. Of the 1,500 printed for the first edition more than half were still in warehouses or on bookshop shelves in the year of Orwell's death.

'Fake news' is generally agreed to have come into being alongside the sidelining of the conventional press by social networks such as Twitter or Facebook. The latter are not subject to journalistic ethics, nor are they subject to the conventions of fact-checking via which newspapers, radio and television can be held accountable. Users of social media are, conversely, unregulated and any notion of what is believable shifts towards a populist consensus and away from documented proof. Orwell's fate indicated that a post-truth environment predated social media by about six decades. The contest between which party was telling the truth about Catalonia in 1938–39, particularly the activities of the POUM and the anarchists, was conducted largely in the print media, but the left-wing organs of news dissemination and ideological polemic had already indoctrinated themselves and their readers regarding what actually occurred in Barcelona and on the Catalonian front line. If President Trump makes a statement on Twitter regarding a peace conference with North Korea, his intention to force Mexico to pay for the border wall or that pro-abortion Democrats advocate 'executing babies AFTER birth', his tweets, however questionable, are protected by his status as a figure who treats 'truth' as the weapon of unpatriotic left-leaning liberals.

But we should not regard the present-day distortion and manipulation of fact as the sole preserve of the American Right. In November 2018 the philosopher and aesthetician Sir Roger Scruton – a man with moderately conservative views on the arts – was appointed as unpaid chair of a government quango on the future of British architecture called 'Building Better, Building Beautiful'. After an interview with George Eaton, a deputy editor of the *New Statesman*, was published in March 2019, Sir Roger was summarily dismissed from the post. This was followed by widespread condemnation of him, in print but mainly online, by figures who transcend the divide between left- and right-wing politics, including Tom Tugendhat and Johnny Mercer (both Conservative MPs), Lord Finkelstein of *The Times* (decidedly liberal-left), George Osborne, ex-Chancellor and now editor of the *Evening Standard*, and many others. In the article Eaton reported that Sir Roger had made antisemitic remarks, commented on how he approved of the policies of the populist Hungarian leader Viktor Orbán – again apparently advocating antisemitism and Islamophobia – and referred to the 'invasion' of southern and central Europe by 'tribes' of Muslims. Eaton had completely distorted the actual content of the interview (and was later obliged to admit to doing so, though he remains in post), but what is striking about these incidents is that once the buttons for automatic condemnation have been pressed – mostly regarding antisemitism and Islamophobia – a group of seemingly sane, rational individuals is transformed into a Twitter-mob. Their notion of Sir Roger's guilt is taken for granted because anyone seemingly transgressing certain codes must be treated as evil and unsuitable for any form of public office, irrespective of the validity of the evidence.

Something similar happened at the end of the 1930s when those who went against the pro-Soviet storyline were presented as traitors. The hard-left media told lies about Orwell as a Trotskyist fifth columnist just as Eaton altered his exchanges with Sir Roger to present him as a racist neo-fascist. In both cases the mob – from both left and right – immediately swooped on its victim. The terrifying atmosphere of *Nineteen Eighty-Four*, in which facts and truth become the property of those who manipulate the official consensus, originated in Orwell's experiences after Spain. In 1942 he wrote an essay called 'Looking Back on the Spanish War' (published in *New Road*, June 1943) in which the following passage leaves us in no doubt that the alteration by the establishment left of his recollections in Catalonia, especially his weeks on the run in what had effectively become a version of Stalin's Russia, would be carried over into his last, most terrifying novel:

> In the past people ... struggled after the truth, well knowing that they must make mistakes; but in each case they believed that 'the facts' existed and were more or less discoverable ... It is just this common basis of agreement, with its implication that human beings are all one species of animal, that totalitarianism destroys. ... The implied objective of this line of thought is a nightmare world in which the Leader, or some ruling clique, controls not only the future but *the past*. If the Leader says of such and such an event, 'It never happened' – well, it never happened. If he says that two and two are five – well, two and two are five.

In late summer 1938 Orwell was advised by consultants that another English winter might trigger a flare up of his illness. L. H. Myers, a novelist whose considerable wealth came largely from his inheritance rather than his book sales, was approached by Dorothy Plowman, wife of the *Adelphi*'s co-editor. The Orwells, she told him, needed money to go abroad and Myers, a communist fellow traveller who lived well but with a guilty conscience, gave Dorothy £300. After leaving the sanatorium on 1 September and spending one day in London Orwell and Eileen boarded the *Stratheden* for Gibraltar, crossed the Strait to Tangier, and took the train to Marrakech. Again, Jack Common looked after the cottage and the animals; since their return from Spain they had also taken in a large black poodle which they named 'Marx'. They first booked into the Majestic Hotel, then took rooms with a Madame Vellet and next rented a spacious villa just north of the town. It was rather like Wallington-in-the-Sahara, with an orange grove, some goats and a servant who came daily to do basic cleaning and laundry. Eileen wrote to Jack Common's wife Mary that 'he [Orwell] has been worse here than I've ever seen him. The country is, or was anyway, almost intolerably depressing ...' (5 December 1938). She did not expand on the exact cause of Orwell's depression but we can infer a good deal. The environment, though hot enough, did not alleviate his bronchitis. He had to deal with incessant gusts of fine sand from the surrounding desert and in December fell seriously ill once again, this time without access to doctors or medicine. He and Eileen found the architecture of Marrakech at once enchanting and saddening, given that it was the legacy of an indigenous population which had to endure conditions of colonial oppression by the French that made the British in India seem enlightened. But it was the gradual stream of news from outside North Africa that contributed most to Orwell's despondency. During their journey to Morocco, Hitler's demand for control of the Sudetenland had resulted in the Munich Conference at which Britain and France ceded control of the region to Germany. In March 1939, shortly before Eileen wrote to Mary of Orwell's dejection, the Nazis invaded the rest of Czechoslovakia and days after that Hitler delivered an ultimatum to Lithuania and effectively forced it to give up the Klaipėda region. On one occasion Orwell had conversed with a group of French troops in Marrakech regarding the likelihood of war and was shocked and rather disgusted at their good-humoured indifference.

All of this explains the temper of *Coming Up for Air*. Orwell began the novel shortly after their arrival at the villa and delivered it to the office of his agent Leonard Moore within a day of their return to London at the end of March. It involves a brief period in the life of George Bowling, who delivers the narrative in the first person. Bowling is a fat, middle-aged insurance salesman, married with two children and putting up, just, with life in an unassuming London suburb. He is the archetype of dull lower middle-class expediency, not particularly happy with his lot but lacking the money or spirit to change it. He wins a small amount of cash from a bet, not sufficient to alter his existence but enough for him to take a glimpse into something he still treasures, his past. Taking a train journey to a small home-counties town very similar to those in which his author had spent his childhood and teens, he recalls the things that have held him enraptured for almost forty years: his youthful sweetheart, the air of unassuming ease that seemed to inform the place, its people and buildings, and the pond where he had fished for carp – which, he imagines, will by now be giants. Everything has changed. The district has been altered by people with a seeming disrespect for taste or heritage, the pond has been filled in and when he encounters his loved one she is serving in a tea-shop, ravaged by age. To his relief she does not recognise him. Bowling confesses that his notion of the past is a delusion:

> … I'd come to Lower Binfield with a question in my mind. What's ahead of us? Well, I'd had my answer. The old life's finished, and to go about looking for it is just a waste of time.

He knew all the time that his mythical lost childhood is a refuge from something he would, if he could, shut out. Throughout his various journeys he is plagued by a vision of something horrible and imminent:

> The train was running along the embankment. A little below us you could see the roofs of the houses stretching on and on, the little red roofs where the bombs are going to drop … Funny how we keep thinking about bombs. Of course there's no question that it's coming soon. You can tell how close it is by the cheer-up stuff they're talking about in the newspapers … that bombing places can't do any damage nowadays. The anti-aircraft guns have got so good that the bomber has to stay at twenty thousand feet.

Orwell had witnessed the effects of air bombardment by the Germans in Barcelona; not so infamous as Guernica but nonetheless equally calculated to cause terror in a metropolitan area. During one Barcelona raid more than sixty civilians died, mostly children. And his prediction of what would happen to British cities during the Blitz, barely eighteen months hence, is chilling.

WAR

The years between late 1939 and 1945 found Orwell busily producing hundreds of articles for a number of journals and weeklies. He served as literary editor of the left-wing *Tribune* between 1943 and 1945 and enabled a large number of previously unpublished writers to get into print. What is notable about this wartime period is that his hyperactivity was matched with a persistent feeling of anger and frustration.

In April he received news from Southwold that his father was terminally ill with cancer, and in late June his sister told him that it would be best if he could return immediately to his parents' home. Later he informed Moore, his agent, that they had become reconciled during these final meetings: 'he had not been so disappointed in me as before'. Avril read to him an early favourable review of *Coming Up for Air* from the *Sunday Times* and he died peacefully the day afterwards.

Soon after war broke out in September 1939 Eileen began work in the Censorship Department at the Ministry of Information. She moved in with her mother and sister-in-law in their spacious house in Greenwich. She would return to Wallington for a weekend every fortnight but Orwell remained there tending the livestock and planting vast numbers of root vegetables, on one occasion more than fifteen pounds of potatoes, as part of what would soon be advertised as 'digging for victory'. He also wrote. *Coming Up for Air* had received good reviews and the first printing sold three times more than *Homage to Catalonia* did in the twelve years following its publication. But he was no longer interested in fiction, at least in producing it. He was preparing the first draft for the title essay of what would become *Inside the Whale and Other Essays*, an astringent assault against literature per se as endemically self-indulgent, ineffectual and generally useless.

In January 1940 Orwell went for a physical examination in the hope of qualifying for military service, which was an unlikely prospect for anyone aged thirty-seven – at that time regarded as well-established middle age. He failed, mainly because of the condition of his lungs and his throat injury. In April he wrote to Geoffrey Gorer that his decision to join Eileen in London was because 'I want to get her out of it, as they [the Ministry] are simply working her to death ... besides it's making it impossible for us to be together.' His true motive was disclosed in a letter, again to Gorer, written after he failed his medical: '... now we are in this bloody war we have got to win it & I would like to lend a hand'. Eileen moved out of the family home and for the following three years they rented bearable but largely austere flats in various parts of West and North London.

Orwell's first option to 'lend a hand' became available six weeks after his arrival in the city. He joined what would formally be known as C Company, 5th County of London Battalion (the St John's Wood Company), of the Home Guard (then known as Local Defence Volunteers). Most of his fellow early volunteers were First World War veterans, wearily and patriotically committed to something they'd already fought for. Soon, however, much younger men were attracted to the Home Guard as an apprenticeship for full-time service. Few arms were available and Orwell felt he was reliving his days as an NCO and instructor with the POUM militia. He sought out locals who owned shotguns to fill in during the period while his platoon waited for Lee Enfield rifles and, drawing on his experiences in Spain, showed his fellow volunteers how to assemble basic fire-bombs. In June, the same month that Orwell joined his unit, his brother-in-law Laurence O'Shaughnessy, then a medical officer, was killed by shrapnel from German artillery while treating wounded infantrymen on the beach at Dunkirk. Eileen was stricken by the loss of her brother. Tosco Fyvel described her as sitting in the garden of one of their flats 'sunk in unmoving silence while we talked'. Everyone who knew the Orwells testified to her falling into a state of depression from which she never fully recovered.

Orwell began filing 'London Letters' for readers of the American political magazine *Partisan Review* and took up irregular scripting and speaking work with the BBC. In October 1940 he became the chief film reviewer for the weekly political and literary magazine *Time and Tide* – he gave up the job in August 1941. There is no record of who was responsible for taking him on but the decision was the equivalent of appointing a radical feminist as a judge for Miss World. In his twenty-six reviews there is no evidence that he actually enjoyed, let alone approved of, any of the movies that he was paid, albeit poorly, to sit through. He was particularly disgusted by the apparent appetite for gratuitous violence fed by American Westerns and gangster films. Of *High Sierra* he comments that '... Bogart is the Big Shot who smashes people in the face with the butt of his pistol and watches his fellow gangsters burn to death with the casual comment, "They were only small town guys," but is kind to dogs and is supposed to be deeply touching when he is smitten with a "pure" affection for a crippled girl, who knows nothing of his past.' He was equally merciless with melodrama, comedy and escapist romance, savaging, amongst others, Noël Coward and George Cukor, as brainless populists. It was not that he had a temperamental aversion to cinema per se – not quite. Rather, he found that everything he watched was made by and for people who existed in a parallel universe, desperate to escape from any notion of their world, not just Europe, on the brink of something close to apocalypse.

This feeling energised the title essay of *Inside the Whale*, published by Gollancz in March 1940. The piece has been assessed and summarised by dozens of Orwell critics and biographers, in much the way that one might attempt to describe the bizarre behaviour of a close friend or relative while avoiding any attempt to explain it. In it he does for literature, from around the middle of the 1800s to the present, what he did to film in the *Time and Tide* reviews. The only writer he admires, begrudgingly, is Henry Miller. Miller's *Tropic of Capricorn* is a celebration of capricious bacchanalia, an inversion of Orwell in Paris, not working to survive but whoring and drinking himself to oblivion. Orwell's point was that Miller had at least been honest about the sheer irrelevance of literature as a medium for improvement, while the vast majority of poets and novelists felt entitled to avoid this question and to closet themselves against what was actually happening around them. He spares no one, aiming particular contempt against the modernists who had become obsessed with the nature of 'writing' immediately following the years when a continent had consumed itself in an orgy of self-annihilation. It is a superbly radical piece of work, which goes some way to explain the reluctance of Orwellian commentators to accept what it says. He does not urge his literary peers to refashion themselves according to a new, unnerving world. He tells them to shut up and accept that while their work might be countenanced as a form of entertainment or high-art diversion it is no longer significant in terms of how we think, behave and make political decisions. A year later he turns his attention specifically to H. G. Wells, who in his opinion epitomises the quintessentially English trend towards literary writing as a form of introverted escapism. Wells' preoccupation with creating pseudo-science fiction utopias had blinded him to the inherent evil of a state run according to any ideological model, to the point that he was incapable of taking Hitler seriously – he called him 'that screaming little defective in Berlin' ('Wells, Hitler and the World State', *Horizon,* August 1941). Soon after the article appeared Wells dined with the Orwells and the evening might have ended with an exchange of blows had Orwell not thought better of striking a seventy-five-year-old man. In his *Diary* of 27 March 1942 he writes: 'Crocuses now full out ... Abusive letter from H. G. Wells, who addresses me as "you shit", among other things.'

Whether we agree or disagree with Orwell is irrelevant, at least in terms of his life and career. He was already thinking about *Animal Farm*, a novel that would be neither enjoyable nor instructive; just a reflection of various levels of human failure. This, as *Inside the Whale* shows, is his personal vision of literature; its only function. His childhood admiration for Swift was coming to fruition in his own work.

In London Orwell began to socialise again with friends and associates from the early 1930s, notably Richard Rees, Max Plowman, Rayner Heppenstall and Cyril Connolly. When working for the BBC, supervising broadcasts to India and Southeast Asia, he got to know Malcolm Muggeridge, also employed by the Corporation. In his memoirs Muggeridge recalled how both felt like unwitting participants in a farce, with Orwell reciting passages from Milton's *Areopagitica*, Eliot's *The Waste Land* and other gems of Western culture to help stiffen the resolve of eager listeners in Kuala Lumpur, Rangoon and Cawnpore. Orwell's contempt for the mindless, stifling BBC bureaucracy would filter into various parts of *Nineteen Eighty-Four*.

In January 1940 Orwell was introduced by Fredric Warburg to Tosco Fyvel. Born in Cologne in 1907, Fyvel spent the 1930s in Palestine, where his Zionist parents had emigrated, and later moved to London to assist in any way he could in the war against Nazism. He would eventually be called up to serve as an intelligence officer specialising in psychological warfare in the Middle East and Africa. Before this he met regularly with Orwell, Warburg and an anti-Nazi refugee, Sebastian Haffner, and they planned a series of short books and pamphlets, largely focused on the evils and dangers of Fascism and other totalitarian doctrines (communism included) but also reaching into a broader agenda of the injustices of colonialism, class division and the various cultural and moral questions raised by the war in Europe. The series was

called 'Searchlight Books'. Fifteen volumes out of a projected
seventeen were published before Secker & Warburg's printing
house in Portsmouth was destroyed by German bombing in 1942.
Orwell and Fyvel were the principal co-editors and would remain
close friends until the former's death.

In December 1941 David Astor asked Cyril Connolly who he
thought was 'good on politics' with a view to transforming the
somewhat leaden and predictable *Observer*. Astor would not take
over as editor until after the war, during which he served in the
Royal Marines, but the paper was owned by his father and he was
determined to recruit people who would energise it in the interim.
Connolly recommended Orwell and the two men got on well from
the start. They took meals together, Astor being obliged to put
up with the kind of ration-only concoctions that Orwell insisted
upon creating in his flat. As a baronet from the landed gentry Astor
regularly dined in the classier black-market restaurants of the city
and concoctions such as eel, potato and larded bread eaten from
Orwell's kitchen table struck him as little masochistic. Orwell
contributed a few largely uncontroversial pieces to the paper,
but was immensely influential behind the scenes. According to
Crick, Astor treated him as his 'surrogate conscience', a sounding
board for ideas on the paper as the left-leaning – though not
quite socialist – voice of liberalism in post-war Britain. Astor was
fascinated by Orwell's observations and questions on what Britain
might become if it survived against Nazi Germany and spent many
nights on Orwell's camp bed rather than miss out on what his
mentor had to say.

Warburg was also responsible for introducing Orwell to Arthur
Koestler. Koestler was rather like Fyvel remade by Rabelais. A
Hungarian Jew, he fell out with communism mainly because he
was equally committed to lechery, drink and adventure. In 1926 he
went to Palestine, worked on a kibbutz and campaigned vigorously
for the foundation of a Jewish state. After founding the Zionist
weekly *Zafon* he was appointed correspondent for the Ullstein

News Agency in Paris and then became an undercover agent of
the German Communist Party, working mainly on orders from
Moscow. During his visits to the Soviet Union in this period he
witnessed Stalinist totalitarianism and the show trials of dissidents.
He reported from Spain, was imprisoned by the Falangists and
escaped execution while every other man captured at the same
time was shot by firing squad. He, as the last condemned man alive,
was exchanged for a valuable Nationalist prisoner, a fighter pilot.
After several months in a French detention camp he joined the
Foreign Legion, deserted, and fled to England, where he was again
incarcerated, briefly, in Pentonville, which he said was his preferred
prison. Orwell reviewed his account of the psychological effects
of the Moscow Purge Trials, *Darkness at Noon* (1940). 'Brilliant as
this book is ... it is probably most valuable as an interpretation of
the Moscow "confessions" by someone with an inner knowledge of
totalitarian methods.'

Orwell first met Koestler in February 1941 and they talked
regularly over the subsequent nine years. Operation Barbarossa,
the German invasion of Soviet Russia, began in June 1941
and despite rapid advances towards Leningrad, Moscow and
Stalingrad it was evident by early 1942 that the Red Army was
capable of absorbing and thwarting the previously successful
tactics of blitzkrieg. On 8 December 1941 America entered the
conflict following the bombing of Pearl Harbour the previous
day, declaring war against both Japan and the Axis forces in
Europe. Inevitably, Orwell and Koestler speculated on the shape
of Europe following what now seemed to be the inevitable defeat
of the Nazis. In particular they were concerned with the likely
influence of the Soviet Union on the continent, post-war. Despite
desperate counter-offensives by the Wehrmacht during 1942 it
was clear that the Red Army would soon be mounting an assault
upon Nazi-occupied areas of central Europe, before the Allies
could launch an invasion from the west. Both men knew from
their experiences in Spain that the Soviets would not so much

liberate these territories as annex them as parts of an expanded communist super-state. The exact nature of their discussions remains unrecorded but when *Inside the Whale* was reissued in 1945 Orwell included in it a profile of his friend, and from this we can appreciate how their dialogues energised *Animal Farm*. On the one hand Koestler 'believes in an Earthly Paradise, the Sun State which the gladiators set out to establish, and which has haunted the imagination of Socialists, Anarchists and religious heretics for hundreds of years'. But 'his intelligence tells him … that what is actually ahead of us is bloodshed, tyranny and privation'. It would be difficult to find a more astute encapsulation of the paradox at the heart of Orwell's novel: it transposes unqualified optimism, a future involving limitless enchantment for all, with an insistence that this is a hopeless delusion.

In *Animal Farm*, the pigs Napoleon (Stalin) and Snowball (Trotsky) are short-term idealists for whom power lends limitless opportunities for egotistical self-advancement. Koestler recognised that these same impulses are an endemic feature of humanity – a demonstration that hardline communism is at odds with who we are – but he was also honest about how they manifested themselves in himself: simultaneously racked by despair and self-doubt while remaining hungry for ideas and political engagement. This is why Orwell enjoyed his company. Painful sincerity of this kind was scarce among those on the left and Orwell used it, or rather perverted it, for the novel: unlike Koestler, Napoleon and Snowball conceal those aspects of their personalities which will ruin the revolution.

Orwell had a particular affinity with deracinated Mitteleuropean outsiders, particularly Borkenau, Fyvel, Kimche and Koestler. All were nomadic involuntary expatriates; Jews who had faced the very real prospect of Fascism as a murderous ideology. None, in this respect, had anything in common with Orwell and it is for this reason that he sought their company and friendship, and why they cultivated his. They had considered communism, notably Soviet communism, as the antidote to the evils of Nazism, unrestrained capitalism and imperialism, but despite the fact that their backgrounds might have caused them to overlook its shortcomings each had recognised it as another brand of totalitarianism. Orwell shared their forebodings and while his first-hand experience of Soviet witch hunts in Catalonia was relatively brief and hardly comparable with that of his friends, all were dumbfounded by the extent to which so many in free countries such as Britain could blind themselves to what was going on in Russia.

At the same time Orwell could not quite suppress his chameleonesque tendencies, his inclination to socialise with groups and individuals from which he'd previously alienated himself. He certainly enjoyed the company of the Astors but equally he took pleasure in testing their credulity regarding his true character and temperament. Inez Holden came from the landed gentry and had been a well-known high-living society beauty during the 1920s. By the time she met the Orwells in 1941 those days were well behind her, her looks were adversely affected by weight gain brought on by a glandular disorder and she had become a louche bohemian, though conspicuously wealthy. Holden, with mischievous calculation, had arranged the dinner party involving the Orwells and Wells, in the full knowledge that the latter had read the article and would arrive filled with explosive rage. She would entertain the Orwells at the best restaurants in the city, notably ones in which black-market food and drink were available, testing George's presentation of himself as a gloomy ascetic figure content with the privations of the war. He would play along, objecting in principle to being able to eat quality fare which ordinary people could never afford, while suggesting that the supposedly rare pre-war Bordeaux vintages might not be what was claimed on the labels.

Soon after Orwell met Koestler in 1940 Holden took George and Eileen to supper at the Café Royal and introduced them to a couple she knew, Anthony and Violet Powell. Powell had published five novels, each informed by his cultural environment, the intellectual branch of the gentry, figures who drifted between their estates in the shires, their London homes and escapades on the continent. Politically he was a moderately liberal conservative who maintained an enduring contempt for the left; socially and ideologically he could be treated as Mosley's second cousin. Inez probably expected that sparks would fly but Orwell outplayed her. Powell had been a year below him at Eton; he had been an Oppidan, one of the rich boys who did not need a scholarship. When they met Powell was wearing the dress uniform of his regiment, the 'Blues', the military equivalent of Eton or Oxbridge, part of the Royal Household Division and the preserve of the upper classes, at least for officers. Powell later recalled, with some puzzlement, that Orwell opened the conversation by asking if his regimental trousers 'strap under the foot' and commenting on how as an imperial policeman he had worn such breeches in Burma and that 'these straps under the feet give you a feeling like nothing else in life'. Was he offering Powell the equivalent of a freemason's handshake: we belong to the same stock? Unlikely, given that he loathed everything about Burma, including his involvement with it, and was equally contemptuous of the culture of entitlement preserved in institutions such as Eton. The Orwells and Powells remained on good terms, but to what extent was this a performance verging upon a caricature on the part of George? Much later, when journalists and biographers interviewed Powell and asked how he could get along with a man with whom he was seemingly incompatible he confessed to bemusement. Understandably; Orwell had played him for a fool.

Orwell later described the atmosphere at the BBC as 'something halfway between a girls' school and a lunatic asylum' and claimed that 'all we are doing … is useless, or slightly worse than useless'. He meant that he had become the instrument of the official propaganda department, which was founded on roughly the same principles as Matthew Arnold's thesis on the benefits of studying literature; that in some pseudo-mystical way, 'great' literature strengthens character and morale. As his merciless attack on the supposed relevance of literature showed, Orwell found this ludicrous, but he worked hard, and aside from doing his own broadcasts recruited some of the most eminent figures to talk about literature and read extracts from their work, including T. S. Eliot (whom quietly he loathed), E. M. Forster (to whom he exhibited tolerance as a Victorian relic), Dylan Thomas, Cyril Connolly, Stephen Spender (who he'd mocked during the Spanish War as a closet pacifist, but almost made up with since), John Lehmann, Herbert Read and V. S. Pritchett.

In June 1942 the propaganda arm moved into premises previously occupied by the Peter Robinson department store which were entirely unsuitable for broadcasting. The smallest room was turned into the canteen, persistently overcrowded and stinking of cabbage, over-stewed tea and gin, which virtually everyone brought to the place as an antidote to relentless boredom. He was aware of the basic statistics. In India only 0.4 per cent of the population of 300 million plus had regular access to a wireless and most of them had better things to do than listen to broadcasts from 200 Oxford Street, London. He was marshalling the greatest cultural presences of the age to spout irrelevances while, almost hilariously, no one was listening. Accordingly Orwell in his own broadcasts adopted a tone of voice that indicated irredeemable boredom and monotony both on his part and what he expected of his largely non-existent audience. Off broadcasts he began to adopt the persona of the dedicated eccentric which included slurping tea from his saucer – the badge of the working classes – followed by comments on its quality in a cut-glass Etonian accent. But he made friends, initially with Muggeridge and later with John Morris, George Woodcock and the literary academic William (Bill) Empson, all of whom shared his opinion on the utter pointlessness of their undertaking.

During his first two years in London Orwell had the impression that he was involved in something by parts bizarre and apocalyptic.

He recalled walking through a park with Connolly in June 1940. Several cricket matches were in progress, mothers were pushing prams and nannies playing games with their infant charges, yet a hundred or so miles south-east more than 300,000 soldiers, the bulk of the army, were making desperate attempts to get off the beaches at Dunkirk. Connolly observed, disdainfully, that panic would set in once the bombs started to drop. The Blitz would begin in three months but Londoners seemed, at least for Orwell, to have chosen make-do stoicism over terror. He recorded in his *Diary* being approached in the street by two women, their faces, hair and clothes thick with black dust from an overnight raid. 'Please sir,' one asked with poised gentility, 'can you tell us where we are?' (21 September 1940). Inez Holden amused him with a story of how she and others had gazed in fascination at the spectacle of a tree in Regent's Park that was hung with silk garments of various colours, stockings and a shining bowler hat. Her friend, an artist, observed that he had once painted 'this sort of thing … it has taken some time to get here'. He was a surrealist, and the tree was decorated with many-hued debris from a hotel bombed the night before. Orwell, according to Connolly, was secretly excited by the Blitz yet at the same time he felt left out; he could observe but not participate. Quite soon after this he would.

Orwell's life and career changed in September 1943 when he resigned from his BBC post. The *Observer* offered him the position of foreign correspondent in the Mediterranean, which would include coverage of the British and American invasion of Sicily and Italy but he declined, reluctantly, knowing that his persistent and recurring bouts of bronchitis would probably kill him in a region beyond reach of reliable medical assistance. Instead he became literary editor of the weekly Labour-supporting newspaper, the *Tribune*. The editor was the Labour politician Aneurin Bevan, son of a Welsh coal miner, who would become one of the most influential figures in the post-war Labour administration. In the summer of 1942 Orwell's sister and mother moved to London, Avril to work in a sheet metal factory, and Ida as a saleswoman in Selfridge's. After only nine months however, on 19 March 1943, Ida died of a heart attack. Orwell was genuinely saddened; he had always been closer to her than to Richard, but his new life as a journalist, or to put it more accurately a controversialist, was already distancing him from his past.

EXPLOSIVE JOURNALISM

Shortly after his mother's death Orwell embarked energetically on two projects that would establish him as the contrarian of his era. One, *Animal Farm*, is well known. It was begun in 1943 and published in 1945. The other is not regarded as a single work. Aside from his editorial duties for the *Tribune* his regular contributions carried a collective title, 'As I Please'. Since 1968 these have been dispersed among many other pieces in *The Collected Essays, Journalism and Letters of George Orwell*, but they have a character of their own, an unflinching temper of irreverence and mischief, and cutting anger.

Orwell was one of the few to defend Bomber Command and its crews against a widespread condemnation, from the left and the right, of what was referred to as 'obliteration bombing'; he mocked those who called for its cessation in their attempt to impose a cosy notion of 'fair play' upon a worldwide struggle against totalitarianism (19 May 1944). Considering how long it has taken the nation to erect a monument to Bomber Command (now regularly vandalised and graffitied) his was certainly a voice in the wilderness. In the same piece he declares that conspiracy theories are feeding some 'obscure psychological need of our time'. In the opinion of all communists every Trotskyist is in the pay of Hitler; every non-member of the Freemasons believes the masons are conspiring against everybody; all Indians are convinced that every Englishman, anti-colonialists included, are machinating against the interests of the sub-continent; and, of course, all Jews are in secret conspiracy against all non-Jews. Orwell doubts that the stress of war is solely responsible for this and what followed the assassination of Kennedy (the FBI and/or the Mafia did it) and 9/11 (engineered by Mossad) suggest he was right.

On 7 January 1944 he published a piece that today would certainly not have appeared in the press and would probably have led to his prosecution had he distributed it on social media. After looking through photographs accompanying the New Year's Honours List it occurred to him that a prerequisite for eminence, even unearned, is a degree of physical grotesquery. And he extrapolates this to the figures currently acting out the enormous drama on the world stage. 'A dictator taller than five feet six inches is a very great rarity,' and shortness is generally accompanied by 'quite fantastic ugliness'; '... Japanese war-lords impersonating baboons, Mussolini with his scrubby dewlap, the chinless De Gaulle, the stumpy short-armed Churchill, Gandhi with his long sly nose and huge bat's ears, Tojo displaying thirty-two teeth with gold in every one of them'. On the recent capture of Ezra Pound (28 January 1944) he hopes that the Americans do not shoot him for treason, given that his martyrdom may cause some to believe that his poems are any good.

In another article, Orwell writes of receiving a letter from a West African on the widespread imposition of the 'colour bar' in pubs and dancehalls. Prejudice originated with white American troops who did not want to socialise with their black fellow servicemen but the English soon backed them up enthusiastically. Orwell had heard that a West Indian infantryman had been brought up before a magistrate for entering a 'place of entertainment' in uniform, though the exact nature of the charge was unclear – would he have been permitted entry in a suit? (11 August 1944). He goes on to tell of how in Paris in the late 1920s black Americans – musicians, singers *et al* – mixed amicably with Parisians, openly courting French women. Objections came only from Britons and Americans. The nastiness that awaited the Windrush generation seemed to be well embedded. A week later, continuing with the theme of home and abroad, he asks why we, in peacetime, attract so few tourists from Europe. There are, he answers, too many rules on what can and cannot be done. Everything closes down on Sunday, 'Trespassers Will Be Prosecuted' signs obstruct access to teasingly beautiful landscapes and pubs are governed by draconian rules on opening and closing, seemingly designed to inflict misery on anyone who simply wishes to while away their time in a bar. Unlike France, Italy or Spain where you can walk for miles without noticing anything proprietorial about the scenery: 'In France, and in various other countries, a café proprietor opens or shuts just as it suits him.' (18 August 1944). As we shall see, Orwell was an Englishman who regarded European mores as something we should aspire to.

One of the most prophetic articles is on the overuse of the words 'fascist' and 'fascistic' ('What is Fascism?', 24 March 1944) to the extent that both had been rendered meaningless. Any given standpoint, state of mind or individual that an opponent finds even mildly disagreeable would be appended with these terms. Times haven't changed.

On 12 May 1944 he opened by dismissing as a myth the belief that modern technology such as the aeroplane and the radio had brought about 'the abolition of distance' and the 'disappearance of frontiers'. In his view the 'effect of modern inventions has been to increase nationalism, to make travel enormously more difficult, to cut down the means of communication between one country and another …' His underlying thesis is that the more that nations become aware of and communicate with each other the greater their tendency to turn further inward. 'Except for a short visit it was [before the war] very difficult to enter Britain, as many a wretched anti-Fascist refugee discovered.' Throughout Europe 'along all the frontiers were barbed wire, machine-guns and prowling sentries …' Which brings to mind the strategy recently adopted by the Hungarian leader, Orbán, in an attempt to seal off his country from the Balkans and Greece, the first point of entry for a vast number of refugees, economic and political, from various parts of the Middle East and North Africa. Orwell continues: 'As to migration, it had practically dried up since the nineteen-twenties. All the countries of the New World did their best to keep the immigrant out unless he brought considerable sums of money with him … Europe's Jews had to stay and be slaughtered because there was nowhere for them to go …' The EU policy of internal free movement was allied to the egalitarian principle of opening up Europe as a refuge for individuals from areas riven by civil conflict, during the post-Iraq war period and the disastrous 'Arab Spring'.

Little more than a year after the end of the war (24 January 1947) Orwell tells of listening in to a conversation in a hotel between two businessmen:

> The younger man remarked that he belonged to several business and civic associations, and that on all of them he made a point of putting forward resolutions that the Poles should be sent back to their own country. The older one added that the Poles were 'very degraded in their morals'. They were responsible for much of the immorality that was present nowadays. 'Their ways are not our ways,' he concluded piously.

The two men agreed that Poles were also 'invading the medical profession', and stealing jobs from 'our lads'. 'Let the Poles go back to their own country.' These foreigners who were taking over the medical and apparently other professions were also responsible for the housing shortage and, for one of the entrepreneurs, made it difficult to profit from buying and selling properties. 'It seemed it was impossible to buy houses or flats nowadays. The Poles were buying them all up … and "where they get the money from is a mystery"'. Orwell considers putting it to them that Poles are probably also responsible for pushing to the head of queues, wearing brightly coloured clothes and displaying cowardice during air raids, stereotypes of Jewishness that became commonplaces during the Blitz. He did not, but he reflects that the most depressing phrase he overheard was 'let them go back to their own country'. The Jews,

the few who survived, didn't have one, and nor did the refugee Poles
who had been betrayed by Churchill's trading off of their nation to
the USSR. The run-up to the 2016 Referendum, and its aftermath,
could have been taking place in 1947. True, our incomers – Poles,
Romanians, Bulgarians, Czechs *et al* – are not refugees but nor are
they, as the two businessmen insist, the enemy. No evidence by
UKIP, Farage's Brexit Party or the Brexit Conservatives has been
offered to show that immigration has damaged the UK economy,
let alone involved the theft of posts from indigenous applicants
for jobs in the medical profession or property from greedy British
speculators. Nonetheless an insidious belief that these foreigners
are the cause of our numerous, sometimes spurious and delusional,
afflictions was the keynote of the anti-EU campaign.

Within the British printed media only the *Guardian* and the
Mirror have taken an astringently anti-Leave stance. *The Times*
plays both points of view against each other but the rest of the
press, particularly since the Referendum result, have presented
those who questioned the wisdom of Brexit as variously enemies
of the people and traitors. Somewhere in the middle we find that
questions are being addressed regarding the 'BBC's impartiality'.
The argument goes something like this. Because the BBC is staffed
at production and managerial level mainly by educated middle-
class, and largely liberal, perhaps left-leaning figures, who also
constitute a large number of its presenters, it will inevitably be
anti-Brexit. Hence it will distort the objective truth, though how it
will do so without telling outright lies that go against undisputable
facts is never explained by its accusers. On 21 April 1944 Orwell
reported that he had received angry letters following his statement
that the BBC was 'a better source of [objective] news than the daily
papers'. Orwell had direct knowledge of how the BBC and the
privately owned newspapers worked. 'You could not,' he contends,
'make an *intelligent* [my emphasis] newspaper pay because the
public wants tripe.' 'In allowing their profession to be degraded
[journalists] have largely acted with their eyes open, whereas, I

suppose, to blame somebody like Northcliffe [British newspaper magnate] for making money in the quickest way is like blaming a skunk for stinking.' Orwell sees the BBC as guilty of no more than the spreading of boredom; verifiable details that are unlikely to distract the beer drinker or darts player when the wireless is on in the background. But if you want to attract their attention, and play the populist card, distort the truth, tell lies. So then with the BBC and the press; and so today, especially with Brexit.

Orwell's thoughts in 'As I Please' on the nature of populism and the character of England originated in *The Lion and the Unicorn* (1941), one of the short books released as part of the Searchlight series, co-edited by Orwell and Fyvel. In Part I, 'England Your England', Orwell tries to tie down the true nature of what it means to be English, without entirely excluding the Scots and the Welsh. The opening section seems to evoke a collective quaintness, 'bound up with solid breakfasts and gloomy Sundays ... winding roads, green fields and red pillar-boxes ... the old maids hiking to Holy Communion through the mists of the autumn morning ...' John Major quoted this in his vision of England, adding his own gently lyrical 'long shadows on county [cricket] grounds, warm beer, invincible green suburbs, dog lovers ...' but Major overlooked the fact that Orwell peppers his wistful compilation with features that we would probably prefer to keep to ourselves. As the old maids make their way to church others are deafened by 'the to-and-fro of the lorries on the Great North Road'. Others are going nowhere, stuck in 'the queues outside the Labour Exchanges' or passing their time at 'pin-tables in the Soho pubs'. The crowds in the 'big towns' are different from their European counterparts partly in their adherence to 'gentle manners' but also because they are uglier, 'with their mild knobby faces, their bad teeth ...' It is, he concedes, a 'muddle' and 'Good or evil, it is yours, you belong to it, and this side of the grave you will never get away from the marks that it has given you.' This call for a sense of unity – drafted in 1940, five months after Dunkirk – was essentially Orwell's preamble to the later parts of the book in which he would emphasise a six-point manifesto for the new socialist England which he is confident will emerge from the ruins following the ongoing conflict; nationalisation of all core industries and utilities; Dominion status (leading to independence) for India and other colonies; the narrowing of the enormous income gap between the ordinary worker and the inordinately wealthy by means of taxation; a reform of the education system to narrow the division between private schools and the poorly provisioned state sector; an Imperial General Council which would ensure that non-whites in the colonies and Dominions would have a say as to their rights and future, at least as long as the Empire endured; and a formal international alliance with all 'victims of the Fascist Powers'. In 1941 it was an extraordinary proposal – less than ten per cent of Labour MPs would have supported such a programme – but astonishingly prophetic, in that it is an almost exact replica of the radical policies adopted by the Labour government of 1945. Everything but the NHS was present, and something of its nature was implied. Moreover, it was this formula which would shape the social and economic landscape of Britain for generations to come. Eileen, somewhat drolly, perfectly interpreted it as a very English combination of radicalism and common sense. She wrote to her friend that 'George has written a little book … explaining how to be a Socialist though Tory' (letter to Norah Myles, 5 December 1940), though Jon Kimche saw it as 'a turning point for people like myself'. During the war years it outsold all of his novels combined – over 12,000 copies – and it is impossible to imagine that some of those who would forge the policies of the 1945 Labour government did not come across it. Indeed, Warburg was convinced that it provided the most convincing propaganda for the election victory.

Even the Thatcher government of the 1980s did not completely undermine the pillars of the mixed economy, most specifically the welfare state, decent-quality education for all and free healthcare. In this respect Orwell was an exceptional soothsayer, but there is also something about the book that foresees the tensions and contradictions which would, post-1945, militate against its ideal. These have been most evident since the 2016 Referendum.

We expect that the 'muddle' described in the opening section of 'England Your England' is a prologue to an exercise in reasoning and insight, that Orwell will show us how the contraries of England disguise some deeper sense of brotherhood, or at least how such a condition might be brought about. But our expectations will be disappointed.

Every time Orwell points up a gross imperfection or imbalance that robs Britain of any claim to respect, let alone unity, we await a foretelling counterbalance, some indication that change is afoot or wished for, but we do so in vain. He puts forward a couple of generalisations about England 'that would be accepted by almost all observers': 'the English are not gifted artistically ... as Europeans go, the English are not intellectual. They have a horror of abstract thought, they feel no need for any philosophy or systematic "world view". Nor is this because they are "practical", as they are so fond of claiming for themselves. One has only to look at their methods of town planning and water supply ...' They also 'have a certain power of acting without taking thought. Their world-famed hypocrisy – their double-faced attitude to the Empire, for instance – is bound up with this.' One is almost prompted to cry out to him: 'stop digging, man!' The qualifier, when it arrives, is that we English, 'in moments of supreme crisis ... can suddenly draw together and act upon a species of instinct, really a code of conduct which is understood by almost everyone, though never formulated'. But quite soon he undoes this reassuring notion of instinctive togetherness by an account of how Chamberlain's policy of appeasement was by far the most popular response to the threat of Nazism, and that even in 1941 the attractions of weekly papers such as *Peace News* indicated that a large number of people would prefer some kind of armistice to continued warfare. Sometimes one feels sorry for Orwell. He has a sharply tuned intellect but he is surrendering it to a lost cause.

On the massive inequality of wealth in England: '... England is certainly two nations ... But at the same time the vast majority of people FEEL themselves to be a single nation and are conscious of resembling one another more than they resemble foreigners. Patriotism is usually stronger than class-hatred, and always stronger than any kind of internationalism.' It is rather like listening to some imaginary Counsel, trying to defend the English people, throwing all of his logistical and rhetorical skills into getting the accused off the hook and then admitting that the case is hopeless: 'Except for a brief moment in 1920 (the "Hands off Russia" movement) the British working class have never thought or acted internationally. For two and a half years they watched their comrades in Spain slowly strangled, and never aided them by even a single strike.'

Which brings us to Brexit. Orwell wrote in 'England Your England' that:

[T]he famous 'insularity' and 'xenophobia' of the English is far stronger in the working class than in the bourgeoisie. In all countries the poor are more national than the rich, but the English working class are outstanding in their abhorrence of foreign habits. Even when they are obliged to live abroad for years they refuse either to accustom themselves to foreign food or to learn foreign languages. During the war of 1914–18 the English working class were in contact with foreigners to an extent that is rarely possible. The sole result was that they brought back a hatred of all Europeans ... the insularity of the English, their refusal to take foreigners seriously, is a folly that has to be paid for very heavily from time to time.

In 1941 Orwell could not have imagined the events that would lead to 2016 and its aftermath – the post-war Common Market followed by the EU was not even a hypothesis – but one can't help noting the similarities between the Tommies who insulated themselves from 'abroad' in the First World War and the overseas home buyers of the television series *A Place in the Sun* – exporting their Englishness but not at all concerned with the culture or history of southern Spain or the Canaries. Orwell certainly diagnosed in Englishness endemic characteristics that would create political and ideological disparities far more savage than those brought to the surface by Thatcherism. He does not try to excuse the English insularity and instead comes up with something that sounds rather like Boris Johnson in the *Daily Telegraph*. Xenophobia 'plays its part in the English mystique, and the intellectuals who have tried to break it down have generally done more harm than good. At bottom it is the same quality in the English character that repels the tourist and keeps out the invader.'

At the other end of the spectrum we have the English 'intelligentsia', who are Europeanised:

They take their cookery from Paris and their opinions from Moscow ... England is perhaps the only great country whose intellectuals are ashamed of their own nationality. In left-wing circles it is always felt that there is something slightly disgraceful in being an Englishman and that it is a duty to snigger at every English institution ...

Few would dispute that among teachers, academics, senior civil servants, 'serious' media figures and those who run the media, Brexit was treated as an act of intellectual bad behaviour by those who should keep their maladjusted prejudices and half-baked opinions to themselves. Suddenly, empowered by a single-issue referendum involving us (the Brits) versus them (the despicable foreigners), they adopted what Orwell referred to as 'a certain power of acting without taking thought'.

In September 1943 Orwell was commissioned by Collins to produce a pamphlet called *The English People*. It was written in May and June 1944 and completed after D-Day at which point the Red Army was advancing towards the eastern border of Germany. The defeat of the Nazi regime would, it was accepted, be costly but inevitable.

While he did not self-plagiarise his earlier piece Orwell managed to rewrite 'England Your England' while preserving the message intact.

The English People would not be published until 1947 and Orwell tinkered with it in the interim. Had his perception of Englishness altered now that the survival of the nation was guaranteed? Not much. The working classes are concerned with 'beer and football pools while scientific research languishes for lack of funds'. We can 'afford greyhound tracks innumerable but not even one National Theatre'. The ordinary people are 'all too ready to listen to any journalist who tells them to trust their instincts and despise the "highbrow".' Substitute 'experts' for 'highbrow' and we are projected forward to post-Referendum Britain and the proclamations of Michael Gove. The post-war intelligentsia has not changed either. 'English intellectuals, especially the younger ones, are markedly hostile to their own country ... the philistinism of the English public alienates the intelligentsia still further.' Once more we find ourselves in Britain, post-2016. Right-wing politicians reframe the anti-intellectual, xenophobic narratives of the popular press as patriotism, a desire for independence from foreign interference, while the pro-Remain metropolitan elite – the intelligentsia – are seen as betraying their country. Orwell diagnoses this as something characteristically English but in the later document, revised when the war was over, he is optimistic for change:

> The English will never develop into a nation of philosophers. They will always prefer instinct to logic, and character to intelligence. But they must get rid of their downright contempt for 'cleverness'. They cannot afford it any longer.

The next two sentences, for which this plea for open-mindedness is a prologue, are quietly stirring. 'And they must stop despising foreigners. They are Europeans and ought to be aware of it.' Churchill is credited as being the first to consider the possibility of a 'United States of Europe', but the thought had occurred to Orwell when he wrote this, in 1943. Less than a year after Churchill's 1946 speech Orwell put together what was effectively the first full-length manifesto for what would eventually become the EU, 'Towards European Unity' (1947). His case is convincing and prophetic. 'The European peoples, and especially the British, have long owed their high standard of life to direct or indirect exploitation of the coloured peoples.' But, he predicts, imperialism will end completely after the war and while the 'advantages we derive from colonial exploitation' will be given up we must seek recovery through our trading relationships, fair rather than exploitative, with post-colonial nations and most significantly within the new community of European States. There will, he concedes, be difficulties. 'The Russians cannot but be hostile to any European union not under their own control.' The Americans will be equally unsympathetic. 'The English-speaking Dominions, the colonial dependencies ... and even Britain's supplies of oil, are all hostages in American hands. Therefore, there is always the danger that the United States will break up any European coalition by drawing Britain out of it.' Four years before the Benelux countries signed the Treaty of Paris, the forerunner to the EEC, Orwell foresaw precisely the external forces that would threaten the EU in the early twenty-first century. Trump certainly wants to 'draw Britain out of it' and Putin saw it as a threat to his continued presence as the Big Brother of central and eastern Europe. The only element of the document that might seem discordant with the unfolding of actual events is Orwell's prediction, albeit 'unlikely', that it will be a 'Socialist United States of Europe'. But, as he makes clear, his notion of a shared concept of 'socialist' principles has very little to do with communism. Instead he envisaged a treaty which allowed its members a degree of autonomy while committing them to shared principles involving social protection and a general impulse to obviate poverty. Orwell's notion of European socialism was based on the model of the mixed economy introduced by the post-war British Labour government. The Common Market, as yet unheard of, would through the 1950s be based almost entirely on trading arrangements, but by the time that the EEC had mutated into the EU in the late twentieth and early twenty-first centuries there was an impulse towards a collective welfare state similar to that envisaged by Orwell fifty years earlier. The most striking manifestation of this was the publication of the draft of the Charter of Fundamental Rights of the European Union in 2000. Along with articles designed to protect civil rights, which included the prohibition of prejudice based on race, gender or sexual orientation and the abolition of torture and the death penalty, citizens of all member states were covered by regulations regarding workers' rights, fair working conditions, protection against unfair dismissal, access to healthcare and social and housing provision. Five decades is a long time but it seemed that Orwell's seemingly fantastic hypothesis had finally come to pass.

Just as significantly Orwell regarded this new European organisation as a vanguard for secularism. He regards the suppression of free speech implemented by the Fascists and Communists as the modern legacy of organised Christianity, notably the Catholic Church:

> But if it [Catholicism] is allowed to survive as a powerful organisation, it will make the establishment of true Socialism impossible, because its influence is and always must be against freedom of thought and speech, against human equality, and against any form of society tending to promote earthly happiness.

EU members such as Spain and Ireland have, over the past thirty years, been transformed by the open, secular atmosphere of the EU, which Orwell foresaw. In both of these and in other European countries in which the power of the Church had long been established as the bedrock for what could be said or done the consensus has shifted towards a tolerance of religious belief and the rejection of established religion as a brand of social authoritarianism.

Orwell was a passionate Remainer long before the EU was conceived of. Every point asserted in his 1947 essay would be seized upon by Leave campaigners, and distorted, as an argument for departure: we should not be accountable to a 'foreign' Court of Human Rights, let alone a colloquy of Eurocentric bureaucrats, MEPs and principles which might threaten our national integrity. Equally, the Leave movement insisted that once we were released from the political and economic constraints of the EU we would renegotiate deals not only with the US but, crucially, with the states we left behind shortly before we joined the Common Market in the mid-1970s. We would renew relationships with the old Empire whose collapse, Orwell predicted, would energise a collective Europe. The concept of 'Empire 2.0' was allegedly invented by sceptical civil servants but the post-Referendum Conservative government saw it as a means of winning support for its policies. The Commonwealth – the politically correct legacy of imperial exploitation and oppression – would now enable Britain to realise its global ambitions, without any commitment to Europe. Boris Johnson, during his brief period as post-Referendum Foreign Secretary, declared that Britain's friends outside the EU would 'jump at the chance' of becoming our trading partners: 'We used to run the biggest empire the world has ever seen, and with a much smaller domestic population and a relatively tiny civil service.' Liam Fox's inability to secure trade deals with countries other than Liechtenstein, Fiji and Papua New Guinea points to the delusional optimism of Johnson's prognosis. Theresa May visited India with a delegation of businessmen in the aftermath of the 2016 Brexit vote. She seemed to believe that Empire 2.0 was a realistic possibility, that she could kick-start the old colonial setup, with Britain as an amenable partner rather than an oppressor and exploiter. She returned with nothing. As Orwell predicted in 1947, the Empire would expire and not all of its states would maintain an indulgent, forgiving relationship with their previous ruler. Our future, in his view, must be with Europe. Providentially, however, he also regarded

Britain as the country least enthusiastic about becoming part of an alliance between post-war European countries. Intellectuals might countenance the idea, but the rest of the electorate, especially the working classes, would instinctively reject any formal association with foreigners across the Channel. 2016 here we come.

Orwell's writings as a journalist and commentator during the closing two years of the war and in the early post-war period are characterised by his willingness to strike out against the orthodoxies of the left and right and populism.

His revulsion for capital punishment is evident in 'A Hanging' and one begins to wonder if this has become touched by a guilty taste for the macabre given that in 1944–46 he writes about it on five occasions. But no, Orwell is now horrified by what appears to be the resurgence of an appetite for judicial killing as a spectator sport. In 'As I Please' on 3 November 1944 he reflects on the depiction of executions, fictional and actual, by literary writers and surmises that there is no anthology of such pieces because the enduring sentiment exhibited by the author, irrespective of whether they have made up or witnessed the event, is horror. But, it seems, this sense of displeasure is not shared by their potential audience, given that popular newspapers have been 'smacking their chops' at the popularity of their accounts of the 'bumping off of wretched quislings in France and elsewhere'. One paper had gone further and achieved record sales by including photographs of the execution of Caruso, ex-chief of the Rome police, which featured rather like a sequence of stills from a film. 'You saw the huge, fat body being straddled across a chair with his back to the … rifle barrels and the body slumping sideways.' On 8 September 1944 he reported that the *Star*, and most other papers, carried photographs of two partially dressed Frenchwomen with heads shaved and swastikas painted on their faces being publicly humiliated in Paris to the evident delight of a large crowd, their gratification shared vicariously, it seemed, by the British reading public. Orwell states that he doesn't blame the French for punishing collaborators but at the same time he senses that justifiable vengeance has become infected by something closer to mob-sadism and prurience, especially among readers of the popular press in Britain.

Even more approval, apparently, was shown for recently published photographs of the dangling corpses of Germans hanged by the Russians in Kharkov which appeared alongside the promise that 'these executions had been filmed and ... the public would shortly be able to witness them at the news theatres'.

On 15 November 1946 Orwell reports on the Nuremberg trials for war crimes. Apparently, as much attention had been given by reporters for the popular press to the nature of the executions as to the evil crimes committed by those convicted. Sly hacks had cultivated their readers' appetites for macabre voyeurism by telling of how a number of the condemned had been subjected to the old-fashioned slow-strangulation form of hanging rather than the drop, designed to make death instantaneous. Orwell points out that 'before the war, public execution was a thing of the past ... Now it seems to be returning ... and though we ourselves have not actually reintroduced it as yet, we participate at second hand by watching the news films.' He remarks that 'a dozen years' ago 'every enlightened person' advocated the abolition of capital punishment as a matter of course. But now we seem to have entered a 'downward spiral' towards an enthusiasm for it. He notes that we have been following this spiral 'since 1933', the year in which the Nazis were elected by a popular mandate. In seeming to take a particular delight in watching the executions of these, now defeated, agents of inhumanity we have, he implies, become as bad as them. During a visit to Germany shortly after the end of the war he witnessed a number of people whom the Germans had repressed taking physical revenge against captured soldiers, particularly members of the SS. It 'brought home to me ... that the whole idea of revenge and punishment is a childish daydream. Properly speaking, there is no such thing as revenge. Revenge is an act which you want to commit when you are powerless and because you are powerless: as soon as the sense of impotence is removed, the desire evaporates also'. ('Revenge is Sour', *Tribune*, 9 November 1945). This should make us think again about his revulsion at the Jew kicking the SS concentration camp guard – he felt pity for the ex-prisoner who had been reduced to the condition of his oppressor. As he frequently states elsewhere, revenge and the spurious notion of justice are what lie behind the current appetite for executions. But revenge is a 'childish daydream' which masks a much darker stimulus: human beings enjoy witnessing the ceremonial killing of their own.

Was this a disillusioned portrait of the human condition, born out of a period when mankind was in a wretched state? Or was it an astute diagnosis of something nasty, endemic and enduring?

Social media and the immediate availability of videos online have revived a passion referred to by Orwell which can best be described as sadistic gratification masquerading as horror or sanctimony. The tape of Saddam Hussein's hanging 'went viral' and according to media sources was the most popular online attraction for young men in the US in December 2006, outpacing top porn sites by several million. It was overtaken ten years later by the selection of beheadings made available by ISIS on YouTube and other sites. In the same year, 2016, the *Sun* got in on the act and warned its online readers of 'One of the most depraved videos ISIS has ever made. Some of the scenes are so disturbing that Sun Online has chosen not to show them.' Which is very thoughtful, given that the more 'disturbed' readers would be able to access the originals from a trail left by Sun Online. It all reminds us of the good old days of Page Three: family porn, but with a smirking nod towards the hardcore available on the newsagent's top shelf. In April 2019 the *Sun* reported on its website the 'barbaric' treatment in Saudi Arabia of thirty-seven citizens charged 'with adopting terrorist extremist ideology' and harming the 'peace and security' of society. No accusations of acts of violence were put forward and according to the human rights group Reprieve the youngest, arrested when he was seventeen, had 'confessed' after torture. The *Sun*'s account is suitably restrained but just in case its website readers are not sufficiently appalled by the verbal facts it makes it easy for them to find a link which will show them the young man having his head chopped off. China leads the world as the most enthusiastic proponent of capital punishment, with a wide variety of crimes, against other citizens or the state, leading to a bullet in the back of the head. The *Daily Mail* website of 14 August 2013 offered a reproachful report on the policy of mass executions carried out by China, one of our major trading partners, adding thoughtfully, 'if you have a sensitive stomach look away now,' while directing readers to the source of the video download.

In the 'As I Please' column of 22 November 1946, a week after one of his laments on the vile tastes of the reading public regarding capital punishment, Orwell sets out two lists of the nine most prominent British newspapers, one entitled 'INTELLIGENCE' and the other 'POPULARITY'. At the top of the former we find, in descending order, the *Manchester Guardian*, *The Times* and the *News Chronicle*. The *Express* tops the list of the most popular followed closely by the *Herald* and the *Mirror*. He explains: 'By intelligence I do not mean agreement with my own opinions. I mean a readiness to present news objectively, to give prominence to things that really matter, to discuss serious questions even when they are dull, and to advocate policies which are at least coherent and intelligible.' The popular papers earn their ranking partly in terms of statistics – they sell the most – but also, as Orwell implies, because they cater for the opposite of INTELLIGENCE: populism, lowbrow tastelessness and distortions of the truth. I will leave it up to you to guess where he sourced the lurid accounts and photographs of executions. Orwell has long been hailed as the champion of the common people but one has to wonder if it wasn't just his height that caused him to look down his nose at them from time to time.

The Cold War ended three decades ago but differences of opinion in the West on the nature of state communism endure. As Orwell affirmed continually, during and after the war, it amounted to heresy to present the Soviet Union as anything other than our heroic ally in the battle against Nazism. The pre-war conception of Russia as a social and political utopia was shared by the majority across the spectrum of left-wing politics, from the CPGB through unaffiliated fellow travellers to the more radical elements of the mainstream Labour Party. Once the Soviets entered the war even Liberals and patrician Tories avowed a grateful and uncritical allegiance to our new friends in the East. Orwell's was a voice in the wilderness. He continually drew attention to the Molotov–Ribbentrop Pact – effectively Hitler and Stalin's agreement to divide up eastern Europe between them – and to the post-1941 realignment of power. He persistently reminded his fellow countrymen of their grotesque hypocrisy. After the Nazi invasion of Russia in 1941 every writer in Britain pretended that the pact had never existed. Typically Orwell pointed out that the British and French press had colluded in falsifying history by claiming that the French communist, Thorez, had deserted the army and gone to Moscow before the outbreak of war and not, as was the case, during the period when Nazi Germany and the Soviet Union were de facto allies ('As I Please', 17 November 1944). The pro-Soviet communists were very influential in France shortly after the war and were keen to rewrite the past.

On 1 December 1944 Orwell remarked how Trotsky's *Life of Stalin*, completed shortly before the former's assassination by agents of the latter, had been suppressed; suppressed in the USSR obviously but also by the US and British press. Orwell took it for granted that it was not an entirely 'unbiased book' but he pointed out that bias, opinion, was synonymous with free speech, a principle that the UK and the US had committed themselves to uphold in the war against totalitarianism. Orwell added that a little while back he had attended a PEN Club meeting to celebrate the tercentenary of Milton's *Areopagitica*, the first English tract in defence of the freedom of the press, and reflected that Milton's phrase about the special sin of 'murdering' a book had suddenly become very relevant in 1944.

The British media did not refuse to cover the Warsaw uprising of 1944 but Orwell was the only writer who dared to present the truth

('As I Please', 1 September 1944). It is an extraordinary article, in which he tells of how the anti-communist Polish government in exile – in London – were presented as traitors because of their antipathy towards the Soviets, and of how the latter had suspended their attack from the east bank of the Vistula to allow the Germans to crush the Poles before they moved in. He admits that he cannot explain why the 'British intelligentsia ... have developed a nationalistic loyalty towards the USSR and are dishonestly uncritical of its policies'. But he decides to offer the intellectual elite two 'considerations':

> Do remember that dishonesty and cowardice always have to be paid for. Don't imagine that for years on end you can make yourself the boot-licking propagandist of the Soviet regime ... and then suddenly return to mental decency. Once a whore, always a whore.

Next, he predicts the consequences of this purblind obeisance. Once Germany has been defeated the Soviets will maintain a regime that equals Nazism in its inflexible totalitarianism and will by various means impose this on most of central and eastern Europe. Orwell goes so far as to predict that there will be two Germanies, with the eastern part a radically extreme version of Stalin's dictatorship. Unless intellectuals banish the 'Stalin is always right' mantra immediately the 'illusions' embedded in it will ensure that it will endure and guarantee support for Stalin's super-state in the post-war years.

In January 1946 he expanded on this in a much longer essay for *Polemic* called 'The Prevention of Literature' on state-censorship of literary writing. He focuses mainly on the Soviet Union but digresses briefly on 'Our own society ... broadly speaking, liberal':

> The big public do not care about the matter one way or the other. They are not in favour of persecuting the heretic, and

they will not exert themselves to defend him. They are at once too sane and too stupid to acquire the totalitarian outlook. The direct, conscious attack on intellectual decency comes from the intellectuals themselves ... the Russophile intelligentsia.

Five months earlier *Animal Farm* had been published but the events prior to its acceptance by Secker had confirmed Orwell's belief that the cultural and intellectual establishment of Britain was capable of imposing its own policy of censorship. The book had been rejected by Gollancz, Jonathan Cape, Faber and Faber and several smaller independent presses. None found fault with its qualities but each, with shameless ingenuity, came up with reasons to distance themselves from it. An unwittingly hilarious letter of rejection came from T. S. Eliot, director of Faber, who struggles to find a reason for not taking the book, continually contradicting himself. His second paragraph is a classic example of evasion and hypocrisy:

> ... we have no conviction ... that this is the right point of view from which to criticise the political situation at the present time. It is certainly the duty of any publishing firm which pretends to other interests and motives than mere commercial prosperity, to publish books which go against the current of the moment; but in each instance that demands that at least one member of the firm should have the conviction that this is the thing that needs saying at the moment. I can't see any reason of prudence or caution to prevent anybody from publishing this book − if he believed in what it stands for.
>
> (13 July 1944)

He goes on and on, without explaining *why* he won't publish it. It is an astonishing piece of prose, as discontinuous and impenetrable as his early poetry. It might well have contributed to Orwell's concept of doublethink. Orwell knew that Eliot would not go against the prevailing pro-Stalin ideology and he also knew that he did not have the courage to say so. Cape initially accepted it but changed their minds after taking 'advice' from the Ministry of Information, exactly the kind of conspiracy between the political establishment and the intelligentsia that Orwell would portray in 'The Prevention of Literature'. If it had not been accepted by Secker & Warburg it might not have been published at all, or at best have been accepted by a very small company whose lack of resources and promotional clout would have condemned it to long-term obscurity. Even its eventual acceptance was a matter of hit-and-miss, with Fredric Warburg going against the almost unanimous opinion in his office that the work was a heretical attack on Britain's allies and, closer to home, his wife Pamela's assertion that it would be seen as a gross act of ingratitude towards the heroic Red Army and ruinous for the company.

CHANGES

Secker & Warburg offered Orwell a contract for *Animal Farm* in July 1944 but it would not go into print until August 1945. Germany would surrender unconditionally in May 1945 and, after the dropping of atom bombs on Hiroshima and Nagasaki, Emperor Hirohito issued a radio broadcast announcing the surrender of Japan on 15 August 1945. A novel that depicted one of the two most powerful of the victorious allied nations as made up of squabbling and corrupt farm animals could hardly have been better timed.

During the same period Orwell's private world would undergo a number of abrupt changes. In May 1944 he began an affair with Sally McEwan, a secretary in the *Tribune* office, which would continue for six months. His marriage was not exactly 'open' in the modern sense but Eileen had grown to accept, somewhat wearily, that her husband was addicted to occasional bouts of infidelity. He had first exhibited this tendency in Spain shortly after their wedding. This time, however, his fling would overlap with their adoption of a son. Eileen was less enthusiastic than George about having a child but was willing, for his sake, to try, and it remains unclear as to whether her failure to conceive was due to his infertility or hers. Gwen O'Shaughnessy, the widow of Eileen's brother, also a doctor, had promised to look out for babies put up for adoption in the area of Newcastle close to her surgery. At the end of May she announced that a boy, born on the 14th, was available, and the Orwells took the train north to make formal arrangements to become the parents of Richard Horatio Blair. They planned to return with him to London on 28 June but the journey was postponed when

a V-1 'doodlebug' fell on Mortimer Crescent, around one hundred
yards from their flat. While not destroyed, the building was rendered
uninhabitable. Walls and ceilings were dangerously unstable, water
and drainage pipes irreparably damaged and electricity cut off. Inez
Holden was recovering from illness at her family's country house so
she offered them her flat in fashionable George Street. Eventually
they found a place of their own at 27b Canonbury Square, Islington,
with two bedrooms, a breakfast room/kitchen and a modest sitting
room. Today it would be difficult to purchase a small flat such as this
in the square for less than £850,000. The houses are mostly graceful
late-Georgian or Regency properties and those not converted to
flats will set you back around three or four million pounds. When
the Orwells moved in the area was a curious combination of the past
and the future. The eighteenth-century buildings had fallen out of
favour with the Victorian middle and upper classes, been taken over
by landlords and let out as flats or single rooms to manual workers
and their families. It had become a version of the East End. Many
of the Orwell's neighbours were living in relative poverty alongside
ornate carved ceiling-work and marble fireplaces. But by the 1940s
the less well-off members of the cosmopolitan intelligentsia who
could not afford to live in Hampstead, Knightsbridge or Mayfair were
beginning to colonise this region of North London as a bohemian
outpost. Orwell relished the bizarre contrast between working-class
residents who had moved there involuntarily and their down-at-heel
intellectual counterparts. It seemed a rerun of his life before the war
when he had continually crossed the boundaries between classes and
states of mind.

Everyone who met and socialised with Orwell at this time agreed
that he was, albeit for a brief period, restored to the happiness of his
first year in Wallington. He was a 'new man' sixty years before the
term gained currency, who would joyously bathe Richard, change his
nappies, and choose the most appropriate pram and carrier for him
with scrupulous discrimination. As a self-taught carpenter he made
toys and miniature buildings for his new son and spent hours walking

him along streets around the square in the hope that his delightful
infant would attract praise from passers-by. At first Eileen seemed
uncertain about her feelings for Richard but by the end of 1944 she
had joined her husband as a committed, if not quite elated, parent.

The Orwells played host to an enormous number of writers
and activists, some left-leaning and others from the opposite end
of the political spectrum. Astor, Koestler, Muggeridge, Powell and
others were regular visitors. According to Paul Potts, a poet and
independent publisher who had offered to bring out *Animal Farm*
when the big houses had all but censored it, the atmosphere in the
flat involved a strange combination of nostalgic Englishness and
chaos. A pot of Gentleman's Relish occupied the centre of the table
while Orwell praised the unimprovable quality of British roast beef,
without telling his guests where this rationed delicacy had come
from. Nor did he explain how he had got hold of the best Indian
teas, London gin and scotch.

At the end of February 1945 Astor asked if he would become
the war correspondent for the *Observer*. He wanted him to cover
the push over the Rhine into Germany and report on the eventual
defeat of Nazism. Despite the new experience of fatherhood
Orwell could not resist this opportunity to relive his Spanish
experiences. He wouldn't be on active service but he would be at
the front line, a witness to the overturning of a regime that had
ensured Franco's victory and become a far more evil manifestation
of Fascism.

Orwell left London for Paris on 15 March 1945, proudly
wearing the uniform of a first lieutenant, war correspondent. He
took his typewriter in a case and one suitcase and, once in Paris, he
persuaded a regular army officer to get him a revolver. It seemed
like 1936 again. Orwell found a room at the Hôtel Scribe, a popular
base for war correspondents, among them Ernest Hemingway. He
didn't know that Hemingway had collaborated with the Soviets in
Madrid and connived in the capture and execution by them of José
Robles, a close acquaintance of Hemingway's erstwhile friend John

Dos Passos. In Paris in 1945 Orwell saw him as a fellow veteran from that first attempt to overthrow Fascism. Orwell later told the story of their meeting to Paul Potts. He went to Hemingway's room, knocked, was asked to come in and introduced himself: 'I'm Eric Blair.' Hemingway stared vacantly at him. 'Well what the fucking hell do you want?' To which this tall English stranger replied 'I'm George Orwell.' Suddenly the man who had fictionalised the Civil War in *For Whom the Bell Tolls* recognised the author of *Homage to Catalonia*, grinned, brought a bottle of scotch out from under the bed and bellowed: 'Why the fucking hell didn't you say so. Have a drink. Have a double. Straight or with water, there's no soda.'

Orwell moved on to Cologne and sent despatches to the *Manchester Guardian* and the *Observer* on the advance of the Allies. He wanted to be there at the fall of Berlin and he hoped that the British and the Americans would arrive before the Soviets. Suddenly, only two weeks after his arrival in Europe, things went horribly wrong. First he was taken ill, again with what seemed to be bronchitis, and sent a letter to his solicitor with instructions for his literary executor. He did not expect to find a lung specialist or a welcoming sanatorium in the bombed-out cities of western Germany but he made do with a ramshackle institution in what was left of Cologne. Just as his condition was improving he received a telegram on 30 March, via the *Observer*, informing him that his wife was dead. Before he left he knew that Eileen was due for an operation which, commendably, she reassured him was only for the rectification of a minor problem in her lower stomach. In truth she was undergoing a hysterectomy after tumours had been detected, but she suffered a heart attack and died under the anaesthetic.

Orwell discharged himself from hospital and returned to London on a military aircraft. The first thing he encountered was an unsent letter from Eileen, which she had written shortly before being taken to the operating theatre. She concerns herself with trifles, mentioning the surgeon, Harvey Evers, as though he is fitting her for a new dress. Apparently she is regarded as a '*model* patient'.

'They think I'm wonderful, so placid & happy they say.' In the final paragraph she seems preoccupied with her surroundings, perhaps as a way of assuring herself that this world, this room, is the one to which she will soon return:

> This is a nice room – ground floor so one can see the garden. Not much in it except daffodils & I think arabis but a nice little lawn. My bed isn't next the window but it faces the right way. I also see the fire & the clock.

Reading the final unpunctuated, incomplete sentence, which she probably jotted down hastily before they took her to the theatre, is a harrowing experience for an outsider, but how would Orwell have felt?

In London, after the funeral, people he knew and met seemed unsettled by his clumsy stoicism, but their descriptions of him give the impression of a man in a state of involuntary numbness. He would open an exchange with a friend with something like, 'You know, my wife has died. Such a shame, she was a good old stick.' Or, to Julian Symons, 'My wife died last week. She was going to have a minor operation and died while having it.' He seemed intent on repeating the same formulaic statement to deal with something he could not properly comprehend. Some others, notably Geoffrey Gorer, Paul Potts and Inez Holden, told of how in private he cried for hours and confessed that he was in unutterable pain. In his memoir Fyvel stated that 'Eileen's death was a blow to [Orwell] from which he never fully recovered.'

Three weeks after Eileen's death he arranged for friends and relatives to look after Richard and set off again for Paris, staying for a few nights with his aunt Nellie. This was an odd choice, since he'd pointedly avoided her for years; it seems he was finally acknowledging her existence. He then went to Germany, followed the Allied advance and sent regular reports on the state of towns and cities effectively occupied by British and American troops. He was a hundred miles from Berlin when the Nazis surrendered. Throughout his time in Europe his despatches, with very few exceptions, are lifelessly factual. He wanted to experience something of Germany as it had been since the rise of Nazism but the Germans he encountered, particularly the civilians, seemed concerned more with food and clothes than the legacy of their recent totalitarian past.

Orwell returned to London in June, reopened the Islington flat, and found a live-in housekeeper who would also act as occasional nanny for Richard. Susan Watson was twenty-five, separated from her Cambridge don husband and had a small daughter of her own. The three of them moved into the flat at the end of June and Orwell paid her £7 a week for herself and £10 for housekeeping on top of free board; Richard would join them soon afterwards.

Avril, Orwell's sister, did not like Susan, probably because she suspected she had designs on a man who, a month after Richard was returned to the flat, would become one of the most celebrated writers in the English-speaking world. Susan did not have any such intentions. Their friendship was quirky but entirely platonic.

Some things endured from his life with Eileen. The same circle of friends would be invited around, though more often for a traditional English tea of cakes and sandwiches than supper. Orwell didn't give up drink but since Susan was following instructions rather than acting as a co-host they often simply ran out of it. One evening he invited the Connollys for what Cyril assumed would be their customary few hours of conversation, whisky and gin and tonic, but when Orwell's guests arrived he hurriedly opened cupboards and confessed to having nothing but tea. Connolly rushed out and returned bearing an unappetising combination of bottles of Mackeson and sweet sherry.

The overall impression from those who knew Orwell at the time is of a man by parts set in his ways but distracted. Susan filled in for Eileen as a chaste wife. She would grow used to his screams through their adjoining wall and devised a way of waking him gently from his regular nightmares. He did not speak of their subjects, and she didn't ask. They breakfasted together at 8.30 a.m., after which he would work, then perhaps browse in second-hand bookshops and have beer and sandwiches in a pub. If there were no guests they would take tea together followed later in the evening by a meal with the children. His favourite, she recalls, was English beef laced with dripping gravy on roast potatoes and Yorkshire pudding. Then he would type in his study, often until 3.00 a.m. Between his return from Europe and early 1946 he produced one hundred and thirty articles. Along with toys for Richard he put together bookshelves, small tables and chairs, though his accomplishments as a carpenter more often drew polite expressions of puzzlement than admiration. Apparently the varied lengths of the legs on one of his chairs enabled it to rock in two directions.

Orwell introduced Inez Holden to Susan as an established friend of the family, but Susan also recalls him entertaining other women, who seemed from his and their manner to be recent acquaintances, notably Celia Kirwan and Sonia Brownell. They were two members of a triumvirate, including Anne Popham, who Orwell dated and courted during the eighteen months after Eileen's death. He proposed marriage to each, randomly, without waiting to find out if the others had considered and decided on the prospect.

Sonia was the most beautiful and quixotic. She had worked with Connolly at the *Horizon*, part of his ménage of intelligent and good-looking assistants. She was from a comfortably-off middle-class family, Catholic, and she carried into her later life a rebelliousness which began with her loathing for the convent schools of her childhood. In this respect she and Orwell were well suited, but she differed from him in preferring the company of louche establishment figures to those advocating left-wing radicalism. Nonetheless they got on, talking and drinking late into the night. She admitted to being attracted to him as an enigmatic outsider but she did not find him handsome. They had a brief affair after which he proposed marriage; she turned him down.

Celia Kirwan was the sister of Arthur Koestler's wife Mamaine. Koestler introduced his friend to his sister-in-law in December 1945 and the Koestlers invited him to spend Christmas and New Year with them at a farm they had rented in Merionethshire. Celia, recently separated from her husband, would be there too and Orwell replied that he, along with Richard, would be overjoyed to come to Wales.

Koestler had heard of his courtship of Sonia and was unashamedly keen to see if Celia would be interested in a long-term relationship. He felt a brotherly bond with his friend and the thought of them as siblings, if only in-laws, appealed to him. Arthur, Mamaine and Celia were amused and astonished by the ease with which he dealt with Richard – bathing, changing and feeding him and carrying him on one arm or his shoulders when they went for walks. They had never come across a man who was so content with tasks routinely allocated to mothers or servants. When later asked how she felt about Orwell, Celia said that he made her recall a sentence at the opening of *Homage to Catalonia*: 'Queer the affection you can feel for a stranger!' She told Crick that over this brief period she felt that there was something special between them. 'If I call it love (as I do) it might give the impression that I was in love with him.' It was 'love', she explained, but not the kind that would prompt her to marry him or have an affair with him. He proposed to her, honestly and clumsily, explaining his bronchitis, how she might soon become a widow, that their age difference – he was thirty-nine, she twenty-nine – might cause problems, and even that he suspected that he was sterile. She was aware that he would soon become famous and wealthy though neither of them mentioned this. They remained close friends until his death.

When Orwell returned to London he was introduced by Connolly to another young woman, Anne Popham, who shared a flat in the same building as him. The Connollys had invited both to a dinner party and the following morning Anne and Orwell met again on the stairs. He asked her about what she did – she was on leave from working for the Control Commission in Germany – and when she returned to her flat later that afternoon she found a note from Orwell, pushed under the door, asking her if she would come upstairs for tea because he had something important to say to her. Was he about to introduce her to someone who might advance her career, or advise her, in general, on the state of the country and the world? She was in awe of him and a little surprised when he opened the conversation by stating that he was attracted to her and then asked if she would consider marrying him. Ten days later he wrote her a long apologetic letter:

> There isn't really anything left in my life except my work and seeing that Richard gets a good start. It is only that I feel desperately alone sometimes … Of course it's absurd a person like me wanting to make love to someone of your age.

She replied, consoling him that she had not been upset by his proposal and hoping she had not hurt him in turning him down. He followed this with a second letter, in which he seems to accept her decision but can't help expanding on what his offer had involved, good and bad:

> What I am really asking you is whether you would like to be the widow of a literary man. If things remain more or less as they are there is a certain amount of fun in this, as you would probably get royalties coming in … I am supposed to be a 'bad life' [susceptible to a life-threatening illness] … and several times in the past I have been supposed to be about to die, but I always lived on just to spite them … if you think of yourself as essentially a widow, then you might do worse … If I can live another ten years I think I have three worthwhile books in me … but I want peace and quiet and somebody to be fond of me.
>
> (no recorded dates for letters – both of which were shown to Crick by Anne Popham)

He certainly hoped Anne might think over his suggestion but one senses that he is addressing himself as much as her. Both letters are far more candid and reflective than anything in his diaries. Ten years was a brief period for a man of his age but as it turned out he was over-optimistic. As for being '*desperately* alone', the term could refer as much to resignation as wretchedness. A few months before he proposed to Anne he began arrangements to rent a ramshackle cottage on Astor's estate on Jura, one of the more remote islands of the Scottish Inner Hebrides.

13

ANIMAL FARM

Before the publication of *Animal Farm* Orwell was a middling literary celebrity, his novels and non-fiction politely respected as blunt, argumentative contributions to the political debates that had raged across Europe from the 1930s onwards. Within a month of the appearance of his penultimate novel, however, he had shot to fame on both sides of the Atlantic. *Animal Farm* would not go into print in the US until 1946 but before Americans had the opportunity to read it they were engrossed by news of a British author who had ridiculed the Soviet Union only months after it had helped the Allies to end the war in Europe.

Apart from the *Daily Worker*, which saw it as further proof that Orwell was a treacherous fifth columnist, the reviews ranged from favourable to ecstatic. The right-wing popular press saw it as a licence to voice anti-Soviet opinions now that the war was over. The moderate-left and liberal papers approved of it for different reasons. Typically, Connolly in *Horizon* saw it as the portrayal of a 'revolution betrayed': it was not an attack on the commendable principles that underpinned 1917 but rather a satirical representation of individuals, by parts loathsome and incompetent, who had attempted to implement them. Most reviewers took the same line: there was nothing wrong with Marxism as an ideology, but the fault lay in its manifestation in the Soviet Union. In later years the book was pored over by critics determined to pin down one-for-one parallels between its animals and humans and real individuals from Marx onwards. A consensus is now served up to schoolchildren and undergraduates which few dispute but which raises a question: why bother reading or thinking about the book if it no longer mystifies us?

Old Major is Marx – with a hint of Lenin – Napoleon is Stalin and Snowball Trotsky. Squealer, Napoleon's second-in-command and minister of propaganda is almost certainly Molotov, who served Stalin in similar roles. The young pigs, who are later executed because of their criticism of Napoleon, are seen as the victims of Stalin's purges, notably Zinoviev, Kamenev, Bukharin and Rykov. Mr Jones, the cruel decadent farmer, is Czar Nicholas II and Mr Frederick, owner of a nearby farm who enters into an alliance with Napoleon, is Hitler, thus invoking the Molotov–Ribbentrop Pact. Boxer, the loyal hardworking carthorse, is supposed to be modelled on Alexey Stakhanov, the miner who Stalin used to advertise the notion of the ideal worker. Unlike Boxer, Stakhanov was not sold to the knacker to fund Napoleon's/Stalin's taste for good food and whisky – he died of natural causes in 1977 – but Stalin's mythologising of him as the dedicated and happy worker was a perversion of the fact that most Soviet manual workers during the 1930s and 1940s endured conditions little better than their pre-1917 counterparts. One could go on but to do so would be the equivalent of turning the novel into a recreational version of 'A' Level Modern History.

One cannot dispute the accuracy of Orwell's account of Stalinist Russia, or at least few would do so today. When *Animal Farm* was published most reviewers treated it as the story of how Stalin had turned Communist Russia into a tyranny, though they wondered whether the minutiae of horror was based on what had actually occurred. Orwell knew about the purges and Stalin's murderous totalitarian regime from witnesses, notably Koestler, but it was not until 1968 that a non-fictional account, based on historical research, caused left-leaning thinkers in the West to revise their delusions about communism in action. Robert Conquest's *The Great Terror* was effectively *Animal Farm* with the names changed back to those of the actual individuals. Orwell told us the horrible truth long before it was begrudgingly accepted by the cultural establishment of the free world. But is it for this that the book should, as indeed it is, be treated as a classic? And is it of political relevance today? Shortly after it was published Stalin was extending his regime beyond Russia towards most of the states of central Europe east of western Germany, Austria and Italy; the Cold War (a term coined by Orwell) was about to begin. Napoleon, during the battle with Mr Frederick of the neighbouring farm – a version of the Second World War – briefly entertains a similar notion of expanding his domain. But the Communist Bloc began to fragment at the end of the 1980s and is now made up of states variously democratised, quasi-liberal and given over to free-market economics. Russia is no longer run by the Communist Party, but the demagogic president Putin maintains the legacy of his predecessors by ensuring that those who stand against him in elections are largely wasting their efforts. There are around five countries on the globe that still bear some resemblance to the model forged by Lenin, Stalin and Napoleon. Cuba's survival depends on support from Putin, who keeps it going as a nostalgic reminder of the days when the USSR had a well-armed ally a few miles from Florida. Venezuela pretends to a form of democratic socialism/communism while most members of its population forage in dustbins for enough food to get them through the day. North Korea, thanks to a hybridisation of Maoism and Stalinism and grudging support from China, is the closest we have to a surviving version of Orwell's dystopian vision and Napoleon's regime at its most murderously repressive. China is still, technically, a communist country with the Party the only existing political body, ensuring censorship and monitoring free speech. It has, however, diluted its previous authoritarian nature with elements of liberalism, mainly to become a major player in global free trade. Vietnam, though far less powerful economically, has modelled itself precisely on China's project of global marketeering anchored to a one-Party state.

One is reminded of the closing pages of Orwell's novel where the humans, led by Pilkington, and Napoleon's pigs celebrate their

new alliance. Pilkington begins the event with a speech and Orwell
sums up his sentiments. 'He would end his remarks, he said, by
emphasising once again the friendly feelings that subsisted, and
ought to subsist, between Animal Farm and its neighbours. Between
pigs and human beings there was not, and there need not be, any
clash of interests whatever. Their struggles and their difficulties
were one.' Quite a large number of present-day British politicians
have echoed Pilkington's words. Supporters of Brexit believe that
our arrangements with Europe have frustrated far more profitable
trading opportunities with the likes of China, presently the world's
second-largest and most rapidly growing economy. Boris Johnson, as
Foreign Secretary, spoke enthusiastically of negotiations for a trade
deal, his planned visit curtailed by his resignation from the Cabinet
over Mrs May's EU Departure Agreement. His successor, Remainer-
turned-Brexiteer Jeremy Hunt, took his place only to be confronted
with a statement that he had made online two years earlier: 'if we
want [Britain] to be one of the most successful countries in the
world in 20, 30, 40 years' time, there is a pretty difficult question
to answer ... are we going to be a country that is prepared to work
hard in a way that Asian economies are prepared to work hard ...'
He was referring mainly to China, and was somewhat embarrassed
by the implications of his comparison: that British workers chose
not to work hard because, unlike their Chinese counterparts, they
were not forced by a largely authoritarian state to do so. Hunt's
clumsy attempt to present the governments of China and Britain as
united in a similar resolve is pre-empted by Pilkington. 'Was not the
labour problem the same everywhere? ... "If you have your lower
animals to contend with," he said, "we have our lower classes!"' The
conclusion of the novel, where the pigs form a precarious alliance
with the human farmers, was completed shortly before the war in
Europe ended. No one dared to suggest that the Allies would soon
turn against each other and no one foresaw that seventy years later
the so-called democracies would be negotiating, cap-in-hand, with
the tyrannical pigs. No one except Orwell.

China has turned communism into State-controlled capitalism, and in this regard Orwell's observation that Hitler's and Stalin's systems had much in common is astute. Even more telling is his prediction of the unsteady relationship between China and the West. Pilkington is a pragmatist and a hypocrite. Privately he feels only contempt for Napoleon and his associates but for the good of his own farm he will, in public, overlook this moral anomaly. At least Pilkington had the confidence to argue with Napoleon. In 2018 when Theresa May visited Beijing to meet Xi Jinping she carried a begging bowl. Her suggestions on export opportunities for British meat and vegetables were less than subtly undermined by Xi's insistence that Chinese agricultural produce was sufficient for the country's demands. Mrs May did, however, secure distribution rights for the sale of the BBC series, *Poldark*. May told reporters that she had, briefly, raised the issue of the deterioration of human rights in Hong Kong, but soon afterwards the *Global Times*, a mouthpiece of the government, stated that she was simply responding to 'posturing' from 'western media outlets' to criticise Beijing, and she knew her comments would have no effect on China's policy.

As to the close of *Animal Farm*, May's humiliation by China shades into insignificance compared with President Trump's recent bouts of intercontinental fisticuffs. The self-contradictions of his Twitter-disseminated policy statements since 2016 are innumerable but he has maintained a stance of foot-forward belligerence against China. He has no concern with the morality of the government's oppressive, sometimes murderous, treatment of its people but he won office by promising to defend American jobs against under-priced imports from Chinese manufacturers. In 2019 Trump began a trade war, imposing large tariffs on Chinese imports, and in May commanded US IT companies to break off trade and collaboration with the giant China-based corporation Huawei. The latter was accused of being an instrument for the Beijing government, enabling it to spy on Western intelligence systems, hack them and, potentially, wreck them. As Orwell puts it, 'Yes, a violent quarrel was in progress. There were shoutings, bangings on the table, sharp suspicious glances, furious denials. The source of the trouble appeared to be that Napoleon and Mr Pilkington had each played an ace of spades simultaneously.' The image captures perfectly the outcome of two individuals, two governments, competing against each other while rewriting the rules of the game to suit their own interests. None of the current Western players acknowledge that their attempts to establish fair, even profitable, trading agreements with China involve deals with a state that is liberal/capitalist in name only. Certainly the success of the Chinese manufacturing and export base is founded on its ability to compete successfully with other free-trade economies. Yet at the same time Chinese free enterprise is a myth. All seemingly independent companies are accountable to and in effect controlled by the Party. Napoleon, in his speech to the humans, is honest enough about this. 'This farm which he had the honour to control, he added, was a co-operative enterprise. The title-deeds, which were in his own possession, were owned by the pigs jointly.' It is unlikely that Trump, May or Hunt are oblivious to this anomaly (although with Trump this might be open to question) yet they appear to have blinded themselves to it, with the result that, in Orwell's words, we regularly listen to 'an uproar of voices … coming from the farmhouse'.

Something that might well have alerted the British politicians to their bizarre situation also finds a place in the closing passages of *Animal Farm*. Napoleon draws the attention of his audience, the human farmers included, to some of the habits that have survived from the recent history of the farm but now seem of questionable significance. 'There had also been a very strange custom, whose origin was unknown, of marching every Sunday morning past a boar's skull which was nailed to a post in the garden.' The mummification and display of Lenin's corpse in Moscow was in 1946 common knowledge in the West. His tomb remains a popular attraction for those with a nostalgic affection for the old days or a taste for the macabre. Until 1961 Lenin was joined by Stalin but the process of de-Stalinisation during the late 1950s resulted eventually in him being buried elsewhere. With admirable prescience Orwell foresaw the ability of the Party to at once manufacture and demystify the relics of its past. Napoleon orders that the skull must be buried. It belonged to Old Major, but ideology, for the sake of contingency and profit, must move on, for some. As our distinguished Western representatives attempt to do deals in Beijing – on an open-market, free-trade basis – with the new China, hundreds of thousands of its citizens troop past the mummified remains of Mao Zedong preserved in a crystal coffin a few kilometres from where the talks take place. Maoism in its purest economic form is no longer the order of the day but Mao's legacy of intransigent Party control and totalitarianism endures.

Earlier I raised the question of why *Animal Farm* deserves its status as a literary classic. Few early reviewers disagreed with its power as a satire, redolent of Swift, on the state of Soviet communism, but Isaac Rosenfeld, following its publication in the US, asked, 'what is the point of *Animal Farm?*' (*Nation*, 7 September 1946). Does it imply that Marxism is by its very nature defective, irrespective of who attempts to implement it, and as a consequence will continue to fail in practice? This is very different from the interpretation of the novel by Connolly and others, that some might succeed where Stalin has not.

It was evident that the revolution and its ideology were fatally flawed even in the opening pages of the novel, before Old Major had completed his speech and Napoleon and Snowball seized control. 'All animals are comrades,' declares Old Major and immediately afterwards the dogs suddenly catch sight of four large rats, entranced by Old Major's words, and attempt to savage them. Old Major declares that there must be a vote on whether all creatures, including wild ones, are 'our friends'. The majority agree that they are, although there are four dissentients, 'the three dogs and the cat, who was afterwards discovered to have voted on both sides'.

Orwell's analogy between animals and human beings is at once transparent and misleading. He does not suggest that we – specified by class or circumstance – are genetically predetermined towards particular and predictable types of behaviour. But this is the precept that underpins Marxism. Just as it is impossible to cause different species of non-humans to act in the same way – the governing principle of the novel's ideology of animalism, aka Marxism – so it is absurd to treat an overarching economic, philosophical and social-political thesis as a means of curing the ills that beset humanity. Orwell believed that freedom of choice was more than a right or aspiration. It was in his view the endemic, defining feature of the human condition, even if prompted by illogic or caprice, as was the case with the dogs and the cat. Marxism and animalism were guaranteed to fail because both subsumed this notion of individuality – albeit sometimes fickle, arbitrary or even chaotic – beneath a constraining doctrine. The fact that Napoleon is inherently unpleasant, power-mad and nepotistic is irrelevant. He did not destroy the dream of animalism; it was damned even when Old Major cultivated it as an abstract ideal.

Orwell's essay 'Catastrophic Gradualism' (*Commonwealth Review*, November 1945) came out shortly after *Animal Farm* and is one of the most convincing arguments that state communism is by its nature doomed and self-destructive. The process of the 'centralised economy' and 'common ownership' are fine as political debating points but in practice necessitate the suppression of resistance and 'pave the way for a new form of oligarchy'. Communism will, inevitably, usher in dictatorship because people, even the oppressed and dispossessed, cannot be expected to fall into line with a new, collective state of mind; they have to be forced to conform. And when they do so a vacuum for ultimate control is created. 'In the minds of active revolutionaries, at any rate the ones who "got there", the longing for a just society has always been fatally mixed up with the intention to secure power for themselves.' And so it is with Napoleon and Stalin. The truths of Orwell's diagnosis, his prediction, have been proved self-evident. Every communist regime since 1917 has involved the vigorous suppression of the autonomy of the individual at the hands of a tyrannical dictatorship. This has not come about because of a 'bad-man theory of history', as Rosenfeld put it; quite the contrary, the bad men, from Stalin to Venezuela's Maduro, have been spawned by communism.

It is seventy-five years since *Animal Farm* presented us with the addictive, self-destructive evil of communism but things seem not to have changed. Venezuela is rather like a Soviet Bloc republic rerun as a macabre pantomime. It is, potentially, one of the most wealthy South American states, with oil resources that merit comparison with those of the Middle East, but under Maduro its citizens have been queuing at every border crossing to find refuge in a country that will pay them money for their labour that is not, in seconds, made worthless by inflation. It will continue to suffer, but its ailments will be mildly alleviated by the fact that the rest of Latin America is – relatively – reformed and democratic. It is like a mad, suicidal person surrounded by wearily indulgent neighbours and friends.

And yet. The leader of Her Majesty's Opposition has refused to condemn the Maduro regime's implementation of press censorship, the arrest and imprisonment of dissidents and the use of what is effectively martial law in response to street protests. He stated that the cause of the country's crisis was outside interference, principally from the US, and that the Venezuelans should be left to tackle their own problems. Underpinning his stance is the enduring belief, which Orwell set out to dismantle in *Animal Farm*, that socialism/communism is a sacred ideal that has failed only because of meddling by outsiders, such as Farmer Pilkington and the capitalist-imperialist President Trump.

'Overnight success' is usually a misplaced exaggeration but it is an accurate enough description of what Orwell achieved following the publication of *Animal Farm*. Secker & Warburg assumed that an initial print run of 4,500 was something of a gamble, especially since Orwell was not much known beyond the London literary intelligentsia. However, the entire run had sold within a few weeks and an extra 10,000 were ordered to go into print by October; these too had sold out by early 1946. Fan letters poured in via the publisher from people Orwell had never heard of and, directly to his Islington address, from the more eminent, including E. M. Forster and Evelyn Waugh. Orwell admired Waugh as a writer but loathed his politics and dedication to Roman Catholicism and he began to fear that the book would become a weapon of British conservatism, not just as an anti-Soviet talisman but as a rallying point for those determined to stop the recently elected Labour government in its tracks. In November, for example, the Duchess of Atholl asked if he would speak at a rally of the British League for European Freedom, a group as dedicated to preserving the Empire as it was to defending European democracy against the far left. He turned her down with calculated discourtesy.

Over the subsequent four years sales would earn him around £12,000 which, given the cost of living and taking inflation into account, amounts to around half a million pounds today. Alongside this, his 'Payment Notebook' for 1945, detailing his income from journalism, shows that he had earned £961.8s 6d (approximately £40,000) that year. He was not outstandingly rich but he would never again have to worry about the hardships that had dogged him since his return from Burma.

Orwell would amuse his friends with the story of how Queen Elizabeth, later the Queen Mother, had been told of the novel by her literary advisor Sir Osbert Sitwell and immediately sent a courtier in full livery, including top hat, to the Secker offices, only to find that all copies had been despatched to bookshops and distributors. Her representative then set off on a search across London in his carriage until he finally located a volume at the anarchist Freedom Bookshop in Red Lion Street. Some thought Orwell was making this up, but the only inauthentic part involved the carriage and the livery. The courtier, in suit and bowler hat, took a taxi.

14

JURA

By mid-1945 Orwell's social life involved regular lunches and dinners with Koestler, Heppenstall, Empson, Muggeridge and Powell. But once the news of *Animal Farm* circulated through London his network expanded, whether he liked it or not. Michael Meyer, a journalist and translator, was recently down from Oxford and well connected, and no one is certain how or why the two men came to meet. But they got on and one evening Meyer took his new friend to dinner with a recently appointed minister in the new Labour government. Neither could recall quite what the politician had to say since what struck them most was his apparent obliviousness to their presence. He talked incessantly, as though they weren't there. His next lunch with Meyer was a rerun of their first: Meyer introduced him to Graham Greene who turned his tribulations with Catholicism and politics into what seemed like a dramatic monologue, while remaining impervious to Orwell's polite display of irritation. Despite this he and Meyer remained on friendly terms and Orwell would see Greene again on several occasions. Overall, Orwell gained the impression that literary celebrity involved the admission to some kind of tacit brotherhood, whose principal qualification for membership was self-regard. Lunching with Muggeridge at the Little Akropolis restaurant, Orwell spotted Kingsley Martin hanging up his coat. After Spain Martin had rejected his review of Borkenau's book for the *New Statesman and Nation* on the grounds that both men were Trotskyist fifth columnists, but he now appeared to be making his way across the restaurant to greet the literary star. Orwell made a point of asking Muggeridge to swap seats with him, effectively turning his back on the approaching Martin, and silently snubbing him.

Orwell took George Woodcock to a celebratory lunch in a restaurant in Fitzrovia fashionable with the literati: *Animal Farm* had been selected for the Book of the Month club. August was hot and after summoning the waiter he was politely informed that customers were expected to wear a jacket and tie. Orwell thanked him, ushered Woodcock across the road to a downmarket eating house and sat happily in his shirtsleeves and braces.

When Tosco Fyvel replaced him as literary editor of the *Tribune* in the autumn of 1945 Orwell no longer had a regular professional connection with London. Throughout the 1940s he would continue to contribute articles and reviews to the *Tribune* and other newspapers but these could be prepared and despatched from a distance. Since 1944 he had been talking with David Astor about Astor's estates in the Inner Hebrides of Scotland and Astor assumed that his friend wished to find the equivalent of a holiday let, an escape from Southeast England for a few weeks when the weather was decent. Only after Eileen's death did he realise that Orwell wanted to become a near-permanent resident of this remotest region of Britain. Barnhill was not owned by the Astors, but Astor found it for Orwell. It was an empty spacious farmhouse close to the sea on the island of Jura, the property of an Old Etonian, Robin Fletcher, whom Astor knew. It was in disrepair but had four bedrooms, a well-sized kitchen, sitting room and dining room on the ground floor and a large garden.

In May 1946 Orwell's elder sister Marjorie Dakin died from kidney disease, and after attending her funeral in Nottingham he took the train to Scotland. In Edinburgh he stayed with the Kopps, his friends from Spain, and bought a small van from Georges which he drove west before crossing by ferry to Jura and Barnhill. Over the next two months he freshened up and redecorated the house and installed some comfortable furniture. Satisfied with the state of the building he went south, collected Susan, her daughter and Richard, and returned with them to his new home.

Some have treated his decision to go to Jura as verging on the suicidal, given his regular lung afflictions, but there was sound wisdom behind it. The west coast of Scotland is not the Mediterranean but it is favoured by moderate temperatures from the Gulf Stream. Even in the depth of winter there is hardly ever severe frost and compared with London, which in a few years would see smog that killed thousands, the air was gloriously pure.

The van Orwell had bought from Kopp took him only to around two miles from the house. After that the lane was heavily pot-holed and impassable to four-wheeled motor vehicles. To negotiate the ruts and crevices Orwell resorted to his old favourite and bought a motorbike, which regularly broke down. Food and mail could be delivered to the Fletcher house, Ardlussa, again around six miles away, and Orwell would use the bike, when it worked, to collect these. The train journey from London, via Glasgow, to the Jura ferry took around forty-eight hours, followed by various unreliable forms of transportation to the beginning of the unmade path. After that, guests were expected to walk. When they first arrived, Orwell had carried Richard, then less than two years old, down the path, followed by Susan and her daughter. Meyer, Heppenstall and Julian Symons received invitations during 1946 but despite being sincerely devoted to Orwell they regarded the prospect as an exercise in masochism and politely found reasons to be otherwise engaged. Later in the year Orwell, Susan and the children were joined by Susan's boyfriend, David Holbrook, a Cambridge graduate who had served as an officer in the tank corps during the war. He brought with him food and an outboard motor for Orwell's rowing boat, and from Susan's account he expected to be welcomed as a potential member of what amounted to an unofficial family. Avril had also arrived and Holbrook later recalled that he was greeted with an 'icy apartness' by Orwell and his sister. The final member of the party was Paul Potts, who vacated his bedroom to make way for Holbrook. Despite Susan's attempt to stimulate conversation neither Orwell nor Avril showed any interest in Holbrook's background, his degree or his war service, let alone his train journey and crossing to the island. Holbrook was intelligent and affable; he was in awe of Orwell and hoped at least for some brief exchanges on the state of post-war England. Instead, he was treated as an intruder, an unwelcome presence. Avril's unexplained aversion to Susan might have played a part in this, but more and more it seemed that Jura had brought to the surface elements of Orwell's character that the conventions of sociability in London had caused him to conceal. Margaret Fletcher, his landlord's wife, remembered him as 'a sad, lonely man' who when offered help 'said he would be all right and preferred to manage himself'. 'Managing' involved a brutal version of life in Wallington. Orwell shot rabbits and birds, geese when he could but seagulls if necessary, and caught fish. The soil was rocky but he managed to grow a few vegetables. Holbrook remembers a particularly horrible evening when Orwell had picked out the lead-shot from a duck and gutted it before his sister cooked it to blackness on a smoky range. No one dared comment on their shared self-imposed misery. In September Susan, her daughter and Holbrook left for London and she informed Orwell that she would no longer be working for him. His behaviour with Holbrook had shown her a different side of him, but despite this she wished him well and they departed on good terms.

Like everyone else, Paul Potts seemed to be become slightly deranged by the otherworldliness of life on Jura. In Soho he was tolerated as an eccentric and irascible British version of Walt Whitman, determined to live differently and record his equally singular observations in verse. On Jura, these inclinations were exacerbated. He started to take over gardening duties, cutting down trees that were vital in protecting vegetables from the wind and during the evenings working on a bizarre epic account of contemporary existence. We will never know what the latter involved since Susan, desperate for a fire in the main room, unwittingly made use of Potts' manuscript to light it. He left the following morning. At the centre of this strange community was Orwell. He was twelve months into his next novel, one that would take him four years to complete, far longer than his previous pieces of fiction. He had become, though not deliberately, a version of Winston Smith, the pitiful and less than endearing anti-hero of *Nineteen Eighty-Four*. Smith is forced into a state of alienated self-loathing. His creator, for reasons we can only speculate upon, forced this condition on himself.

Orwell returned to London for Christmas 1946, reanimated the 'As I Please' column, lunched with Graham Greene again, and met with figures from Secker & Warburg to discuss the demand for translations of *Animal Farm*. The novel was sought after in all major European languages, and nations of Africa and Asia began negotiations for translation rights. Warburg was so impressed by sales that he wanted to launch reprints of earlier Orwell volumes and buy the copyright for his pre-war novels with a view to a 'Collected Works', including fiction and non-fiction. The project was sidelined partly because Gollancz saw a similar opportunity for profit and was reluctant to sell for the amount that Secker envisaged. The main problem though was Orwell himself, who refused to allow *A Clergyman's Daughter*, *Keep the Aspidistra Flying* and *The Lion and the Unicorn* to be reissued. His aversion to a new edition of the latter is curious given that it was the foundation for his opinions on Britain and England that permeated his post-1941 journalism. Jettisoning the novels was even more extraordinary. He was aware of their shortcomings but at the same time he was proud of shedding so much 'bloody sweat' to earn himself a place in the literary establishment. It seemed that he was determined to rewrite his legacy, beginning to accept that *Animal Farm* and the novel on which he was working might be his last and he did not want them to be obscured by blueprints for something very different.

A year later he told friends that his winter in London had worsened his health problems considerably. The winter of 1946–47 was one of the coldest for twenty years. Tosco Fyvel remembers having dinner with Orwell at the flat of a *Tribune* colleague in Bayswater. The fog, effectively freezing smog, and ice were so bad that the Fyvels thought it best to abandon their car and as conditions deteriorated welcomed their hosts' invitation to stay the night.

Orwell had walked from his Islington flat and was able to return home on foot, and Fyvel later recalled the 'grim, sad-faced figure' bidding them good night and disappearing into the gloom.

The dreadful weather made people reluctant to leave their homes for anything other than vital tasks but just before the New Year Orwell, for no obvious reason, decided to return to Jura. During the ferry crossing the conditions abated for an hour, the sun shone and it seemed spring-like, but by the time he reached Barnhill the island was beset by gale-force winds, sleet and rain. He tried desperately to plant fruit trees and drew some diagrams of the garden he hoped to restore in the spring; the cabbages and non-root vegetables that he hoped would still be there from the autumn had been eaten by rabbits. His *Diary* entries ended on 5 January 1947 so there is no record of why he decided to return again to London but one might reasonably assume that he had accepted that an attempt to survive alone on Jura for the rest of winter verged on the insane.

Soon after he got back to Islington on 9 January, the BBC Third Programme began its adaptation of *Animal Farm*. Press coverage was enthusiastic, fan mail began to arrive once more, often via Broadcasting House, and sales of the book increased. The horrible weather continued into February, accompanied by power cuts. The lack of regular coal supplies for power stations reflected a broader shortage, and as a substitute Londoners were foraging among bombsites for timber that would sustain a fire for long enough to defrost a room. The privations of war had been bad enough but peacetime London seemed worse. All the time Orwell was absorbing minor details that would make their way into the urban landscape of *Nineteen Eighty-Four*, a city seemingly unable to recover from a global conflict. He dragged upstairs a battered oak bedstead from the ruins of the building down the road that had been hit by a V-1 rocket. It only lasted a couple of days and by mid-February he was burning wooden toys he'd made for Richard.

He left for Scotland on 10 April and in early summer he ended the lease on the Islington flat. He planned to treat Barnhill as his permanent home, visiting London occasionally and staying with Avril. The political commentator James Burnham had recently predicted another war, between the Western democracies and the Soviet Union, and Orwell, in 'You and the Atom Bomb' (*Tribune*, 19 October 1945) contemplated a nuclear conflict. At the time, the Soviets did not have nuclear weapons but Orwell expected that they would soon acquire the knowledge and technology to build a bomb. There is a passage in the essay that offers an extraordinarily accurate account of how global power bases would develop over the next few decades:

> More and more obviously the surface of the earth is being parcelled off into three great empires, each self-contained and cut off from contact with the outer world, and each ruled, under one disguise or another, by a self-elected oligarchy. The haggling as to where the frontiers are to be drawn is still going on, and will continue for some years, and the third of the three super-states – East-Asia, dominated by China – is still potential rather than actual.

By the beginning of the 1960s the Communist Bloc was split between the USSR and its enforced allies and the growing influence of Mao's China. The triangulated 'parcelling' of tensions would also involve nations aggregated as compatriots of America, some less enthusiastically than others. Militarily this untidy alliance would become NATO in 1949. In *Nineteen Eighty-Four* the essay would be fictionalised with the three power blocs becoming Oceania, Eurasia and Eastasia.

In 1947 Orwell was convinced that global warfare, involving nuclear weapons, was all but inevitable. A member of his Home Guard platoon, whom he came across in London just before travelling north, remembered him saying that Richard would be 'safer' from the forthcoming apocalypse in the remoteness of the Inner Hebrides.

During the first eight weeks back on Jura he seemed to give as much attention to turning Barnhill into a smallholding as to writing.

He built a hen-house, planted bulbs and ploughed up for vegetables what had been a rough lawn. Nonetheless, he wrote to Warburg at the end of May with news that he had completed roughly a third of the first draft of the novel.

The house was spacious enough and by late summer it was overflowing with family and friends, including Richard Rees. Impressed by Orwell's self-sufficiency project, he invested money in equipment so that the surrounding land covered in the leasehold could be properly farmed. Gwen O'Shaughnessy arrived with her children, and the recently widowed Humphrey Dakin allowed his teenage daughters Lucy and Jane to travel north. They were soon to be joined by their elder brother Henry, on leave from the army where he had recently been commissioned as a subaltern.

Orwell proposed a boat trip to a headland where there were sparkling white beaches, caves and enough fish for them to eat well for several days. The weather prospects were good so they would camp. Avril and Jane decided to walk while Orwell, Henry, Lucy and Richard, or Ricky as he was now known, took the boat. They pitched tents, and some slept in an abandoned shepherd's hut. After two days they loaded the boat for the return trip.

The strait of Corryvreckan is a series of whirlpools that seem to have a mind of their own; the deadliest is the one that gives the strait its name. On their outward journey they hardly noticed them but coming back they were thrown from one to another and eventually into Corryvreckan itself; the boat was twisted 360 degrees, hurled twelve feet upwards and the outboard motor ripped off. Were it not for Henry's youthful strength with the oars it is likely all would have drowned. They reached a rocky shoreline and waved a shirt, flag-like, from the fishing rod. Lobster boatmen spotted it and picked them up. Much later Henry recalled that Orwell 'seemed to keep his normal "Uncle Eric" face ... We had not been there [ashore] three minutes when he said he would go off and find some food. A slightly ridiculous thing, it struck me afterwards, because we had had breakfast only two hours before ... When he came back the first thing he said was "Puffins are curious birds, they live in burrows. I saw some baby seagulls, but I haven't the heart to kill them." "I thought we were goners," he concluded. He almost seemed to enjoy it.'

All, on and off the boat, continued to enjoy the company of their eccentric life-endangering uncle. Rees stayed on but by September the rest of his guests had gone back to England and Orwell committed himself to completing a first draft of *Nineteen Eighty-Four* before the end of the year. In early November he was a few hundred words short of a provisional conclusion but, as he had informed Moore in a letter at the end of October, he was now confined to bed with an 'inflammation of the lungs', an optimistic self-diagnosis given that he had not seen a doctor for more than a year. In early December a Glasgow chest specialist was persuaded to take the ferry to the Fletchers' home at Ardlussa where he confirmed that Orwell was suffering from TB, with complications. The doctor was so concerned that he urged that, at best, Orwell must remain with the Fletchers and if possible move to a Glasgow hospital. Orwell refused and Rees reluctantly drove him back to Barnhill. A fortnight later he accepted that his already serious condition had further deteriorated and agreed to be moved to Hairmyres Hospital just outside Glasgow, where his consultant, Bruce Dick, diagnosed his TB as 'chronic'. The only treatment, he announced, was to pierce the worst affected lung, collapse it and reinflate it with oxygen. It would be 'rested' for a period which would enable the lesions to heal, or so it was hoped. The treatment was reasonably successful initially but it did not bring about a long-term cure. Word was out of a drug developed in the US called streptomycin, which might eradicate the causes rather than just suspend the devastating symptoms. Dick was optimistic that the drug would live up to its reputation but there were problems: it had not been licensed in the UK and it was extremely expensive. The 1946 National Health Service Act would not come into effect until 1948, and the vast institution would take years after that to be fully organised. Nonetheless, Orwell found allies amongst those who supported the establishment of this 'free at the point of delivery' service. He telegraphed and wrote to David Astor, whereupon Astor told Dick that money was not an issue. Astor had given an account of Orwell's condition and possible cure to his old *Tribune* editor Aneurin Bevan, now Secretary of State for Health in the Labour government. By mid-February 1948, roughly a fortnight after Astor contacted Bevan, the first ever 70 mg shipment of the drug was on its way across the Atlantic. But Dick now had reservations, particularly since there were no proven methods of safely administering streptomycin. Orwell and his friends insisted that he should improvise, and dreadful side effects ensued, notably a dry and inflamed throat that made drinking and swallowing painful and talking all but impossible, and a skin complaint that combined flaking with a persistent itch. But his worst-afflicted lung improved and by April he was breathing easily, had gained three pounds in weight, despite a commensurate reaction that now included rashes, ulcerations and hair loss. On 29 July 1948 he was allowed to return to Barnhill, where again he was joined by a legion of family members, Richard included, and friends.

There is in his *Diary* a striking passage entered when the streptomycin treatments were having their worst effects:

> ... you have the impression that your brain is quite normal. Your thoughts are just as active as ever, you are interested in the same things, you seem to be able to talk normally, & you can read anything that you would read at any other time. It is only when you attempt to write, even to write the simplest & stupidest news-paper article, that you realise what a deterioration has happened inside your skull ... Your mind turns away to any conceivable subject rather than the one you are trying to deal with ...
>
> (30 March 1948)

Read *Nineteen Eighty-Four* and you will find that this is a concise description of the ordeals and terrors that beset Winston Smith, particularly in the closing parts of the novel when nothing, particularly O'Brien, is what it first appeared to be. When Orwell began his rewritings of the first draft in late summer his period of private torment would become a vital element of the book. He never treated Bruce Dick with anything other than respect and gratitude but it must have occurred to him over these months that the man who was desperately attempting to save his life was also, obliquely, a torturer. All of this was framed by the darkly comic disclosure that Dick had fought with the Falangists during the Spanish Civil War. Perhaps the horrid spectacle of O'Brien being not who he claimed he was grew out of this.

By December Warburg had secured for him a typist for the longhand revision of the final draft and soon afterwards he despatched it to London. Around the same time his condition deteriorated once more and early in the New Year of 1949 he set off by train with Rees for Cranham Sanatorium in the Cotswolds. This time his doctors administered para-aminosalicylic acid, like streptomycin a revolutionary treatment. The side effects were equally acute, with only a slight improvement in his condition. He remained optimistic about his prospects but he would never again experience the world beyond the walls and windows of medical institutions.

Warburg's advisors were devastated and horrified by the manuscript. Warburg himself declared it 'amongst the most terrifying books I have ever read' and closed his report on the draft with: 'It is a great book, but I pray I may be spared from reading another like it for years to come.' Others found it incomparably depressing and ghastly, but Warburg's associate David Farrer predicted that it would sell more than anything they had previously published, insisting that they must issue at least 15,000 or they 'ought to be shot'. In the end they went for 25,000, and less than a year after publication 50,000 had been sold in Britain. During the same period 170,000 of the Harcourt Brace edition had been purchased in the US.

15

NINETEEN EIGHTY-FOUR

Nineteen Eighty-Four is the most important literary work of the past hundred years, for the simple reason that no other has caused so much debate and controversy. It was banned in the Soviet Union immediately after publication and throughout the 1950s and 1960s copies smuggled over the Iron Curtain caused readers to assume that 'George Orwell' was the pseudonym of a Soviet dissident, gone underground or defected. No one else, they thought, could have conceived so accurate a model of the Soviet regime.

Reviewers in the West, particularly America, reached a similar conclusion; that it was the recantation of a one-time left-winger who had come to regard Soviet communism as at least as bad as Nazism. Orwell disagreed:

> It has been suggested by some of the reviewers of NINETEEN EIGHTY-FOUR that it is the author's view that this, or something like this, is what will happen inside the next forty years in the Western world. This is not correct. I think that ... something like NINETEEN EIGHTY-FOUR *could* happen. This is the direction in which the world is going at the present time, and the trend lies deep in the political, social and economic foundations of the contemporary world situation.
>
> (Statement made for Warburg for a potential press release, but not published until after his death.)

He expanded on this in a letter to Francis A. Hanson, an American Trade Union leader, who wanted to recommend the book to his members but was uneasy about it receiving such unreserved praise in the conservative press. Orwell begins by stating that it is 'NOT ... an attack on Socialism or on the British Labour Party (of whom I am a supporter) ...' as was claimed by several American reviewers and journalists. 'I do not believe that the kind of society I describe *will* necessarily arrive, but I believe (allowing, of course, for the fact that the book is a satire) that something resembling it *could* arrive.' He states that one version of his dystopian political vision had been created by the Nazis and another was well established in areas controlled by our erstwhile allies, the Soviet Union, but that he was also asking a question about liberal democracy. It had defeated Fascism, and was now steeling itself against the threat posed by the Soviet Bloc, but was there an endemic failing that would eat away at it from the inside and potentially turn it into something similar to the world that destroys Winston Smith? The novel was, in this respect, the summation of issues Orwell had confronted over the previous twenty years.

When researching *The Road to Wigan Pier* he had seen how Mosley's fake promises had triumphed over reason and credulity at his rallies in the poverty-stricken North of England. The proles of *Nineteen Eighty-Four* are oblivious to the nature of the world in which they exist, content with a sufficient supply of drink, pornography and the opportunity to breed. Despite himself Orwell had detected something like this mixture of apathy and poundshop hedonism in his tours of the most deprived areas of Lancashire and Yorkshire. The inhabitants had better lives than the proles but were equally preoccupied with feckless consumption, albeit upmarket, involving such cheap luxuries as fish and chips, artificial silk stockings, tinned salmon, chocolate, strong tea, the pictures, the wireless, beer and the football pools. Unlike the proles they had the vote, which raises questions about Winston's belief that, if empowered, the proles would alter the status quo.

Orwell remained dedicated to liberal democracy and the Labour Party but perhaps he also foresaw the lower classes as the motor for populism, essentially right wing, where a sense of community and the opportunity to think would be sidelined by a blend of instinct and self-interest. His articles and pamphlets published during the war and shortly afterwards are permeated by themes that would resurface in the novel. His pieces on the prospect of a unified Europe present the British working classes as the most likely to hinder the project: inward-looking, innately xenophobic and hostile to alien ideas and lifestyles. This clearly was the grounding for the proles as rooted in a barely remembered notion of the past, of which only an ill-defined concept of Englishness survives. Consider this:

> ... rubbishy newspapers containing almost nothing except sport, crime and astrology, sensational five-cent novelettes, films oozing with sex, and ... songs which were composed entirely by mechanical means ...

It is a concise description of material, including the books, produced by Julia's Fiction Department for the proles as low-cultural conspicuous consumption, a diversion from such activities as thinking. O'Brien explains to Winston that the proles will never rebel because of their overwhelming preoccupation with trash. 'The proletarians will never revolt, not in a thousand years ... ,' because a collective wish for change of status involves 'The secret accumulation of knowledge – a gradual spread of enlightenment ...' This will be stifled by mass recreational stupidity. In *Nineteen Eighty-Four* sensationalist fiction is written by a machine, and though we have not yet replaced popular novelists with computers, Julia's Department anticipates the formulaic nature of bestsellers such as *Fifty Shades of Grey*. James's name might be on the cover, but repetitive mass production is her raison d'être, rendering her redundant as an intelligent creative presence. Machine-produced trash as supervised by Julia seems to have become a reality.

Orwell, in 'Good Bad Books' (*Tribune*, 2 November 1945), foresaw this. He treats writers of popular fiction as the equivalent of literary tradesmen, skilled artisans but certainly not artists. He goes so far as to suggest that intelligence and popularity are mutually exclusive. In such works 'the author has been able to identify himself with his imagined characters, to feel with them and invite [for the reader] sympathy on their behalf, with a kind of abandonment that cleverer people would find it difficult to achieve. They bring out the fact that intellectual refinement can be a disadvantage to a story-teller ...' Tellingly, he adds that such an author 'only partly grasps the pathetic vulgarity of the people he is writing about, and therefore does not despise them,' implying that a similar bond of empathetic stupidity links such an author with his or her target readership. In *The English People* (1947) we come across an account of the culture of ordinary England that could have been an early draft of the function of Julia's department: 'England tolerate[s] newspapers ... of unheard-of silliness, and these [produce] further stupefaction in the public, blinding their eyes to vitally important problems'. Orwell concedes that stupefaction was at its height during the inter-war years, that war had focused attention on 'vitally important problems', but that by 1947 the general public had regained its apathetic condition. He goes so far as to venture that 'the survival of free speech in England is partly the result of stupidity'. As an island nation we are 'protected by geography from major disaster' which encourages 'the narrow interests of the average man, the rather low level of English education, the contempt for "highbrows"'. He could be writing about the current demographic and the xenophobic, Anglocentric mindset that some believe led to Brexit. If we accept the whispered consensus of the left-leaning media and intelligentsia then the Leavers decided to detach themselves from Europe for the same reason that Orwell's proles refused to revolt. Head-in-the-sand insularity was preferable to the challenge of anything else. *Nineteen Eighty-Four* is routinely treated as an attack on Soviet totalitarianism, and so it is – to an extent. The closer we look at the parallels between the novel and his journalism the more we have to wonder if he was predicting a country, his own, gone bad without the assistance of Stalin. He had observed the real proles and forewarned us of of their twenty-first-century successors long before he invented their enslaved counterparts.

In Catalonia Orwell had witnessed something quite different, a willingness among everyone from the illiterate farmhand to the skilled artisan to overturn orthodoxy and fight those who wished to restore it. He also encountered a real-life version of the Party. Within a few months the Soviet factions of the Republican coalition subjected their fellow anti-Franco compatriots in Catalonia, principally the POUM and the anarchists, to a regime of imprisonment, show trials and executions. Orwell and Eileen only just escaped, and their sense of a revolution transformed into totalitarianism would have stayed in his mind when he created the scenario of Smith finding that O'Brien belongs to the Inner Party and discovering that Charrington is a member of the Thought Police. Throughout the novel the satirical searchlight shifts unnervingly from the horrors of regimes abroad, notably Stalin's, to things equally distasteful but closer to home.

One day Winston has to endure the ghastly company of the Parsons and their horrible children. They are Outer Party but only slightly superior to proles. The children are hideously noisy and demanding, visceral versions of their parents. '"They do get so noisy," she said. "They're disappointed because they couldn't go to see the hanging, that's what it is."... "Want to see the hanging! Want to see the hanging!" chanted the little girl, still capering around.' It is evident from Orwell's *Tribune* pieces on the widespread appetite for photographs of executed war criminals at the close of the Second World War that he suspects that among the general population, public hanging, if made available, might well become as popular as football as a spectator sport.

In 'As I Please' (28 April 1944) he tells of a night in 1940 when, during an air raid, he had taken cover in the Café Royal and come upon a young man 'making somewhat of a nuisance of himself with a copy of *Peace News*,' the pacifist journal. He was an artist and pacifist, and seemed unconcerned about his prospects if the Nazis invaded and occupied Britain. 'You don't suppose the Germans are going to encourage Fascism in this country, do you? They don't want to breed up a race of warriors to fight against them … That's why I'm a pacifist. They'll encourage people like me.' The young man seemed to believe that while Nazism was a distasteful spectacle it would have nothing to do with what he chose to get up to in private, where he would be able to paint and more importantly think as he wished. Orwell comments that 'the fallacy is to believe that under a dictatorial government you can be free *inside* … [that] up in the attics the secret enemies of the régime can record their thoughts in perfect freedom …' Winston Smith entertains the same fallacy as he escapes for moments of freedom, sometimes with Julia, in the 'attic' above Charrington's shop. After being captured and tortured he no longer has access to that private 'inside' that is the last refuge of individuality. The young man in the Café Royal remains anonymous but he sowed the seeds for Winston Smith's moments of pathetic naiveté. He also encapsulated Orwell's anger against the apparent alliance between complacency, indifference and self-absorption bred out of liberal democracy; such citizens took for granted their entitlements so long as there seemed no danger that they'd be taken away. Most importantly, advocates of the Soviet utopia who were based comfortably in the West shared the mindset of the self-deluded artist.

Orwell said very little about the novel, but when Fredric Warburg visited him in the Cranham Sanatorium on 15 June 1949 he dictated a statement which did not go into print until after his death. 'The moral to be drawn from this dangerous nightmare situation is a simple one. *Don't let it happen. It depends on you.*' So, over the past seventy years, how have we done?

Until the end of the Cold War, and to a lesser extent since, there was an unseemly dispute over what exactly the 'it' we should prevent from happening involved. The hard left, in Britain and elsewhere, pilloried Orwell not as a Trotskyist but as a disciple of capitalism and even neo-Fascism. The *Daily Worker* saw the book as pro-Western Cold War propaganda and its American counterpart, *Masses & Mainstream*, presents Orwell as an apologist for colonialism, based on his record in the Burma Police, who transforms his loathing for the lesser races into a contempt for indigenous white 'proles': 'who are described with fear and loathing as ignorant, servile, brutish'. For *Pravda*, the organ of the Soviet Communist Party, it was a 'squalid ... misanthropic fantasy ... [a] filthy book,' that has, apparently, justified the revolution it was held by others to have satirised. 'The living forces of peace are uniting ever more firmly into an organised front in defence of peace, freedom and life,' and on and on, in an unwitting replica of Orwell's Newspeak.

The conservative and moderate-left commentators of 1949 and 1950 concurred on it as being a searing attack on totalitarianism in general and Soviet Russia in particular. As the 1950s rolled on and the Cold War turned even frostier the novel was subjected to its more grotesque features, notably doublethink. It could mean two very different things simultaneously, depending on each reader's bias.

On 12 December 1954 those who owned a television set were treated to the first on-screen adaptation, with Peter Cushing as Winston Smith. The book was still selling an impressive 150 copies per week but the majority of viewers who tuned in to the screening, roughly seven million, had heard of but not read it. Letters of complaint to the BBC flooded in with one licence payer saying that he 'felt like putting a hammer through my TV set'. It even featured on *Panorama*, with a Home Counties magistrate claiming that it would create a crime wave and inspire widespread degeneracy. A group of Conservative MPs put forward a motion condemning it as pandering to 'sexual and sadistic tastes'. This was ironic given that six years later the Tory MP Charles Curran declared that the novel 'probably had more to do than any other single factor with the socialist defeat in the 1951 General Election'.

George Orwell, a shipping clerk in South West London, spent the evening of the play's screening answering his telephone to appalled viewers. The following day his wife, Elizabeth, asked for their phone to be disconnected until George's name could be removed from the directory.

Prince Philip later disclosed that the recently crowned Queen had enjoyed the production greatly. Seemingly she had followed her mother into the Orwell fanbase.

A year earlier, in 1953, Ealing Studios had released a black comedy called *Meet Mr. Lucifer* which presents the television set as a socially harmful tool of the Devil (played by Stanley Holloway). Despite the joviality of the film, movie studios were becoming genuinely worried about the threat that television posed to their business and they borrowed the idea of a demonic presence lurking in the set from the horrid telescreens of a 1949 novel. *Nineteen Eighty-Four* was becoming a multi-stranded cultural phenomenon.

Communists, particularly those in the West, were busily building a case against Orwell as a man who had been plotting against all forms of socialism and Marxism since the 1930s. They presented it over twelve months between early 1955 and the beginning of 1956. In *Heretics and Renegades* (1955) Isaac Deutscher stops short of accusing Orwell of plagiarising Eugene Zamiatin's 1924 novel *We* (acknowledging that he had praised the novel in the *Tribune* in 1946), but he claims that he turned Zamiatin's story of totalitarianism into a gross distortion of the inherent qualities of Marxism. On 5 January 1955 R. Palme Dutt, one of the leading figures in the British Communist Party, had written to the *Manchester Guardian*, as if to prepare the ground for Deutscher's more substantial assault:

> The ideas which Orwell depicts as dominating the world in *1984* reflect the ideas not of communism, of which he knew very little, but of present-day Western monopoly capitalism ...

Dutt goes on to explain some key aspects of communism, of which Orwell 'knew little'. Winston Smith's axiom that 'reality exists in the human mind and nowhere else' is 'the characteristic standpoint of all current Western idealist philosophy, favoured by the ruling class'. All literary works are, of course, open to interpretation but Orwell makes it unambiguously clear that Smith's notion of inner 'reality' is his final refuge against forces apparently set upon extinguishing his sense of identity. In January 1956 James Walsh published an article in *Marxist Quarterly* in which he quotes Deutscher and Dutt and, with some savagery, closes the case for the prosecution. Orwell is a propagandist for the ruling classes who present workers, proles, as all but sub-human and 'he throws in everything he has learnt in his longish career as a petty colonial dictator and as a minor official in the main capitalist propaganda agency [the BBC], together with many unconsidered trifles from the Nazis'. The assault of 1955–56, which some suspected to be planned and choreographed, was followed by a measured but perhaps more effective campaign led by the academic Marxist historian Raymond Williams, who was certainly not as loud-mouthed as Walsh but over three decades, up to his death in 1988, employed a strategy of damning Orwell with faint praise, treating him as might a head tutor his bright but rather misguided pupil. William's enduring point is that Orwell was incapable of properly understanding communism because he had alienated himself from it. Only those who are part of the community of Marxism can be allowed to ponder, let alone criticise, its essential features – which sounds rather eerily like the working manifesto of the Inner Party in *Nineteen Eighty-Four*.

Also in 1955 the CIA found that a day in late April was entirely suitable for their own drive to act as intermediaries between Orwell and readers who, unlike Deutscher, Walsh, Dutt *et al*, had been denied access to the novel. The night was cloudy, the wind, from the west, moderate but not too gusty or strong, as tens of thousands of balloons were launched across the Iron Curtain. Each carried a copy of *Nineteen Eighty-Four*.

It is notable that the most vociferous anti-Orwell spokesmen (and alongside Williams we should include figures such as the Marxist historian E. P. Thompson and the literary critic Edward Said) published their uncensored invectives from within societies whose overthrow they enthusiastically advocated. One might compare their case, and circumstances, with those of Czesław Miłosz whose *The Captive Mind* was published in English translation in 1953. Miłosz, Polish and previously a communist, had fled Warsaw for Paris in 1951 after finding that Stalinist totalitarianism had effectively seized control of post-war Poland. His book's title indicated its and his affinity with Orwell's novel. The 'inner' reality, so despised by Dutt, is the final retreat of a mind otherwise broken by the implacable forces of ideology:

> ... it [*Nineteen Eighty-Four*] is both difficult to obtain and dangerous to possess [in the Soviet Bloc], it is known only to certain members of the Inner Party. Orwell fascinates them through his insight into details they know well, and through his use of Swiftian satire. Such a form of writing is forbidden by the New Faith because allegory, by nature manifold in meaning, would trespass beyond the prescriptions of socialist realism and the demands of the censor.

Miłosz respectfully borrows terminology from Orwell (notably 'Inner Party') to emphasise the uncanny parallels between *Nineteen Eighty-Four* and the world from which he had recently escaped. He also points out that behind the recently constructed Iron Curtain Orwell has caused members of the Inner Party to agree with dissidents on one thing: 'The fact that there are writers in the West who understand the functioning of the unusually constructed machine of which they themselves are a part astounds them and argues against the "stupidity" of the West.' The purblind 'stupidity' referred to is also known, in a phrase allegedly coined by Lenin, as the credulity of 'useful idiots', those in the West who continue to accept the delusion of a Marxist utopia fed to them from the East: Dutt, Walsh, Deutscher, Williams *et al*. Miłosz's was not a lone voice. Other Soviet Bloc dissidents – including Václav Havel, Miklós Haraszti and Milan Šimečka – have cited Orwell as their inspirational guide.

By 1984, the actual year that is, the novel had become a magnet for media enterprises and celebrities who had small concern for its artistic and political import. David Bowie was allegedly fascinated and influenced by the novel. In the mid-1970s he planned a rock-music adaptation which Orwell's second wife treated with awestruck contempt, with some wisdom. Bowie approached Richard Branson with a view to investing in the film, an opportunity that, mercifully, Branson turned down. One wonders what a drug-addicted, hedonistic rock star who had given little attention to recent history and literature would have done with the book. The word mutilate comes to mind.

1984, the year, opened with individuals of doubtful intelligence planning events, television programmes and films which they hoped would make money out of the book's reputation as an apocalyptic prophecy. It was as if some obscure verse in the Gospels had suddenly been found to give a specific date to the Second Coming. Bernard Crick, whose authorised biography of Orwell had come out in 1980, predicted a 'black plague' of Orwelliania: tee shirts, calendars, board games, stage and film adaptations *et al*. His warning was echoed by Paul Johnson in the *Spectator* who predicted that the new generation of Orwell-acolytes would become 'a kind of Orwellian obsession in themselves'. The main cinema event of the year was a film, directed by Michael Radford, in which John Hurt starred as Winston Smith and Richard Burton, in his last on-screen performance, portrayed O'Brien.

The political resonances of the film are vague, mainly because 1984 was a very unsuitable year for the revisitation, let alone the interpretation of *Nineteen Eighty-Four*. Thatcher's Conservatives had won the 1983 election and were pressing ahead with a policy of privatisation that seemed intent on dismantling the managed economy established by Labour just before Orwell's novel was published. The miners' strike represented the hard left in direct conflict with the Conservative establishment – by the end of 1984 the latter had become the victors. Virtually everyone in the media and the film industry was affiliated to liberal-left politics but now they faced a dilemma.

Orwell's terrible apocalyptic prognosis seemed like a piece of pro-Tory propaganda. Under Michael Foot the Labour opposition was infiltrated by individuals, especially members of Militant, who believed in a purist brand of socialism that was effectively communism diluted with minor concessions to liberal democracy. Labour's manifesto in the 1983 election was described by the Labour MP Gerald Kaufman as 'the longest suicide note in history', involving as it did mass nationalisation and unilateral nuclear disarmament. The Conservatives presented it as an application for membership of the Soviet Bloc (it also stated that the UK would leave the then EEC, presented as an abominably capitalist alliance). Michael Radford faced the prospect of dramatising the nightmare that the Conservatives had presented as the inevitable outcome of a Labour victory the year before. Labour's vote was their lowest since 1918. As a consequence the film is a peculiarly apolitical piece of science fiction that shies away from reconciling Orwell's message with the complications of the real 1984.

So: where are we now? Orwell's Eurasia was based on the Soviet Bloc which in the novel included all nations of continental Europe. Five years after the making of the film the Soviet Bloc began to collapse.

Oceania, which includes the UK, North and South America, Southern Africa and Australia/New Zealand, is today comprised mostly of free-trade democracies. The 'Disputed Territories' of North Africa, the Middle East and Southwest/Southeast Asia are, as Orwell predicted, divided in their allegiances to the super-states of the rest of the globe and riven by internal divisions of their own.

When Orwell was completing *Nineteen Eighty-Four* it was evident that the pro-Stalin Communist Party of China would be victorious in the civil war that followed the defeat of Japan in 1945. Most political commentators saw it as likely to follow Stalin's policy after the surrender of Germany and expand communist China into a Bloc that would include a number of recently decolonised states on its western and southern borders. Hence we encounter the super-state of Eastasia, which in Orwell's fictionalised world occupies the northern part of India, along with zones close to North Korea and North Vietnam.

Eastasia, or to be blunt, China, is the equivalent of *Nineteen Eighty-Four* seventy years after the author's death, but before we consider this in detail let us look at some other aspects of Orwell's status as a soothsayer.

The invasion of Iraq in 2003 coincided with the centenary of Orwell's birth, and catchphrases from *Nineteen Eighty-Four* became talismanic for left-leaning critics of the alliance between Blair and Bush. Paul Foot described the justifications for the war put forward by the US and Britain as a classic case of 'doublethink' (*Guardian*, 31 December 2002). In 2004, after the war, an aide to President Bush, apparently oblivious to the parallels with Orwell, stated that the administration would not be troubled by critics who believe that 'solutions emerge from [their] judicious study of discernible reality ... we're an empire now, and when we act, we create our own reality.' (*New York Times*, 19 October 2004). 'Fake news' became a commonplace term during Donald Trump's election campaign in 2016 but it has evidently been an unnamed feature of political discourse since the turn of the twentieth century.

In March 2019 the *Washington Post* estimated that since his inauguration almost two years earlier Trump had made just over 9,000 false claims – essentially told lies – in his tweets and in speeches and interviews. In January 2017, shortly after he took office, his advisor Kellyanne Conway unapologetically coined the phrase 'alternative facts'. During his campaign, Trump had treated disputable allegations against Hillary Clinton as verifiable truths and whipped up frenzy in his crowds of admirers who would repeat his chant 'Lock her up!' More recently in July 2019 he took against four ethnically diverse Congresswomen – collectively referred to as the 'Squad' – who had presented his speeches and policies as racist. All but one of the Squad had been born in the US; the fourth had come to the country as a baby with her refugee mother. Trump lashed out at them: 'Why don't they go back and help fix the … crime-infested places from which they came.' Within days crowds at his rallies had adapted his call to a new version of the anti-Hillary Clinton chant. This time it was 'Send her back! Send her back!' Apparently President Trump does not read books, but one wonders if his more literate advisors had instructed him on the effectiveness of Orwell's Two Minutes Hate.

On 25 January 2017 *Nineteen Eighty-Four* went to the top of the Amazon bestseller list in the US with Penguin USA ordering 75,000 new copies of the book the following week. Craig Burke, Penguin USA's Publicity Director, told the *New York Times* (25 January 2017) that over the previous seven days the book had peaked at a 9,500 per cent increase in sales. The dramatic jump followed the news coverage of the claim by White House press secretary Sean Spicer that President Trump had attracted the 'largest audience ever to witness an inauguration'. NBC's 'Meet the Press' asked Kellyanne Conway why Spicer had made a provably false statement. Ms Conway did not deny the statement was false but explained that Spicer had chosen to give 'alternative facts'. Everyone who had even a remote knowledge of the novel, perhaps from high school, recognised similarities between her statement and the process by which 'Newspeak' and 'doublethink' caused listeners to accept contrary versions of reality. Even those who couldn't recall exactly what had happened in the book googled summaries, and social networks went berserk with people proclaiming their fear that Big Brother personified had taken control of America. Hence the rush to Amazon to see if Orwell had indeed prophesised the nightmare.

There are some extraordinary parallels between Winston Smith's world and America during and after Trump's election campaign. The controversial report by Special Counsel Robert Mueller (March 2019) found that there was incontrovertible evidence of Russian interference in the election. Specifically, a programme of misinformation was conducted by the St Petersburg-based Internet Research Agency which involved the use of blogs and other social media platforms. Many of the allegations against Hillary Clinton regarding her misuse of government emails when in office originated from blogs from this organisation which had no claims to authenticity and were disguised as originating from US-based forums, some linked to the American government. In 2018 an ex-employee confessed to the *Washington Post* (17 February 2018): 'I immediately felt like a character in the book *1984* by George Orwell – a place where you have to write that white is black and black is white. Your first feeling, when you ended up there, was that you were in some kind of factory that turned lying, telling untruths, into an industrial assembly line.' These could be the words of Winston Smith, and the sense of the Agency as having been modelled on the Ministry of Truth is reinforced by the disclosures of Lyudmila Savchuk, a former employee at the Internet Research Agency, who in 2015 sued her employer for labour code violations amounting to psychological abuse. She later became a whistle-blower on their practices, which were the equivalent of psychological abuse. She commented ('Disinfo News: Working in Russian Troll Factory Pushed Reporter to "Edge of Insanity"', *POLYGRAPH info*. Retrieved 19 October 2018): 'The realisation that you can invent any fact, then watch it absolutely synchronised with the media outlets as one massive information outflow and spread worldwide – that absolutely breaks your psyche.' As it did with Winston Smith.

Truth used to be something that could be ascertained through the provision of verifiable evidence. This was the prevailing norm three decades ago when authors of printed media and books would cite archived material – records of parliamentary debates, witness reports by groups of journalists, documented court cases, scientific papers and so on – as the foundation for their case. Checking claims against evidential detail was laborious and time-consuming but its existence as an option for a reader who suspected the authenticity of a report was a deterrent against journalists and writers who told lies. One of the last instances of verifiable proof defeating falsification was in 2000 when the Holocaust denier David Irving brought a case against the academic Deborah E. Lipstadt for libel. The evidence presented by Lipstadt's legal team won the case, but only just. Later the journalist Jonathan Freedland, who witnessed the proceedings, recalled that '… one afternoon, as I left the court, I had that strange sensation. It was physical, like seasickness. The ground beneath my feet seemed unsteady, as if the earth itself was falling away … He [Irving] was trying to dispense with something human beings find essential for life – the ability to draw conclusions from evidence. He was saying that we can't trust anything – neither records nor the testimony of tens of thousands of witnesses. And if he was right, where did that leave what we call history?' (*Guardian*, 9 March 2019). Winston Smith could have answered that question: we could dispose of it via the 'memory hole'. Freedland said he felt relief at the verdict against Irving:

> But by 2016 … it was now clear that the truth was under assault once again. Not from a crank who called himself a historian, but from Trump, from the Brexiters, from the Kremlin, all of them united in their disregard for whether a statement is true or false.

This was made possible by the sidelining of evidence-based discourse by social media, in which 'truth' is infinitely malleable and subject only to popular consensus and collective delusion rather than verification.

But let us not be carried away with notions of Orwell as the foreseer of a post-2016 American *Nineteen Eighty-Four*. Trump is the utter antithesis of Big Brother. For one thing the latter never actually appears in the novel. He is quoted and his image represented on billboards but Orwell subtly implies that he might well be an invention of members of the Inner Party, a presence which enables them, by the cult of personality, to maintain power through a combination of fear and loyalty. Trump certainly exists and was, albeit narrowly, elected in a democratic vote, though he does sometimes sound as though he has been invented by an employee of the Ministry of Truth. On a CNN programme (4 June 2019) the presenter compared key doublethink axioms from the novel – 'War is Peace', 'Freedom is Slavery', 'Ignorance is Strength' – with films of some of Trump's speeches, notably his comment on the news media: 'What you're seeing and what you're reading is not what's happening.' This might sound like doublethink, but consider Orwell's/Goldstein's definition of it:

> To know and not to know, to be conscious of complete truthfulness while telling carefully constructed lies, to hold simultaneously two opinions which cancelled out, knowing them to be contradictory and believing in both of them, to use logic against logic, to repudiate morality while laying claim to it ... to forget whatever it was necessary to forget, then to draw it back into memory again at the moment when it was needed, and then promptly to forget it again, and above all, to apply the same process to the process itself.

The clipped, frequently quoted, three-word examples of doublethink from the novel are distillations of something far more complex. As Orwell puts it, it is a 'process' and the most horrible example of it in practice comes close to the end of the novel in the dialogue between O'Brien and Winston Smith. O'Brien is the unsurpassed practitioner of doublethink as a 'process', a means by which it is used to wear down and undermine all notions of what Winston previously took for granted as truth and actuality. O'Brien is evil but he is also a verbal and intellectual genius, implementing

Orwell's specification of doublethink with the adeptness of a linguistic chess player.

Short quotations from Trump, usually little more than a sentence, might seem to echo doublethink, but we should see them instead as examples of an individual struggling to translate his already unsteady grasp of meaning, concrete or abstract, into a chain of words that makes sense.

As Orwell puts it, the doublethink specialist is 'conscious' of the demanding procedures of assertion and cancellation, contradiction, forgetting and remembering, using logic against logic. They belong to an elite, members of the Inner Party selected because of their intellectual adroitness. In comparison Trump's team is constantly fighting a rearguard action against his unwitting neologisms, malapropisms and moments of incomprehension disguised as populist bombast. They do not, unlike O'Brien and other members of the Inner Party, 'consciously' practise doublethink. Rather, it has become the equivalent of a virus spread by the President through the various press releases from the White House.

In early June 2019 Trump visited the UK, Ireland and France to discuss matters of mutual interest, dine with the Royal Family and commemorate the seventy-fifth anniversary of D-Day. In a press interview he stated that a post-Brexit trade deal with the UK would involve the NHS 'being on the table', seeming to agree with a statement made days earlier by Woody Johnson, the US Ambassador to the UK, that all of Britain's utilities would be subject for discussion in future trading relationships. A day later Trump was interviewed by his fawning acolyte Piers Morgan and performed a U-turn, but not because he had softened his stance. His initial comprehension of what the 'NHS' means was roughly that of an American four-year-old, and his advisors had subsequently explained to him why his comments had provoked cross-party outrage among British politicians. Things grew farcically worse later that same day when he visited Ireland to meet the Taoiseach, Leo Varadkar. During their televised exchange Trump commiserated with Varadkar on his problems with the 'wall'. On the post-Brexit situation he was reassuring: 'I mean, we have a border situation in the United States, and you have one here ... I think ... it will all work out very well, and also for you with your wall ...' (*Guardian*, 5 June 2019). His wall between the US and Mexico had been a key element of his election campaign. It would, he declared, be an impregnable barrier against hordes of criminals, rapists and drug dealers, and be paid for by Mexico. Varadkar looked uncomfortable and updated the president on the dissimilarities between Mexico and the Six Counties. This was not calculated 'fake news' or doublethink; it was the spectacle of the leader of the free world incautiously disclosing his stupidity.

Anthony Scaramucci was the most perversely Orwellian figure in the Trump camp, and his performance was unintendedly hilarious. Employed as the senior White House communications director in 2017, he matched operatives of the Inner Party with his outpourings of threats and scorn-flecked vilifications, but his attempts at doublethink were skewed by a condition somewhere between Tourette's and coprolalia (the involuntary and persistent utterance of profanities, obscenities and abusive remarks). He affirmed that his chief White House rival Steve Bannon was of slight significance as a competing ranter since he was 'always sucking his own cock', and more pertinently that 'He is literally [sic] the pig in George Orwell's *Animal Farm* that stands on his two legs the minute he gets power.' (*Vanity Fair*, 1 February 2018). Oddly no one commented on either the appropriateness or irony of Scaramucci's appearance in 'Celebrity Big Brother' following his sacking by Trump.

Orwell in *Nineteen Eighty-Four* does not mock the Inner Party. Its strategies are planned and enforced with scintillating acumen; he does not suggest that profound intelligence and evil are mutually exclusive. In comparison, the Trump administration is a conspiracy of dunces.

By the time this book goes to press the British government, or less likely the electorate, might well have decided on the future of the UK for the coming generation, especially regarding our triangulated relationship with the EU and the rest of the world. Calculated doublethink – rather than Trump's improvised, buffoonish brand – has been a commonplace of Brexit since before the Referendum, and while Remainers have sometimes played games with the truth their transgressions pale into insignificance in comparison with those of the Leave campaign. The most famous was the £350 million a week side-of-the-bus claim. Any later attempt to treat this as an innocent miscalculation was nullified by Nigel Farage's vainglorious admission to *Good Morning Britain* (*GMB*) on the morning after the vote that everyone connected with Leave knew it was a lie. Daniel Hannan MEP had reassured voters before the vote that 'absolutely nobody is talking about threatening our place in the single market' and shortly after the result Boris Johnson promised that 'there will continue to be free trade, and access to the single market'. Michael Gove, amongst others, had claimed that Turkey would soon be a new EU member, with seventy-nine million of its citizens (i.e. the entire population) likely to head straight to the UK. Anyone remotely familiar with Turkey's EU membership bid was aware that it had been hopelessly stalled since 1999, and thereafter ruled out by the contravention of EU conditions of membership by Erdoğan's authoritarian regime. The problem of the Irish border was despatched to the 'memory hole', at least until its re-emergence in negotiations following the Referendum. At present the new prime minister affirms that the UK will leave the EU on 31 January 2020, no matter what, if necessary with no deal. In June Mr Johnson had claimed that the odds against no deal were 'a million to one' and that some new settlement could be reached (despite the fact that the EU parliament and executive would effectively be in recess until 1 November). In March 2019 Gove reassured those anxious about the immediate future that 'We didn't vote to leave without a deal. That wasn't the message of the campaign I helped to lead.' Presently (November 2019), he is the cabinet minister overseeing preparations for a no-deal. One difference between Orwell's doublethink and the Brexit version is that the former is designed to deny citizens access to the truth while the latter involves the campaigners and the voters in a co-operative exercise in open self-deceit and delusion. The shifts between lying and forgetting, the holding simultaneously of two contradictory opinions, the replacement of logic by illogic, all comply with Goldstein's notion of a 'process', but while the Inner Party withheld proof, the Brexit campaign seems to have triumphed via its assumption that the electorate would regard as a democratic right its gleeful acceptance of lies as preferable to facts. As Orwell privately feared, Smith's dream of an empowered, enfranchised proletariat seems to have ushered in something almost as nightmarish as the regime it replaced.

A particularly fascinating aspect of this jamboree of falsehood is the way that participants seem able to treat the present and past rather as a conjurer deals with a pack of cards. All of those referred to above appear to have acquired customised memory holes to dispose of what they might have once have said and to erase any conflict between presently held opinions and previously expressed promises or statements of fact. Few, if any, are able to explain how or why their views on the likely effects of Brexit have not so much changed as mysteriously disappeared. In terms of doublethink and in order to maintain the trust and affection of a seemingly gullible electorate they will 'forget whatever it was necessary to forget, then ... draw it back into memory again at the moment when it was needed, and then promptly ... forget it again, and above all ... apply the same process to the process itself'.

From the ridiculous to the sublimely awful. As Orwell said to Warburg, it '*could*' happen, and it has, in the region of East Asia which in 1945 he foresaw as having the 'potential' to become the third super-state: China. As to North Korea, China's maniacal subsidiary, it is as if *Nineteen Eighty-Four* has been rewritten by a modern-day Bram Stoker with a taste for noir surrealism. As I have already made clear, China is an unceasingly successful anomaly. It competes on equal terms, and often cheats, as a player in free-market global capitalism, and has risen to number two in the league of the most powerful economies on earth. Its decisions and fluctuations in fortune cause all other nations, the US included, to watch it anxiously. What happens in China will affect everywhere else. But every company and organisation in China is, if not directly owned by, then controlled by or answerable to the Communist Party.

In *Nineteen Eighty-Four* Orwell created the first, fictionalised, system of electronic mass surveillance. Apart from the proles, everyone has a telescreen which they can watch and which constantly watches them; it cannot be switched off. The screens do not have night-vision technology but compensate with the use of minutely sensitive microphones. Spoken exchanges and whispers are recorded, and even bodily movements – a heartbeat or the twitch of a muscle – can be translated into an image of what the monitored person is doing in the dark. Some early readers thought this was dystopian prophecy gone mad, based as it was on the benign recreational toy, the TV set. In 2018 in Rongcheng, a city in the eastern province of Shandong, some citizens were refused tickets at their local railway station. When they asked why, they were given a full account of transgressions that had led to the state revoking their right to travel, including jaywalking or failing to pay a parking fine. In this respect the new system – for which Rongcheng is the testing ground – seems like a rather unpleasant version of what goes on in the West with, for example, credit scores permanently logged online and thus limiting the ability to purchase goods or services. But the Chinese version goes deeper than this. Monitors placed everywhere in Rongcheng are also programmed to record socially unacceptable behaviour, including the lip-reading of remarks that amount to political dissent. A seemingly innocuous argument with a neighbour might earn a citizen debit points, and if more are accrued the result would be punitive regulations on what they can or cannot do. Criticising the local government, and by implication the Party, would mean that the transgressor could face criminal charges. Authoritarianism of this kind in China has been a routine feature of existence since Mao but the state has now developed technology that makes it all but omnipotent. The sophistications of facial recognition sensors in the Rongcheng experiment mean that every person in the city is being monitored and listened to every minute of the day. The data gathered on them is used as a means of regulating the 1,000 'social credit' scores awarded to each individual at the beginning of the operation. To adapt the analogy of our system of points on a driving licence, a Chinese citizen who is recorded as, say, spreading dissenting rumours and who fails to take heed of warnings would eventually lose all of their social credit and have their licence to exist revoked. 'Big Brother' is indeed 'Watching You', if you are a resident of Rongcheng. As with most tests, the plan is for the system to be implemented throughout China, and so far there is no record of it proving to be unsuccessful. (See *We Have Been Harmonised: Life in China's Surveillance State*, by Kai Strittmatter, 2019.)

Nineteen Eighty-Four first became available in China in 1979, but the translation was effectively a rewriting by Party specialists to distort any obvious resemblances between Orwell's creation and the Maoist state. It was kept in special sections of libraries and bookshops accessible only to licensed Party members. In 1985 it was decided that the *laobaixing* – essentially China's proles – could have access to it, a token gesture of false liberalisation which coincided with the strategy of competing economically with the West. It was assumed that members of the *laobaixing* had never heard of it – it was certainly never mentioned in the education system or the media – and would have no interest in it. Since 2018 English-language editions have been made available, on the assumption that a large number of the better-off, better-educated bilingual citizens who now have access to foreign travel would come across it abroad. This was not so much liberalisation as careful choreographing of the tastes and allegiances of the population. The people most likely to buy it are those whose past and present success depends on their allegiance to the Party. Even if they do recognise parallels between Orwell's prediction and China today they are unlikely to sympathise, publicly, with his standpoint. Equally, university students taking courses abroad in, say, comparative literature are likely to have access to it, but their status as cultural tourists testifies to their position as part of the Party elite and when they return home they are unlikely to voice opinions on Orwell's novel. To do so might endanger their investment in the preservation of the State and the Party as a route to a good standard of living for themselves.

There is a grimly ironic similarity between the policies implemented by China to neuter the impact of the novel and the ways in which Orwell's Inner Party ensures its survival by manipulating the impressions and responses of members of the Outer Party.

The only means by which *Nineteen Eighty-Four* might spark debate on its significance as a horrible mirror image of China today is via social media. Google, Facebook and YouTube are banned outright and if a Chinese citizen attempts to type in the title of the book on other sites in letters or as digits – '1', '9', '8', '4' – their access to a site or their attempt to communicate a message is blocked.

This could be regarded as a mark of esteem for the novel, given that the massacre at Tiananmen Square, which took place just over thirty years ago in 1989, has been subjected to a similar fate. In China Tiananmen Square still exists as a place but the killings which took place there on 4 June 1989, along with the movement of political protest which preceded them, have been expunged from history, at least for the Chinese. Any attempt to locate the name or events remotely related to Tiananmen online results in the equivalent of 'nothing known'. All other records, in print or in the recollections of those involved have also been erased. A considerable number of Western journalists witnessed some of the killings, and the photograph of the so-called 'Tiananmen Man' facing down a tank is a commonplace feature of Western presentations of China today and of recent Chinese history, online and in the print media. It is impossible to imagine that the favoured elite of China do not, during their trips abroad, come upon this image, along with innumerable accounts of what actually happened when the Party suppressed and murdered dissenters. They might, temporarily, become aware of what occurred, but the Party assumes that on their return to China they will erase this knowledge. The Rongcheng surveillance trials show that technology will be able to detect potentially subversive sharing and discussion of this secret knowledge, and in this respect Orwell's telescreens which can decode breathing and movement as forms of communication are extraordinarily prescient. As is Winston Smith's day job. He is one of many who are expected to rewrite the past and dispose of what actually happened via the so-called 'memory hole'. At one point he comes upon an authentic article from an edition of *The Times* which proves that three of the men subjected to show trials as traitors were not guilty. He knows that he has access to the truth but realises that sharing or publicising this would be futile and probably suicidal. This is how privileged travellers feel about their acquired knowledge of Tiananmen Square when they return to China. It reminds us of the concluding pages of *Animal Farm*, a novel also excluded from online discussions or access in China. Napoleon and other members of the Party are arguing with the humans in the farmhouse. The outcome of the exchange is unclear but its cause is evident enough. The farmers want to trade with Napoleon's empire and are prepared to hold their noses regarding their contempt for it. And so it is with the capitalist 'liberal democracies' who wish to improve their economies through trade deals with a horribly totalitarian state. Consider: Every statesman or woman who enters into negotiations with Beijing is fully aware of what actually happened at Tiananmen Square and of how China leads the world as the practitioner of capital punishment for political crimes. Would any of them raise these uncomfortable topics during negotiations? Of course not. Kai Strittmatter states that 'The Party is feeding on the weaknesses of the West.' And winning. Let us revisit Orwell's words to Warburg in Cranham Sanatorium: *'Don't let it happen. It depends on you.'* We have failed him because we won't, or daren't, concern ourselves with a version of his novel being acted out in East Asia.

The expansion of 'tech' and social media in the West has prompted an upsurge of hysteria on the opportunity for liberal democratic states to erode privacy and freedom. In the 2017 film version of Dave Eggers' novel *The Circle* (2013) Mae Holland is initiated into a giant Silicon Valley company and feels she has joined her fellow workers, and surfers, in utopia. Slogans from Orwell are inverted as celebrations of a new openness which technology will offer the consumer: 'Secrets are Lies'; 'Sharing is Caring'; 'Privacy is Theft'. But the breaking down of barriers leads to a form of voluntary totalitarianism-by-narcissism: a culture absorbed by IT causes us to be concerned only with ourselves. Eggers was astute. Also in 2013 Edward Snowden, previously employed by the CIA and the National Security Agency (NSA), leaked details of how the latter had been gathering massive amounts of online details on US and British citizens. Recipients of the leak – notably the *Guardian* and the *Washington Post* – went into panic-attack state. Everyone, seemingly, was being spied on and Orwell citations swamped the press and media. 'Are We Living in 1984?' asked the *New York Times* (11 June 2013). The fact that the NSA was trying to detect evidence of imminent Islamic terrorist activity in order to prevent attacks rather than ensure that all citizens followed the edicts of the Party was not mentioned by those convinced that the West had become, as Senator Bernie Sanders put it, 'very Orwellian'. We seem to be so consumed with our own sense of hysterical entitlement (they're after '*us*') that we turn a blind eye to what is going on in China.

Texting and Twitter are today's most fashionable, one might say addictive, modes of exchange and while Orwell had no conception of electronic media he foresaw with eerie accuracy the manner in which tweeting and text messaging would compress and mutilate language. Winston's Ministry of Truth colleague, Syme, rejoices in the advances being made. 'It's a beautiful thing, the destruction of words. Of course the great wastage is in the verbs and adjectives, but there are hundreds of nouns that can be got rid of as well … After all, what justification is there for a word which is simply the opposite of some other word? A word contains its opposite in itself. Take "good," for instance. If you have a word like "good," what use is there for a word like "bad"? "Ungood" will do just as well – better, because it's an exact opposite, which the other is not.' Short Message Service (SMS) was piloted in – would you believe it? – 1984, and Syme's description perfectly captures the means by which 'wastage' is eradicated to cut each message to 280 characters on Twitter and to simply facilitate immediacy on text messages by opting out of the tiresome conventions of syntax and semantics. The 280 limit amounts to tokenism in that only one per cent of users come close to it: the current average is thirty-three characters. Technophiles have celebrated these developments as part of a new world order, where old-fashioned communication barriers – meeting face-to-face, posting and waiting for letters, telephoning, even emailing – have been replaced by succinct immediacy. Syme saw things differently. 'Don't you see that the whole aim of Newspeak is to narrow the range of thought? In the end we shall make thoughtcrime literally impossible, because there will be no words in which to express it. Every concept that can ever be needed will be expressed in exactly *one* word, with its meaning rigidly defined and all its subsidiary meanings rubbed out and forgotten.' There have been numerous debates on whether social media, which compresses language and suffocates the kind of expansive, speculative freedom that is a commonplace of speech and prose, damages its users, especially the young. Syme's grotesque glee regarding the extinction of free expression is disturbing but his diagnosis seems horribly accurate. An addiction to a medium which encourages, even compels, the avoidance of linguistic sophistry – nuance, studied ambiguity, syntactic inflection, etc. – seems to me to leave us, as Syme put it, with language which 'narrow[s] the range of thought'. I hardly need remind you of the most famous and powerful addict of Twitter.

Twitter and texting enable us, in the free world, to treat electronic free speech as a licence to publicise injudicious comments that we might once have kept to ourselves. Winston offered an unnervingly accurate prophesy of what might happen if telescreens were democratised. 'The horrible thing about the Two Minutes Hate was not that one was obliged to act a part, but that it was impossible to avoid joining in … A hideous ecstasy of fear and vindictiveness, a desire to kill, to torture, to smash faces in with a sledge hammer, seemed to flow through the whole group of people like an electric current …' 'Fear' is no longer part of the ecstasy, at least in the sense that Twitter users have ceased to be in terror of the Party, but in other respects they seem capable of forming themselves into a collective of 'vindictiveness'. As we've seen, the virus of antisemitism that has been infecting the Labour Party for several years works in the same way that Winston described Two Minutes Hate. Even the mildest suspicions regarding Jews and their tribal inclinations are whipped into a frenzy by the 'electric current' of social media which encourages people to stand out from the mob as those most inclined to 'kill', 'torture', and 'smash faces'. Let us remember that Luciana Berger and many others who accused the Corbyn inner circle of allowing proven antisemites to remain in the party were threatened online with physical violence, even death. Outside the odious spectacle of Labour antisemitism there is a growing obsession with the use of social media as a means of imposing some vaguely agreed consensus on what can or cannot be said, what opinions are either publicly admissible or deserving of suppression. There are no given rules which govern this new mood of hysteria involving threats against individuals and the silencing of apparently unsuitable comments, opinions or ideas. Any objection can be sparked by a single person or a group and the inclination to become part of the vengeful online horde becomes addictive, even if those involved have little in common. Look what happened to Sir Roger Scruton once he was accused, falsely, of going against the code of liberal respectability. He was selected as a legitimate target for everyone, left and right, and lynched online. Social media is a form of narcissistic recreation and by the same token it enables users to become unaccountable for the damage they do to others.

Telescreens were technologically crude but they looked forward to a time, now, when our addiction to social media shows us for what we are: grotesquely selfish and malicious beyond our worst expectations. Orwell was an extraordinarily shrewd forecaster.

In totalitarian states social media is regarded by the security forces as a gift to mass-monitoring and suppression. In China Twitter and texting exist in a grey area between an outright ban and ruthless Party scrutiny. The Party security services rejoice in the fact that these imports from the West encourage self-servingly compressed messages. They make what Orwell called 'thoughtcrime' much easier to spot: '... the fact of having very few words to choose from ... the Newspeak vocabulary was tiny, and new ways of reducing it were constantly being devised ... Each reduction was a gain, since the smaller the area of choice, the smaller the temptation to take thought.' (Appendix to *Nineteen Eighty-Four*, 'The Principles of Newspeak'.) And, as Chinese spotters might have added, the greater the likelihood of being singled out as a potential dissident who cannot hide beneath linguistic obfuscation. The Chinese authorities openly admitted that text exchanges by cell phone, because of their brevity, made it easier for them to pick out 'key words' which indicate 'unhealthy content' ('China to Scan Text Messages to Spot "Unhealthy Content"', *New York Times*, 19 January 2010).

One of the functions of the proles in *Nineteen Eighty-Four* is to breed and to provide a sufficient stock of supine manual workers to maintain the basic industries of the state. This, initially, was the policy of Mao's China. Later, it became evident that unregulated population growth would lead to chaos for a still largely agrarian economy and in 1970 the Party declared that two children was the maximum for each family. This was later reduced to one and the system – involving obligatory abortions and fines for giving birth – was only eliminated at the end of 2015. However, the Party maintains the option to intervene if procreation rates threaten the general economic plan. Orwell's novel foresaw the Chinese

State's treatment of the common people as the equivalent of cattle. The Chinese Communist Party has not published a rationale for this. It does not need to; such explanations imply the existence of opposition to policies undertaken, and none is allowed to exist. But O'Brien would happily provide the Chinese Party with a manifesto: 'We control life, Winston, at all its levels … perhaps you have returned to your old idea that the proletarians or the slaves will arise and overthrow us. Put it out of your mind. They are helpless, like the animals. Humanity is the Party. The others are outside – irrelevant.' On procreation he is more specific. 'But in the future … Children will be taken from their mothers at birth, as one takes eggs from a hen … Procreation will be an annual formality like the renewal of a ration card.'

The proles, and by implication members of the Outer Party, will also be disempowered as human beings by the gradual undertakings mainly by the Ministry of Truth: the rewriting of history so that the past forbids any alternative perception of the present as decreed by the Party. Since the 1950s the Chinese communists have embarked on a gradual policy of linguistic centralisation in an attempt to ensure that diversity does not spark dissent. Mandarin is the language of the Party and its officials throughout the country with Cantonese as its closest competitor in Southern China and Hong Kong, along with the language of separatist Tibetans and Muslim Uighurs. The history of the country pre- and post-revolution will be reinvented in Mandarin but variations on this will inevitably occur in translation so it is preferable to have, as Orwell puts it, 'meaning rigidly defined and all … subsidiary meanings rubbed out and forgotten'.

Aside from the official removal of Tiananmen Square from the past, the Party History Research (PHR) Office headquarters in Beijing has for some time been busily altering what was consensually agreed as the history of China from the seventeenth to the early twentieth century, the so-called Qing period. Essentially the PHR has been excising all evidence that China was effectively an empire which violently suppressed all attempts by Xinjiang,

Tibet, Taiwan and Mongolia to achieve independence, and at the same time built an infrastructure of achievements in architecture, philosophy and the arts to rival any European dynasty, especially in the eighteenth century. The motive of the Party is clear enough: it wishes to disguise any parallels between its own policies and those of its brutally colonialist predecessor. We might look on with a mixture of horror and distaste and feel confident that outside this authoritarian regime truth is available, much as Orwell did when he wrote about the Soviet Union in the *Tribune* and elsewhere. But communist China's new status as a global economic powerhouse has changed things. Scholars who wish to have access to original archive material which offers incontrovertible material on what actually occurred in China from the seventeenth century onwards are free to inspect these documents online. The trouble is that the PHR has rewritten the archive. Writers in the West might claim to know the truth but Party officials can accuse them of lying and authenticate their claims with documents from the digitised archive. Chinese students – effectively members of the Outer Party – provide British and American universities with a valuable source of income during a period in which higher education, especially in the UK, has become as much a service industry as a forum for the study of the arts and sciences. They also enable the Chinese Communist Party to undermine some of the West's bastions of free speech. Recently Cambridge University Press was ordered to block articles in its journal *China Quarterly* which might contradict the Party's rewriting of the past and the present day. The Press concurred and only backed down when put under pressure by outspoken academics from Britain and America. We seem to be back to the days in which our press and publishers voluntarily suppressed criticism of an authoritarian regime: the persistent refusal of publishers to accept *Animal Farm* comes to mind. One has to wonder what happened when *Nineteen Eighty-Four* was available only to select members of the Chinese Communist Party. Consider this passage from Goldstein's 'Book': 'The mutability of the past is the central tenet of Ingsoc. Past events, it is argued, have no objective existence, but survive only in written records and in human memories. The past is whatever the records and the memories agree upon. And since the Party is in full control of all records, and in equally full control of the minds of its members, it follows that the past is whatever the Party chooses to make it.' Perhaps the Chinese Communist Party treated Orwell's novel as an instruction manual.

But beyond the reach of China, Western society can protect itself from the rewriting of history for the simple reason that statements based on falsehood can be overturned by the citation of verifiable facts. We should not be in fear of the destructive power of the 'memory hole': surely the *Irving v Lipstadt* case demonstrated that. Didn't it? The French novelist Claude Simon was awarded the Nobel Prize for Literature in 1985 largely because of the impact of his experimental novel *The Georgics* (1981). Part IV of the novel involves a systematic refutation of Orwell's *Homage to Catalonia* as a truthful account of what Orwell experienced and what occurred in Barcelona. Simon prefers his own Stalinist narrative, casting Orwell as an untrustworthy spokesman for the bourgeois establishment. Commentators, including the Nobel Committee, treated this as an instance of art as radicalism, an aesthetic of competing versions of reality – at least until Christopher Hitchens pointed out that it was a ghastly calumny (*Why Orwell Matters*, 2002), using undeniable evidence to establish that Orwell was telling the truth. A minor example was a photograph of the POUM Lenin Barracks in Barcelona, where Orwell signed up and trained as a volunteer. Simon claimed that the barracks did not exist, and as such the rest of Orwell's story must be regarded as questionable. We are back to the moment when Winston Smith discovers the photograph of the three prosecuted dissidents which proves them innocent. At least Hitchens did not feel terrified and despatch his evidence to the memory hole. But the fact that it took over two decades for someone to challenge Simon's 'artistic licence' and expose him as a falsifying ideologue tells us something about a prevailing consensus in Western culture. It might

not involve outright authoritarianism but it favours the opinions of
the left. Here it is worth reminding ourselves of a sentence from
Orwell's 'Looking Back on the Spanish War': 'The implied objective
of this line of thought is [that] the Leader, or some ruling clique,
controls not only the future but *the past.*'

More recently the celebrated historian and cultural theorist
Naomi Wolf, in *Outrages: Sex, Censorship and the Criminalisation of
Love* (2019), gave an account of how a number of men were hanged
for homosexual offences in mid-to-late-Victorian Britain. Almost
by accident a Radio 3 interviewer checked some court records
which showed that while these named individuals had indeed been
prosecuted none was sentenced to death. Wolf claimed that it was an
innocent mistake on her part. Others might regard it as a deliberate
avoidance of evidence that might disrupt the theoretical sweep of
her book. In 2009 the American academic Professor Ray Douglas
published a brief article in the *Journal of Modern History* (4 December
2009) in which he presented decisive archived proof that the British
had not used chemical weapons against Iraq's rebels in the 1920s.
For several years a number of eminent commentators – including
Tony Benn, Noam Chomsky, John Simpson and Robert Fisk – had
claimed in print that they had (see David Aaronovitch, *The Times*, 30
May 2019). Why were they so convinced of something for which
proof was uncertain? Because colonialists (Britain) are bad and
entirely capable of using gas against anti-colonial rebels (good). For
the same reason Wolf overlooked the fact that homosexuals had not
been hanged because she believed that during the period in question
the establishment was vilely reactionary and intolerant: they might
not actually have done the things she accused them of but they were
the sort of people who would; as would members of the British
government of the 1920s, Churchill included, who gassed civilian
Iraqis in the 1920s. Even if they didn't, they were guilty by virtue
of their nastiness. I wonder if a book written by a Trump supporter
on mass rapes sanctioned by senior Mexican officers against Texan
women in the Mexican–American War of the nineteenth century

would have gone unchallenged by determined researchers for as long as did the cases referred to above.

On a lighter note, those of you who have studied literature at university over the past few decades might well have come across Orwell on the curriculum. But I wonder if, even at a subliminal level, you might also have sensed that you had actually entered the dystopian universe of *Nineteen Eighty-Four*. In Goldstein's laborious, jargon-ridden explanation of doublethink we encounter such passages as 'To make sure that all written records agree with the orthodoxy of the moment is merely a mechanical act. But it is also necessary to *remember* that events happened in a desired manner. And if it is necessary to rearrange one's memories or to tamper with written records, then it is necessary to *forget* that one has done so.' He continues: 'To pretend, I actually do the thing: I have therefore only pretended to pretend ... What cannot be said above all must not be silenced but written.' Actually the second quotation is not from Goldstein but from Jacques Derrida, the founder of deconstruction. Anyone obliged to plough through, say, Derrida's *The Gift of Death* will have been struck by the observation that, 'the question of the self: who am I not in the sense of who am I but rather who is this that I can say who?', largely because of its sadistically contorted syntax. O'Brien, addressing Winston, put it far more pithily: 'You do not exist.' If you suspect me of facetiousness, consider the objective of the Inner Party as specified by both Syme and O'Brien: the extinction of individuality through the suffocating illogic of language. Orwell invented deconstruction.

The Appendix to the novel, which seems to have been written by a Party spokesman, offers us an account of plans for the future, including the destruction of literature or to be more accurate a transformation of original books into something utterly unrecognisable. Literary theory, of which deconstruction is but a constituent feature, has achieved something very similar. The book, or rather the text, is regarded more as the product of cultural circumstances than of an individual author, a space in which the interpreter practises various forms of critical activity involving race, gender, class, history, ideology *et al.*

At the 2005 conference of the Modern Language Association, novelist Ariel Dorfman presented a beguiling paper, based, he claimed, on personal experience. He told how CIA agents had recently detained him in a windowless room in Miami International Airport. One of his interrogators, the silent one, bore a disturbing resemblance to Trotsky while the other more loquacious agent bombarded him with endless questions and accusations designed at once to depress and unsettle him. Dorfman quoted from memory the interrogator's verbal assaults, which echoed passages from the likes of Derrida, Lacan, Lyotard, Foucault and so on, and adopted as a routine critical dialect by academics in the US and the UK. Disturbingly or hilariously, depending on your viewpoint, none of Dorfman's audience appreciated that the paper was a joke and appeared confused by being presented, within a most unusual context, with a discourse that was their professional currency. The lexicon, mannerisms and intellectual hauteur of literary theory has very little to do with literature in its own right: as the Appendix to *Nineteen Eighty-Four* predicted, it has all but abolished it.

Read the closing parts of *Nineteen Eighty-Four* in which O'Brien reduces Smith to petrified confusion by his verbal and intellectual gymnastics. This was Dorfman's inspiration, but his stupefied audience of academics were unable to appreciate the darkly comic punchline: that their intellectual inaccessibility had turned them into versions of O'Brien and Dorfman's interrogator in literary theory's room 101.

Orwell detested intellectual inscrutability and elitism, and saw them as early symptoms of authoritarianism. Emmanuel Goldstein's book contains a frightening message but it is also tediously difficult to read. It was Derrida before his time and, as Dorfman showed, *Nineteen Eighty-Four* is alive and well in the academic community of the free world.

One has to ask: if Orwell could rejoin us in 2020 what would he make of it? He would be fascinated, and horrified, by China's ability to maintain implacable totalitarianism while playing and beating liberal-democracy capitalist states at their own game. Few were willing to take seriously Orwell's prediction that the Soviet Union would impose proxy dictatorships on much of central and eastern Europe. He would not have been surprised by the suppression by the Soviets of anti-authoritarian protest movements in Budapest and Prague. Today he can point us to the spectacle of the mainland Chinese Party preparing its military jackboot for use against democracy campaigners in Hong Kong and he will tell us, once more, 'told you so'. Trump, and the alliance between the Tory hard right and proletarian xenophobia, would have struck him as both repulsive and grimly recognisable. He would regard Boris Johnson as by parts Oswald Mosley and Billy Bunter, and he'd wonder why there are still so many rough sleepers on our pavements. One can imagine a wry smile beginning to form as he stares up at his statue outside BBC Broadcasting House, but it might fade as he reads the quotation chiselled into the wall, words that never went into print but were intended for a preface to *Animal Farm*: 'If liberty means anything at all, it means the right to tell people what they do not want to hear.' Seventy years ago the West, for all its failings, could at least be proud of its status as the global bastion of free speech but today, particularly in seats of learning, the insidious spread of safe-spacing and no-platforming reflects a generation that wishes to deny others the right to speak to them for fear of their becoming distressed at 'what they do not want to hear'. The bubble in which the millennials are intent on sealing themselves off seems farcical in comparison with the policies of the Chinese Communist Party which, through technology, has all but eradicated communication that displeases it. Among the top ten countries which practise state censorship, particularly online, five are communist or carry a legacy of communism without significant reforms (China, Cuba, Vietnam,

North Korea and Azerbaijan). The rest (predominantly Iran, Saudi Arabia, Eritrea and Pakistan) belong within a very different brand of totalitarianism, but Orwell would detect in them something that bears a disturbing resemblance to communism both as an ideology and a form of tyranny. A brief encounter with the work of Sayyid Qutb (1906–66), albeit in English translation, will cause one to feel that Marx has been converted to Islam. Qutb's style is a remarkable example of doublespeak, or dialectical materialism placed in the service of Allah. It is wearily incomprehensible but it has an ineluctable purpose. For Marx, the state will wither away and history will end, and for Qutb a society will be created in which politics is irrelevant, equality of wealth and position are givens and all of these developments will follow predictions from the Koran. In each case violence and revolution will be necessary preconditions for transformation and these will be overseen by an elite who are, respectively, agents of historical inevitability or who properly understand the words of Mohammed. In both dispensations man is supposed to become more human, far better than through such minor improvements as dispensed by, say, the Enlightenment. Which seems odd given that we'd be dispossessed of the opportunity to think, especially if our thoughts, and words, go against the orthodoxy. ISIS and Al-Qaeda are Qutb's modern affiliates but even among the more indulgent Islamic states his sense of a society both proclaimed and inevitable endures. Qutb, his more recent followers, and the Marxists who hated Orwell, had one thing in common: you could not be allowed to disagree with their prognostications and eventually the statutes of their dictatorial regimes. In the latter, fickle individuality or the inclination to 'tell people what they do not want to hear' will almost certainly merit imprisonment and sometimes a death sentence: look at what happened to Salman Rushdie, who was effectively condemned to house arrest by his protectors, the security forces of the 'free' West. When *Animal Farm* and *Nineteen Eighty-Four* were published the intelligentsia of the West was predominantly left wing, and many thought that communism would be good for the working classes, irrespective of their opinions on it. Most of these activists were delusional; too comfortably off and part of the establishment to seriously consider giving up their privileges. For that, Orwell detested their hypocrisy. What would he make of an ideology – my apologies, a religion – just as deeply embedded in our precariously liberal culture and far more forthright and determined in its contempt for it?

EPILOGUE

Orwell waited for the publication of *Nineteen Eighty-Four* and read of its reception in Cranham Sanatorium, a set of damp huts which could have been designed to worsen lung conditions.

In April he was visited by Celia Kirwan, to whom he had proposed marriage almost five years earlier. This time she was present in her capacity as part of the Information Research Department (IRD), a branch of the Foreign Office primarily concerned with Soviet propaganda. The Department was recruiting figures – mainly respected journalists, historians and writers directly involved in key global events from the 1930s onwards – who would be prepared to combat the issuing of what we now call 'fake news' from various parts of the Soviet Bloc. She asked him to recommend conscripts and also asked if he knew of any whose sympathies for the Soviet cause might bias their support for the West. He gave her thirty-eight names. The so-called 'List' was first disclosed by the *Sunday Telegraph* in 1991 but few seemed to notice it, at least until 1996 when the *Guardian*, *The Times*, the *Evening Standard* and the *Independent on Sunday* provoked a frenzied witch hunt. Left-wing commentators who had previously treated him with begrudging respect formed a queue to damn him as 'an informer to the secret police' (Alexander Cockburn) as having 'given in' to the Tory establishment (Tony Benn) and even as a 'McCarthyite' (Paul Foot). Foot, Benn and Cockburn were joined by Christopher Hill ('I always knew he was two-faced ...'), Gerald Kaufman MP and Paul's uncle Michael, one-time leader of Labour and Orwell's colleague at the *Tribune* in the 1940s, amongst others.

Orwell had been assured by Celia that those named would simply be left to themselves by the IRD and that they would certainly not be treated as threats to national security. They could continue to hold and express whatever opinions they wished without this causing any damage to their lives and careers. She was telling the truth, and those who condemned him almost half a century later were fully aware of this. They had quietly loathed him for fifty years for daring to expose the Soviet utopia as the vilest form of totalitarianism and now sought their revenge by aping the mannerisms of the Thought Police in *Nineteen Eighty-Four*.

When Orwell met with Celia the Soviet Union occupied most of central and eastern Europe and was planning to expand its sphere of influence. Just over a year after their exchange Russia and China became involved in the invasion of South Korea by the communist North. The threat posed by communist countries against Western democracies in 1949–50 was comparable to that faced by Britain in 1940. Would Orwell have been later reviled if during that year he had offered the Foreign Office a list of establishment figures who might not be entirely trustworthy or competent as anti-Fascist broadcasters? And what would have happened to writers in the Soviet Union who had been marked up as liberal-capitalist sympathisers? Would they have been allowed to ply their trade unhindered by members of the NKVD/KGB? Cockburn, Foot, Hill *et al* were incapable of recognising that freedom of speech and action were allowed in the countries they inhabited but not in those whose ideologies they espoused.

In June 1949 he remarked to Astor that 'Apart from other considerations, I think I should stay alive longer if I was married & had someone to look after me.' Sonia Brownell went to Cranham several times later that summer, though it is unclear who initiated these visits. She, like Celia, was one of the three women to whom he'd proposed marriage shortly after Eileen's death. He asked her again and this time she accepted. Shortly after their engagement his weaker lung collapsed once more, he developed pleurisy and at the beginning of September was removed by private ambulance to University College Hospital in London. On 17 September 1949 the society pages of the *Star* and the *Daily Mail* reported that:

> Blue eyed 30 year old Miss Brownell, assistant editor of the literary magazine 'Horizon', became engaged to Mr Orwell some two months ago but their engagement was not disclosed until today. They have known each other for five years. In her Bedford Square office today Miss Brownell, in a white lace-work blouse, and grey flannel skirt, was wearing her Italian engagement ring of ornamental design with rubies, diamonds and an emerald. She chose it herself because she thought it pretty. Her hope is that her husband-to-be – his real name is Eric Blair – will be well enough to leave hospital so that they can go abroad in the new year.

During autumn and winter Orwell, Sonia and others who witnessed events appeared to flit between states of delusion, fantasy and pathos. Muggeridge noted that Sonia 'is what Tony [Powell] describes as an "Art Tart"', a good-looking hanger-on, who in order to join the 'set' made herself available to cultural celebrities. Shortly before she began visiting Orwell she had broken up with the French philosopher Maurice Merleau-Ponty. Muggeridge predicted that it 'will probably be a rather macabre wedding,' implying that Sonia knew it would soon be followed by a funeral.

There is a moment in *Nineteen Eighty-Four* which has more to do with Orwell's enduring strangeness than politics, when Julia hands Winston a piece of paper, even before they know each other's names. Nervously, he first decides to despatch it to the memory hole and then stops himself and opens it:

I love you.

Impulsive, seemingly unmotivated gestures such as this were Orwell's counterbalance to rationality. Despite the gender-reversal the similarities between Julia and the habits of her creator are striking. He seemed compelled to declare love or propose marriage to women he hardly knew – eight times in my estimation – but not as a preamble to a strategy of seduction. Orwell simply needed to reach out to form some sort of bond, however brief, that would separate the two of them from the rest of the world. Jacintha Buddicom's most vivid memory of him when they were children was when he declared that perhaps all other people were illusions and that they, by virtue of their being together, were the only two who properly existed.

The ceremony took place on 13 October 1949. Orwell was forty-six and she thirty-one. A 'special licence' was required for marrying in a hospital and David Astor, ever useful for contacts, obtained one directly from the Archbishop of Canterbury. Astor and Janette Kee, wife of broadcaster and writer Robert, were witnesses and Powell and Muggeridge were present. Orwell could not get out of bed but he exchanged his pyjama top for a crimson smoking jacket that would not have been out of place in a rather louche gentlemen's club. The guests and Sonia repaired to a wedding luncheon at the Ritz, at Orwell's insistence, and Sonia returned later that afternoon with the menu, signed by all present.

Over the winter visitors arrived like ghosts from the past. Heppenstall and Julian Symons were regulars and Stephen Spender kept Orwell company almost once a fortnight, in a successful attempt to repair their differences from the 1930s. Jacintha Buddicom, his almost-girlfriend from adolescence, wrote him numerous letters. Andrew Gow, still fellow of Trinity Cambridge, came to see him unannounced. It was the first time they had met since Orwell had paid his ex-Eton tutor a similarly unannounced visit in Cambridge thirty years earlier. Stafford Cottman, his teenage comrade from the Catalonia battles, telephoned to arrange a visit with Eric Blair, but the hospital said they had no record of such a patient. Eventually he was connected to the room occupied by one 'George Orwell'. Orwell had invested his future in a scheme to move to a Swiss sanatorium at the end of January and promised to meet Cottman after his return.

Avril and Sonia brought Richard to see him almost every day and made an attempt to present themselves as a genial partnership of aunt and step-mother.

The plan for Switzerland was more than a fantasy born out of Thomas Mann's *The Magic Mountain*, a novel set in an alpine sanatorium where health is restored in a seemingly miraculous way. Specialists at University College Hospital had recommended it and specific arrangements had been made, once more by Astor, for a private aeroplane to take him there. But at the same time Orwell was urgently preparing documents that would specify what would occur after his death. Sonia and Richard would be joint literary executors. A considerable insurance policy was guaranteed to ensure a good education for his son and he requested that Richard should be sole beneficiary of the entire estate after Sonia's death. There was no provision for Avril or for his nieces and nephews. He requested that he be buried 'according to the rites of the Church of England,' that his stone should bear the inscription 'Here lies Eric Arthur Blair, born 25th June 1903, died ...' and insisted on no memorial service. He also instructed his executors – effectively Sonia, at least until Richard attained adulthood – to ensure that no biography of him was written, by withholding rights to quote printed material or have access to archives. Sonia followed his instructions until 1972 when she decided that the historian Bernard Crick could be trusted with unlimited rights to both.

By mid-January visitors were becoming far more frequent, and it was evident to each that plans for the immediate future were at odds with the likelihood of Orwell ever leaving the hospital. Richard Rees noted that the fishing rods for the trip to Switzerland stacked conspicuously in the corner of the room contrasted cruelly with the man in the bed who was all but skeletal. Denzil Jacobs, who had been in his Home Guard platoon, visited and was told by Orwell that his doctors agreed on how the Alps would improve his condition. But

Orwell suddenly paused and stated, 'I've made all this money, and now I'm going to die.' Jon Kimche was of Swiss extraction and used a contact at the embassy to speed up the paperwork. The flight and documentation were arranged for Orwell's removal on Wednesday 25 January. Tosco Fyvel spent time with him on the previous Friday and Paul Potts later the same day. They were the last to see him alive. In the early hours of Saturday 21 January a lung haemorrhage caused him to die, alone.

Orwell was buried in a plot secured for him by David Astor in the churchyard of All Saints, Sutton Courtenay, close to the Astor family estate in Berkshire. Orwell had no direct connection with the village but Astor, ever the facilitator, thought it a suitable resting place for a man whose affection for rural England had endured from his youth. Sonia agreed. The village is on the Thames, the river he loved to fish.

BIBLIOGRAPHY

PRIMARY WORKS

George Orwell's major works

Down and Out in Paris and London, Gollancz, London, 1933
Burmese Days, Harper and Brothers, New York, 1934
A Clergyman's Daughter, Gollancz, London, 1935
Keep the Aspidistra Flying, Gollancz, London, 1936
The Road to Wigan Pier, Gollancz, London, 1937
Homage to Catalonia, Secker & Warburg, London, 1938
Coming Up for Air, Gollancz, London, 1939
Inside the Whale and other Essays, Gollancz, London, 1940
The Lion and the Unicorn, Secker & Warburg, London, 1941
Animal Farm, Secker & Warburg, London, 1945
Nineteen Eighty-Four, Secker & Warburg, London, 1949

Editions

Peter Davison (Ed), *Nineteen Eighty-Four: The Facsimile of the Extant Manuscript*, Harcourt Brace Jovanovich, San Diego, 1984
—, (Ed), *The Complete Works of George Orwell*, 20 volumes, Secker & Warburg, London, 1998
—, (Ed), *Diaries*, Harvill Secker, London, 2009
—, (Ed), *The Lost Orwell*, Timewell Press, London, 2006
Orwell, Sonia and Angus, Ian (Ed), *The Collected Essays, Journalism and Letters of George Orwell*, 4 volumes, Harcourt, Brace & World, Inc, New York, 1968

SECONDARY SOURCES

Anisimov, I., 'Enemies of Mankind,' *Pravda*, 12 May 1950
Atkins, John, *George Orwell: A Literary Study*, John Calder, London, 1954

Benney, Mark, *Almost a Gentleman*, Peter Davies, London, 1966

Bloodworth, James, *Hired: Six Months Undercover in Low-Wage Britain*, Atlantic, London, 2019

Bounds, Philip, *Orwell and Marxism: The Political and Cultural Thinking of George Orwell*, I.B. Tauris, London and New York, 2009

Bowker, Gordon, *Inside George Orwell: A Biography*, Palgrave Macmillan, London, 2003

Brander, Laurence, *George Orwell*, Longmans, Green & Co., London, 1954

Brunsdale, Mitzi M., *Student Companion to George Orwell*, Greenwood Press, Westport, CT, 2000

Buddicom, Jacintha, *Eric & Us*, The Postscript Edition, Finlay, London, 2006

Connolly, Cyril, *Enemies of Promise*, Garden City, New York, 1960

Coppard, Audrey and Crick, Bernard, *Orwell Remembered*, Facts on File, New York, 1984

Crick, Bernard, *George Orwell: A Life*, Little, Brown & Co, Boston, 1980 (Revised edition, 1992)

Cushman, Thomas and Rodden, John (Eds), *George Orwell: Into the Twenty-First Century*, Paradigm Press, Boulder, CO, 2004

Davison, Peter, *George Orwell: A Literary Life*, Palgrave, New York, 1996

Fyvel, Tosco, *George Orwell: A Personal Memoir*, Macmillan, London, 1982

Gottlieb, Erika, *The Orwell Conundrum: A Cry of Despair or Faith in the Spirit of Man?*, Carleton University Press, Ottawa, 1992

Gross, Miriam (Ed), *The World of George Orwell*, Simon & Schuster, New York, 1972

Hitchens, Christopher, *Why Orwell Matters*, Basic Books, New York, 2002

Holden, Inez, *It was Different at the Time*, The Bodley Head, London, 1943

Holderness, Graham, Loughrey, Bryan and Yousaf, Nahem (Eds), *George Orwell: Contemporary Critical Essays*, St Martin's Press, New York, 1998

Hollis, Christopher, *A Study of George Orwell*, Hollis & Carter, London, 1956

Hopkinson, Tom, *George Orwell*, Longmans Grace & Co, London and New York, 1953

Howe, Irving, *Politics and the Novel*, Ivan R. Dee, Chicago, 2002

—, (Ed), *Orwell's Nineteen Eighty-Four*, Harcourt Brace Jovanovich, New York, 1982

Judt, S. 'I Once Met George Orwell,' in Richard Ingrams (Ed), *I Once Met: Unexpected Encounters with the Famous and Infamous*, Oldie Publications, London, 2008

Katz, Wendy, 'Imperialism and Patriotism: Orwell's Dilemma in 1940,' *Modernist Studies: Literature and Culture*, 3 (1979), 99–105

Kogan, Steve, 'In Celebration of George Orwell on the Fiftieth Anniversary of "Politics and the English Language",' *Academic Questions* (Winter 1996–97), 15–29

Lebedoff, David, *The Same Man: George Orwell and Evelyn Waugh in Love and War*, Random House, New York, 2008

Lucas, Scott, *Orwell*, Haus, London, 2003

Lutman, Stephen, 'Orwell's Patriotism,' *Journal of Contemporary History*, 2/2 (1967), 149–58

Meyers, Jeffrey, *George Orwell: The Critical Heritage*, Routledge, New York, 1997

—, *Orwell: Wintry Conscience of a Generation*, W. W. Norton, New York and London, 2000

—, *A Reader's Guide to George Orwell*, Littlefield Adams, New York, 1977

Michéa, Jean-Claude, *Orwell, Anarchiste Tory. Suivi de: À propos de 1984*, Climats, Paris, 2008

Newsinger, John, *Orwell's Politics*, Palgrave Macmillan, Basingstoke, 2002

Patai, Daphne, *The Orwell Mystique: A Study in Male Ideology*, University of Massachusetts Press, Amherst, 1984

Rees, Richard, *George Orwell: Fugitive From the Camp of Victory*, Southern Illinois University Press, 1965

Rodden, John, *Every Intellectual's Big Brother: George Orwell's Literary Siblings*, University of Texas Press, Austin, 2008

—, *The Politics of Literary Reputation: The Making and Claiming of 'St George' Orwell*, Oxford University Press, 1989

—, *Scenes from an Afterlife: The Legacy of George Orwell*, ISI Books, Wilmington, DE, 2003

—, *The Unexamined Orwell*, University of Texas Press, Austin, 2011

—, (Ed), *George Orwell: Critical Insights*, Salem Press, Amenia, NY, 2012

—, (Ed), *The Cambridge Companion to George Orwell*, Cambridge University Press, 2007

—, (Ed), *Understanding Animal Farm: A Student Casebook to Issues, Sources and Historical Documents*, Greenwood Press, Westport, CT, 1999

Rose, Jonathan (Ed), *The Revised Orwell*, Michigan State University Press, East Lansing, 1992

Saunders, Loraine, *The Unsung Artistry of George Orwell: The Novels from Burmese Days to Nineteen Eighty-Four*, Ashgate, Aldershot, 2008

Shelden, Michael, *Orwell: The Authorized Biography*, HarperCollins, New York, 1991

Smith, David and Mosher, Michael, *Orwell for Beginners*, Writers and Readers, London, 1984

Spurling, Hilary, *The Girl From the Fiction Department*, Counterpoint, London, 2002

Stansky, Peter and Abrahams, William, *Orwell: The Transformation*, Knopf, New York, 1980

—, *The Unknown Orwell*, Stanford University Press, 1972

Strittmatter, Kai, *We Have Been Harmonised: Life in China's Surveillance State*, Old Street, London, 2019

Symons, Julian, 'Orwell: A Reminiscence,' *London Magazine,* 3 (September 1963), 35–49

Taylor, D. J., *Orwell: The Life*, Henry Holt, London, 2003

Trilling, Lionel, *Introduction to George Orwell's Homage to Catalonia*, Beacon Press, Boston, 1952

Troppi, Victor, '"1984": Full Circle,' *New Times,* December 1983

Tyrell, Martin, *The Politics of George Orwell (1903–1950): From Tory Anarchism to National Socialism and More Than Half Way Back*, Cultural Notes, 36, Libertarian Alliance, London, 1997

Wadhams, Stephen, *Remembering George Orwell*, Penguin, London, 1984

Walter, N., *George Orwell: At Home and Among the Anarchists*, Freedom Press, London, 1998

West, William J. (Ed), *Orwell: The Lost Writings*, Arbor House, New York, 1985

—, (Ed), *Orwell: The War Commentaries*, Pantheon, New York, 1986

Wilkin, P., *The Strange Case of Tory Anarchism*, Libri, London, 2010

Williams, Raymond, *George Orwell*, Prentice-Hall, Englewood Cliffs, NJ, 1974

Woodcock, George, *The Crystal Spirit: A Study of George Orwell*, Little, Brown, Boston, 1966

Zwerdling, Alex, *Orwell and the Left*, Yale University Press, New Haven, 1974

INDEX